Music and the Forms of Life

Music and the Forms of Life

Lawrence Kramer

UNIVERSITY OF CALIFORNIA PRESS

University of California Press
Oakland, California

© 2022 by Lawrence Kramer

Earlier versions of chapters 1 and 4 were published, respectively, in *Experimental Affinities in Music*, ed. Paulo de Assis (Leuven: Leuven University Press, 2015), 147–167, and *Thresholds of Listening: Sound, Technics, Space*, ed. Sander van Mass (New York: Fordham University Press, 2015), 30–50. My thanks to the publishers for permission to reprint the previously published portions here.

Library of Congress Cataloging-in-Publication Data

Names: Kramer, Lawrence, 1946- author.
Title: Music and the forms of life / Lawrence Kramer.
Description: Oakland, California : University of California Press, [2022] | Includes bibliographical references and index.
Identifiers: LCCN 2022003775 (print) | LCCN 2022003776 (ebook) | ISBN 9780520389106 (cloth) | ISBN 9780520389113 (paperback) | ISBN 9780520389120 (ebook)
Subjects: LCSH: Music—Philosophy and aesthetics—History—19th century. | Music and technology—History—19th century.
Classification: LCC ML3845 .K8129 2022 (print) | LCC ML3845 (ebook) | DDC 781.1/7—dc23
LC record available at https://lccn.loc.gov/2022003775
LC ebook record available at https://lccn.loc.gov/2022003776

31 30 29 28 27 26 25 24 23 22
10 9 8 7 6 5 4 3 2 1

CONTENTS

List of Musical Examples and Figures vii

Introduction: Music and the Life of Statues 1

1 · From Clockwork to Pulsation I: Intensity and Drive 13

2 · From Clockwork to Pulsation II: Action and Feeling 33

3 · From Clockwork to Pulsation III: Metabolism 51

4 · 1812 Overtures: *Wellington's Victory* and Live Action 78

5 · "Dear Listener"...: Music and the Invention of Subjectivity 100

6 · Waltzing Specters: Life, Perception, and Ravel's "La Valse" 123

7 · The Musical Biome 144

Epilogue: Sound and the Forms of Life 166

Notes 171
Index 191

MUSICAL EXAMPLES AND FIGURES

MUSICAL EXAMPLES

1. Haydn, Symphony no. 94 in G Major, Andante, "Surprise" *15*
2. Haydn, Piano Sonata no. 33 in C Minor, mm. 9–14 *26*
3. Beethoven, Piano Sonata no. 5 in C Minor, op. 10, no. 1, opening *28*
4. Mozart, Fantasy in D Minor, K. 397, mm. 12–13, 20–21, 23–24 *45*
5. Beethoven, Piano Sonata no. 10 in G Major, op. 14, no. 2, opening *49*
6. Haydn, String Quartet no. 53 in D Major, op. 64, no. 5, "The Lark," opening *54*
7. Mozart, Symphony no. 39 in E flat Major, K. 543, Andante con Moto, opening *69*
8. Mozart, Symphony no. 39, Andante con Moto, mm. 30–34 *70*
9. Wagner, *Parsifal*, Titurel's voice *116*
10. J. S. Bach, *Goldberg Variations*, no. 10 (Fughetta) *161*

FIGURE

1. Title page, J. S. Bach, *Goldberg Variations* *153*

Introduction

MUSIC AND THE LIFE OF STATUES

SO IS CORDELIA DEAD OR NOT? Shakespeare's King Lear desperately poses this question over the body of his only loyal daughter, whose death has consummated his tragic folly. The audience knows the answer even as Lear refuses to know it. But as the eighteenth century drew near, the cruelty of this ending was more than some playgoers could stomach. In 1680 the playwright Nahum Tate rewrote the ending and brought Cordelia back to life. His version of the play held the stage throughout the eighteenth century. I don't know whether music had a role in the reanimation scene, but Shakespeare himself calls for music in a scene in which he, too, brings someone back to life, or at least her statue, or at least the pretense of her statue, symbolically real if empirically false. Like Cordelia, the figure is motionless, wishfully suspended between life and its lack. This is from *The Winter's Tale*:

> PAULINA:
> Quit presently the chapel, or resolve you
> For more amazement. If you can behold it,
> I'll make the statue move indeed, descend
> And take you by the hand. . . .
>
> LEONTES:
> Proceed:
> No foot shall stir.
>
> PAULINA:
> Music, awake her; strike!
>
> *Music*
>
> 'Tis time; descend; be stone no more; approach;
> Strike all that look upon with marvel.[1]

Why music? Why statues?

Take music first. In 1733, the English physician George Cheyne likened the principle of sentient life to the production of music by resonating bodies: "The brain, where all the nerves, or instruments of Sensation, terminate, [is] like a Musician in a finely-fram'd and well-tuned Organ-case.... [The] nerves are like keys, which, being struck or touch'd, convey the Sound and Harmony to this sentient Principle, or Musician." The metaphor would be reechoed throughout the century, to the point where it became something more than simple metaphor. Étienne de Condillac, writing in 1781, says virtually the same thing Cheyne had: "The exterior organs of the human body are like the keys, the objects that strike them are like fingers on the keyboard, the interior organs are like the body of the harpsichord, the sensations or ideas are like the sounds."[2] For Cheyne, Condillac, and many others, the life of a sentient being depended on the elemental music of vibrating nerves. This animate and animating music, moreover, was not merely resonant; it was harmonious, more like the stuff of a composition than of accidental euphony. Music and life were at bottom coextensive.

In 1803, the German psychiatrist Johann Christian Reil took the prevailing metaphor to a new level, in a book with the musical if cumbersome title *Rhapsodies on the Application of Psychological Methods of Cure to the Mentally Disturbed*. Reil represents the brain as a kind of symphony and the link between the brain and the nervous system as a temple filled with unlimited resonance:

> The brain may be conceived as a complex work of art, composed of many sounding bodies that stand in a purposeful relationship (rapport) with one another. If one of these is excited from outside by means of the senses, its tone excites the tone of another, this one another again; and so the original excitement continues in meandering trains through the wide halls of this temple until a new stroke cancels *[aufhebt]* the previous one or flows together with it.[3]

For Cheyne, the near identity of music and life was primarily physiological. For Condillac it was also intellectual. For Reil it had become psychological. The integration of the personality depended on an "equally determined distribution of forces in the brain and throughout the nervous system" modeled on the harmony of sounding bodies in a resonant space. The corporeal music of life had expanded, "in meandering trains," into the sphere of subjectivity.

One likely reason for this development is that, as we will see in the early chapters to follow, composers in the later eighteenth century began to return the compliment of the physicians and philosophers. They experimented with music that simulated the processes of sentient life. It would thus make perfect sense for Reil to recommend music as a therapeutic device, which he did; its harmonious composition could quell mental disturbance, the dissonance of the sounding bodies, by assuring the orderly operation of the "soul-organs" (*Seelenorgans;* the English, though not the German, affords a nice pun on Cheyne's musical organ). As we will also see, however, the musical modeling of life could also be quite rambunctious.

Now to the statues, or statue-like figures: mannequins that also had an intimate relation to the concept of life in the eighteenth century and, in that capacity, to music as well. During the eighteenth century, statues that came to life, both real and imaginary, became tools for theorizing the operation of life in sentient beings. The principal hypothetical example occurs in Condillac's *Treatise on the Sensations* of 1754, the centerpiece of which is the story of a statue brought to life as a tabula rasa but drawn by sensation into learning how to become aware of its own life and person.

Condillac may have inspired the scenario of the ballet *Creatures of Prometheus,* staged in 1810 with music by Beethoven; the association may extend further to the Finale of the *Eroica* Symphony, which famously takes the theme of its variations from the Finale of the ballet.[4] There is no evidence that Beethoven was familiar with Condillac, but the ballet scenario by Salvatore Vigano is virtually a staging of Condillac's theories. The prototypical humans appear first as statues, after which the benign Prometheus gradually educates them, leading them from the senses to understanding, art, and morality.

It is fair to speculate that Condillac may have been inspired by a real statue, an android or "moving anatomy" built by Jacques de Vaucanson in 1737 with the express purpose of simulating human life—a life the android would verify by playing the flute. The animated flute player was widely hailed as a modern marvel.

Vaucanson coined the term "moving anatomies" as a paradox. "Anatomies" at the time referred to elaborate wax mannequins with cutaway parts that showed the interior of the human body. "Moving anatomies" were automatons, primarily humanoid figures capable of moving in ways that allowed them to simulate the actions and even the feelings of living beings—and in so doing to blur the boundary between living and nonliving forms. As chapter 1 will explain, the flute player was only the first of a series of Enlightenment androids, the best known of which all testified to their virtual life with acts of musical performance. Some of them are still intact and operative. You can still hear them perform.

The technique of simulation first employed by the flute player was a conceptual as well as a technical innovation. Its novelty can best be measured by comparing it with imitation—an apt comparison because in at least one important sphere, that of the arts, imitation declines as simulation advances. An imitation depends on its difference from what is imitated; a portrait merely *looks like* its sitter. But simulation depends on a degree of resemblance that overrides the effect of difference, at least initially. Simulation exceeds illusion without becoming reality. The result may strike all who look upon with marvel—the flute player did that—but it may also make them uncomfortable. In present-day robotics this discomfort has become familiar as the "uncanny valley" effect; when artificial humanoids become *too* lifelike, the border between the living and the nonliving blurs and makes the observer queasy.

As Annette Richards has shown, the abilities of Vaucanson's flute player did prompt hostility in some of the era's musicians—and, one might add, some anxiety.[5] The android, while remaining seated, acted as a kind of Pied Piper leading some observers straight into the uncanny valley. This problem did not arise when the source of machine-made music made no pretension to life; thus the clockwork mechanical organ for which Mozart in 1790 composed funeral music—the subject of Richards's study—enjoyed that immunity. But one person's uncanny valley is another's marvel, and the flute player seems to have affected most observers as the work of genial Prometheanism on the Condillac/Vigano model. Between imitation and the uncanny valley, simulation opens up the prospect of the virtual—the realm of things that *almost* are. Vaucanson's flute player, with music as its credential, presented those who marveled at it with the first genuine case of virtual life.

The parallel development in the arts gave music the power to transform its scientific role as a metaphor of life into an aesthetic experience. The development of the concept of the aesthetic in the eighteenth century had the unexpected consequence of breaking down the traditional concept of art. Changes in artistic practice quickly followed. The story of this change is long, uneven, and complicated. Suffice it here to say that the idea of understanding the arts primarily on the basis of the kind of experience they induced, over and above their empirical characteristics, redefined the phenomenon it had only sought to explain. The concept of the aesthetic did away with the need for the work of art to meet the criterion that had ruled it since classical times: to be a (good) imitation. The subsequent collapse of the "representative regime of art," as Jacques Rancière calls it, subordinated imitation to free-standing form, often making imitation inoperable despite its continued presence.[6] Art could still be mimetic or representational, but it was not mimesis or representation that made it art. The situation was tailor-made for music, especially instrumental music, which had plenty of forms available and would invent plenty more without any need of representation.

Some of those forms were simulations of life, built of real music and virtual embodiment. Music began to invent acoustic surrogates, auditory metaphors, for the primary elements of life as the century's science understood it: pulse, vibration, irritability, sensibility. It also began to investigate the affinities and antagonisms between life and mechanism and the questions of whether and how mechanisms could some to life. At first this enterprise was confined to a small series of experimental compositions; the major canonical figures of the time, Haydn, Mozart, and Beethoven, composed a good number of them. We will touch on many of these in the first three chapters to follow as we move along the meandering train of metaphors started here—a process that will continue throughout the book.

The train continues because in relatively short order music comes to be heard as able to simulate life without needing to form specific metaphors for it. The later chapters of this book will look at some of the forms this simulation assumed in the nineteenth and twentieth centuries. Like the androids, music came to life by acting as if it were alive. The character of this *as if* is not primarily logical or semiological; it is ontological. When music learns to simulate life, it undergoes a fundamental change. What changes is not only how music sounds but what it is. In one of its many aspects, music becomes life made audible.

The possibility of hearing it this way is what allowed Wallace Stevens and Langston Hughes, both writing in the early twentieth century, to add new forms to the still-growing train of metaphors. In both cases the keyboard reappears (as it will again).

> Just as my fingers on these keys
> Make music, so the selfsame sounds
> On my spirit make a music, too.
>
> Music is feeling, then, not sound;
> And thus it is that what I feel,
> Here in this room, desiring you,
>
> Thinking of your blue-shadowed silk,
> Is music.[7]

> Droning a drowsy syncopated tune,
> Rocking back and forth to a mellow croon,
> I heard a Negro play.
> Down on Lenox Avenue the other night
> By the pale dull pallor of an old gas light...
> He made that poor piano moan with melody.
> O Blues!
> Swaying to and fro on his rickety stool
> He played that sad raggy tune like a musical fool.
> Sweet Blues!
> Coming from a black man's soul.[8]

Stevens's Peter Quince plays on his spirit by touching the keys of his instrument; Hughes' blues singer, also at the clavier, transfers the burden (the weight, the melody) of his soul to the keyboard mechanism. The mellow croon of his voice becomes the piano's moan.

Closer to the present, we can find Jorie Graham subtly continuing the train by taking music as the metaphor that joins external perception to internal sentience. The sound, as in Hughes, has become raggy, but the harmony remains. The musical sound of raindrops "breaking / without breaking" parallels the play of tone to tone in Reil's temple of resonance:

> The slow overture of rain,
> each drop breaking
> without breaking into
> the next, describes
> the unrelenting, syncopated
> mind.[9]

Closer still is this plainspoken avowal by the philosopher Kathleen Higgins: "We hear music as a manifestation of vitality and part of our enjoyment is empathy with its liveliness."[10] What is perhaps most striking about this statement is its assurance, the implicit expectation that no one will doubt it. It no longer even needs the long train of metaphors that meander behind it.

Music is feeling, then, in sound.

But why music? Why is it music, of all things, that came to stand for, and then to embody, the passage from the sphere of inanimate mechanism to the sphere of living organism? Why, to put the question from a wider angle, does music become the expression of the answer to what the philosopher David

Chalmers calls "the hard problem"—not "a" but *"the"* hard problem, the one for which no good answer has ever been found and may never be found?[11] For Chalmers, this is the problem of consciousness: How does matter become sentient and self-aware? The hard problem is heir to Descartes's infamous separation of mind from body (overcome, according to Descartes, by the passage of superfine "animal spirits" through the pineal gland).[12] For scientists like Cheyne and philosophers like Condillac, solving the problem of consciousness first required solving the problem of the life that is (or used to be) the condition of possibility for consciousness.[13] The train of musical metaphors brought to bear on this problem, eventually by music itself, forms a kind of placeholder for the answer. To vary the sentence found earlier in this paragraph, music becomes the expression of the wish for an answer, the promise of an answer, the fantasy of an answer. Above all music gives, or "is," the *feeling* of an answer. Expressed musically, the answer is something that, just because we can feel it, does not need to be spelled out further.

Although the nexus of music, life, and the animation of bodily forms takes its proximate origin in the eighteenth century, its prehistory is a long one. The fantasy of bringing statues to life is ancient, going back through the myth of Pygmalion and Galatea to the Homeric passage about the androids—that's essentially what they were—created by Hephaestus:

> In support of their master moved his attendants.
> These are golden, and in appearance like living young women.
> There is intelligence in their hearts, and there is speech in them
> and strength, and from the immortal gods they have learned how to do things.[14]

Hephaestus, the only artisan/artist among the Olympians, occupies the role assigned to Prometheus in the benign version of the latter's myth; he creates the possibility of further creation. His automata are endowed all at once with the curriculum of Condillac's or Vigano's statues. They are explicitly presented as intelligent machines who have been invested with human attributes also shared by the gods. They move, feel, speak, and do things.

The primary criteria for this animation are also ancient, already present in Hephaestus's androids and both of them reflected in Ovid's account of Galatea: the body must move and the body must feel. Pygmalion's sculpture, unnamed by Ovid, is so lifelike that "you might believe, [she] lived / and wished, were it not irreverent, to move." When she comes alive in the act of returning a kiss, she knows life first as feeling; when Pygmalion "presses his mouth / to a mouth no longer feigned, the maiden felt the kiss, / and blushed, and, lifting her gaze to the light, / Saw both her lover and the sky."[15] The story takes on added resonance because it is not recounted by Ovid's primary narrator but by Orpheus, who sings it to the accompaniment of his lyre after failing to retrieve Eurydice from the Underworld.[16]

The Pygmalion myth itself took on a second life in the eighteenth century. In 1762 Jean-Jacques Rousseau wrote a "lyric scene" on the subject, combining music with speech and pantomime. First performed in 1770, the work became a sensation. As Ellen Lockhart observes, in the 1770s and 1780s it "accumulated at least thirty editions and an even greater number of performances."[17] Rousseau's *Pygmalion* became in effect its era's paradigmatic musical-dramatic representation of the link between the life of persons and the life of statues. The chisel of its Pygmalion draws back upon meeting yielding flesh; touch follows as the chisel is replaced by the sculptor's hand. Like Ovid's, Rousseau's Galatea responds with a kiss to the onset of feeling; like Shakespeare's Hermione, she steps down from her pediment to assume the matter of life.

The criteria of motion and feeling took on new significance from the eighteenth century onward as they became the potentialities that empirical science sought to explain—initially, as we will see, under the categories of "irritation" and "sensibility." Since then motion and feeling have persisted informally as the primary signs of life even as the science has grown vastly more complicated. They can be found, for example, in Kazuo Ishiguro's novel *Never Let Me Go* (2005), which is populated by human clones brought to life in order to make organ donations until they "complete," that is, die, while still young.[18] But there is no difference between "real" humans and the clones—the biological machines, the androids by fiat—except the source of their generation. The novel continues the train of metaphors binding music to life. Its title is that of a fictional song, the refrain of which is linked in the narrative to both the desire for life to go on and despair that it will not.

There is, however, an asymmetry between the criteria of moving and feeling that helps explain why the fantasy of animation in its later varieties is so closely associated with music. The same asymmetry also helps explain why music's cultural value rose so rapidly at the end of the eighteenth century, kept on rising throughout the nineteenth, and has persisted ever since. The asymmetry, like the criteria, is still with us, especially in debates over the possibility of consciousness in artificial intelligence (a topic, however, that falls outside the scope of this book).

The asymmetry is simple but powerful. Moving bodies are easy objects of observation, but feeling is observable only by the one who feels. It is not, as Wittgenstein long ago showed, that I, as an observer, must *infer* that someone else is feeling or what the feeling is like; in some sense I actually do know it.[19] It is not something that I doubt unless I believe it is being faked. But feeling, nonetheless, cannot be observed from outside, which means that it cannot be *observed* at all.

But why does that summon music to the scene of animation? When I see a body as having been animated, when the question "What makes it live?" is presented to me in the metaphorical form of animating a statue, effigy, homunculus, mannequin, or moving image, why does the answer come back with music attached? The reason, perhaps—but this is a strong *perhaps*—is that music is the only one of our cultural productions that simultaneously embodies observable motion and direct sensibility. Music seems both to move as it passes through time and to evoke familiar forms of bodies in motion. Concurrently, as the earlier quotation from Stevens reminds us, music affects our feelings so directly that it becomes the tangible, discernible form of feeling itself. To hear music closely is not to observe it but to transfer to oneself the feelings it embodies.

Music, moreover, like all those animated figures, comes to us as something that rises from potential to actual being. Until it is performed, a piece of music, whether it is preserved in notation or recording or collective or individual memory, is dormant. It may persist in memory or understanding, but it eludes the senses; the act of performance audibly summons it to quicken. Between performances music enters a state of palpable potentiality, a suspended animation that, like Shakespeare's Hermione, waits for the right notes to be struck. Music and the dream of coming to life are galvanized by each other, conjoined by a metaphorical force that passes reciprocally between them. The manifold ways in which this has happened over the past three centuries is sampled—only sampled, to be sure, but in exemplary, even iconic ways—by the conjunctions studied in the ensuing chapters.

As we will see throughout, the train of metaphors sampled in this introduction has a life of its own; its acts something like a vine. The metaphors proliferate, they keep on going amid changing times, and as they do they become increasingly substantive, or, if you will, increasingly true. Their reiteration alters the conditions of perception as much as it reflects them. A recent example (it is late 2020 as I write) comes from Eric Motley, a Black political conservative and a longtime friend of a historic white liberal: Ruth

Bader Ginsberg. Motley's remarks, celebrating Ginsberg shortly after her death, require a longish quotation:

> People often asked both of us how we became friends. Last December, at dinner one evening she succinctly replied: "A common love for ideas, for music. It was really the Goldberg Variations that brought us together."
> When I listen to Bach's marvelous, deeply stirring music, I am reminded that in all of these variations—all this flux of life, especially in the inner ups and downs—there is an exquisite order I can actually experience, which is so beautiful that it must be real. In that one piece of music, so beautiful and complex, both she and I discovered that these Variations had become a fixture in our lives.
> On the night of her death, like thousands of others, my fiancée, Hannah, and I visited the Supreme Court. We climbed those marbled steps of majesty, and at the great bronze doors we left a single white rose.... Then we came home and put on the Goldberg Variations.

The *Goldberg Variations* form the center of this book's final chapter, where the twentieth century discovers their proximity to the genetic code. By the time the willing reader gets to that point, this book should have shown that Motley's association of the "exquisite order" of the *Variations* with "this flux of life"—and death—is more than just an evocative moment in a moving eulogy. It is to be taken literally. The flux of life and the order of music are inseparable. Again.

In method this book continues the practice of "open interpretation" that I have sought to develop in the train of its predecessors, weaving back and forth between description and metaphor, cultural and musical practices, historical events and their aesthetic embodiments.[20] Following the twists and turns of music as life will require giving selective but close attention to individual pieces of music. One reason why the association of music and life has been so strong for so long is that the sense and sensation of life do not merely form a general halo around particular compositions and their performances. On the contrary, they inform the fine-grained detail of the musical event. The music reciprocates by helping shape what vitality is and means. More than only an occasion of aesthetic absorption, the music becomes historical agency and historical evidence.

In her posthumously published *The Secular Commedia,* Wendy Allenbrook shows that various French Enlightenment thinkers from Denis

Diderot to the Baron D'Holbach understood the continual flux of sound and feeling in comic opera as a literal sign of life. Writing in praise of Giovanni Pergolesi's popular opera *La serva padrona* (1733), D'Holbach reports with approval "someone's" judgment on the music and its "extraordinary portrayals": "'It is life itself; and at the same time these melodies are divine.'"[21] Implicit in the observation is the question of how to account for the music's vitality. These melodies are divine: it may be true that the music portrays us "to the life," but it is not enough to say only that. We need to know in each case what creative agency is involved and how it comes to life in the sounding. This is perhaps even more true of instrumental music, to which this mercurial vitality quickly migrates (shows, indeed, that it had already migrated), than it is of opera. In order to suggest how music came to reflect, and reflect on, its own "biotic" aspect, as Holly Watkins calls it—the sphere of "vitalities" that extend beyond the human to animals, plants, and even nonliving materials and that inform "two of music's most cherished aptitudes: to stimulate and simulate life"[22]—it is necessary to suggest how one might listen biotically. That is one of the main aims of this book. Accordingly my primary concern here is with neither the reception nor the performance of the music at hand but with its affordances: what it makes available to us in the way of knowledge and pleasure.[23]

At this point it is important to acknowledge that the life made audible by the canon of classical instrumental music is as much a symbolic as it is a biotic process, and that it projects the experience of a select group of Western men. This general historical limitation is now widely recognized, but in this instance it may point to something specific about the identification of music and life. The possibility is speculative, and it will be only latent in the chapters to follow, but it is worth keeping in mind. Why, we might ask, are figures such as Hermione, Galatea, and Hephaestus's androids so prominent in our train of metaphors when the metaphors assume narrative form? Could it be that the particular appeal of artificial life to men during this era points to something like a fantasy of virile birth? That idea is perhaps discernible in the work of one of the few women of the time to devote a work to the topic— which turned out to be the most famous and enduring example of the kind. The woman was Mary Shelley; the work was *Frankenstein*.

When Victor Frankenstein discovers "the cause of life and generation," he also acquires "the capacity of bestowing animation" on lifeless matter. Circumventing pregnancy and childbirth, he becomes capable of creating life without recourse to a female body. The discovery inspires an open fantasy of male parthenogenesis: "A new species would bless me as its creator and source; many happy and excellent natures would owe their being to me. No father could claim the gratitude of his child so completely as I should deserve theirs."[24] Suffice it to say that things don't exactly turn out that way. After scavenging body parts for his creature and assembling them into a kind of fleshly mannequin, Frankenstein uses "the instruments of life" to "infuse a spark of being into the lifeless thing that lay at [his] feet." The results famously horrify him; he quails at the living gaze of the creature's "dull yellow eye." Disaster ensues.

Mastering the mechanism of life is one thing; mastering its aesthetics is another. Frankenstein has tried to make his creature beautiful, but to make his own work easier he has built on too large a scale. He has fashioned a body large enough to induce repugnance in him precisely by being too alive: "His yellow skin scarcely covered the work of muscles and arteries beneath." The creature shows all too transparently what life is made of.

Unlike Frankenstein's creature, Vaucanson's first-born automaton—a flute player—was not a lifeless thing that had come alive. But it had not exactly *not* come alive, either. As chapter 1 will explain, the flute player differed from strictly musical automatons, which had long been popular in Europe and would have a real vogue in the early nineteenth century. This almost living statue was not a mechanical device that made music, but an artificial being that simulated life by the *way* it made music. The difference is not absolute, but its occurrence marks an epochal change. That change is the subject of this book.

ONE

From Clockwork to Pulsation I

INTENSITY AND DRIVE

WHAT IS EXPERIMENTATION IN MUSIC? Like most such terms, this one is very loose. But it seems fair to say that music is experimental in the broadest sense when something about it is obviously set outside mainstream practice. Experimental music asks if something unlikely can become the stuff of art. Can one write intelligible polyphony in forty or even sixty independent parts? Thomas Tallis's motet "Spem in Alium Nunquam Habui" (1575) and the piece that may have inspired it, Alessandro Striggio's *Missa sopra Ecco sì beato giorno* (1565–66), say yes—in forty and sixty voices, respectively. Can a classical symphony end with a choral movement? We all know the answer to that one. Is it possible to compose with "twelve tones related only to each other"? Schoenberg's Five Piano Pieces (1923) show how to do it. Can two pairs of hands clapping generate a polyphony that makes music of bodily sound? Steve Reich's "Clapping Music" figures out a way and produces a mirror inversion of Tallis's and Striggio's polychoral tapestry. Examples abound in every phase of musical history, in every musical culture and subculture. Many of these experiments end by generating new norms. Experiment, for better and worse, is the childhood of routine.

There is, however, another, more historically bounded form of musical experimentation with quite a different logic. This type belongs to the dawning age of empirical science, preeminently in the eighteenth century, and it operates on the same basic principle as the classical scientific experiment. That principle is the setting up of an artifice to reveal a natural truth or law. Explicit musical experiments on this model form a small but significant part of the era's musical canon. Just as significantly, the experimental attitude persists in implicit form throughout the period and continues into the early nineteenth century. In most cases, the aim of the experimental venture is to test whether music can simulate life. It remains to be seen just why that should be so. To begin addressing that question, we might consider a famous musical experiment, one that its composer explicitly described as an attempt to do something new. But to conduct our own experiment we will have to try to un-hear this music, which has been so encrusted by its own fame that its import has largely been lost.

Largely, but not entirely. The slow movement of Haydn's Symphony no. 94, composed in 1791, contains a loud chord in the wrong place—a shocking surprise, as the symphony's familiar nickname announces. First we get a singsong, tick-tock statement of a naïve theme, or more exactly a theme too naïve to be believed; then we go *kaboom!* (See example 1.)

According to Daniel Chua, "The surprise . . . is in the human hand that comes to tamper with the self-wound motions that the music signifies with its clockwork tune. Conscious life ha[s] seeped into the score, and the mechanical [is] merely a play of signs for the organic."[1] The continued force of Haydn's vital outburst became unexpectedly apparent during the presentation of an early version of this chapter at the 2013 Orpheus Academy in Ghent, Belgium, when technical difficulties prevented me from playing the music. Everyone present knew the tune; someone suggested we sing it together; and I thus ended up conducting an *a capella* performance of the first sixteen measures. At the end, several participants redoubled the loud "surprise" with resounding *whomps!* on the tables in front of them. Everyone in the room knew what was coming, but everyone seemed to make a spontaneous leap from formal measure to bodily exuberance. A more convincing or more pleasurable "argument" would be hard to imagine.

Except for the choice of sound, the reaction of my audience repeated that of Haydn's at the London premiere of the symphony in 1791. Haydn described the event by saying that "enthusiasm [*Enthusiasmus:* elation, frenzy] reached its highest level in the Andante with the drum stroke. *Ancora, Ancora!* resounded *[schallte]* from every throat." Although Haydn did not, as Emily Dolan notes, attribute the effect of the movement entirely to the one chord, the effect he did attribute to it is notably physical: a double outcry from a throng of throats.[2]

But why, we might ask, identify the organic with a sudden jolt? Does it come to life like the creature in Mary Shelley's *Frankenstein?* Does it subdue the mechanical or does it just make an entrance, take a bow, and leave?

A good answer rests with what comes after the initial surprise. This movement is a theme and variations, and it follows Haydn's usual custom of

EXAMPLE 1. Haydn, Symphony no. 94 in G Major, Andante, "Surprise."

preserving the theme almost intact in each variation while letting change come from alterations in expression and/or the addition of ornaments. In the "Surprise" Symphony this procedure leads to a grand climax in the third and last variation in which the whole orchestra blares out the no-longer-mechanical theme with big contributions from the brass and timpani—the biggest contributors to the "surprise" chord. The organic manifests itself as a surge of intensity. It is less an expression of consciousness than of bodily excitation at the limit of consciousness. The effect of the music is ultimately more quantitative than qualitative. And it is precisely in its changeable intensity that the music achieves its most lifelike effect and most clearly links its expressiveness to the simulated presence of an animated subjective being. The era understood living bodies as bodies of excitation. For well-informed listeners in 1791, we might speculate, Haydn's "surprise" would really have been an announcement of something that should be no surprise at all, but, on the contrary, a demonstration of the latest scientific models of the principles of life. The music would be one experiment amid a long parade of others. It made the audience feel how life strikes up.

In supposing as much, we encounter an important ambiguity. The life simulated in the "Surprise" Symphony slow movement is *interior* life: that is, it is not life observed from without but life revealed as if from within. Haydn's account of the premiere pinpoints the effect of animation: the audience felt the music's jolt as their own, and they wanted to be jolted again—and again: "*Ancora, Ancora!*" This interiority, however, is divided along lines that had vexed European thought about life since Descartes. It is both a mental and a bodily interiority, and its existence raises the perennial question of how to bridge the gap between mind and body, or more exactly of how to experience the music's implicit claim that its sonority in performance does bridge that gap.

How, indeed? My answers to that question will themselves be somewhat experimental. They will emerge from a free oscillation—in light of what follows, "vibration" might be the better term—between free speculation and the close examination of historical artifacts. In the end, I will be suggesting not only ways to hear life and the body in an important segment of the classical repertoire, but also ways in which such music draws us—again in light of what follows "drives us" might be the better term—to revisit historical forms of embodiment kept alive primarily by that repertoire itself.

VITAL SIGNS

The place to start is once again the train of metaphors linking life and music observed in the introduction. We will continue along that train in this chapter, but with a difference in emphasis. Cheyne, Condillac, and Reil all focus on the vibratory element in sentient life, which corresponds to the ability to sense, perceive, and understand. But Cheyne and Condillac also observe the need to touch or strike a key to release the vibration. This need corresponds to what the era's life science identified as excitation or "irritation," the need to prod living matter into feeling and action.³ The sensibility associated with vibration was partnered by the excitability associated with a kind of blow. Hence the sudden jolt in Haydn's symphony. This pairing is already latently present in the scene from Shakespeare that voiced our first metaphor. In the course of "awakening" what seems to be a statue, Paulina twice issues the imperative "strike": once to the unseen musicians, who are to strike their instruments—presumably lutes—so that the resulting resonance impels the statue to move, and once to the living statue herself, who repeats the stroke of the musicians to awaken the spectators' sensibility with wonder. Reil traces a similar progress when he describes how the excitation of one tone by another ripples across the nervous system.

These ways of hearing attach especially to instrumental music, which had come to stand for music in general. The metaphor that in the eighteenth century treated sentient life as an extension of such music had evolved, by the nineteenth, into a metaphor that treated such music as an extension of sentient life. Both metaphors depended on the paradox that the sounding bodies associated with the production of life were not themselves alive.

In his *Lectures on Aesthetics*, Hegel goes a crucial step further. Reflecting on the fact that music arises through the vibrations of tone, Hegel begins in the same place as Cheyne, Condillac, and Reil had. For Hegel, however, the auditory vibration awakens the immediacy of subjective presence and its rich, endlessly communicable resonance; vibration is primal sympathy. The "oscillating vibration" of sound becomes the material of music when its tone is refashioned as a note. In music "the ear ... listens to the result of the inner vibration of the body through which what comes before us is no longer the peaceful and material shape but the first and more ideal breath of the soul."⁴ Although the breath of the soul is ideal, it manifests itself by disturbing the inert sleep of a material reality. Music is matter rudely awakened—matter that quivers as a result. "The notes only resonate in the deepest soul which in its ideal subjectivity is seized and set in motion."⁵ The touch on the key of Cheyne's or Condillac's keyboard becomes a blow that releases the ideal breath of the spirit in the form of musical sound. Irritability and sensibility combine, and the result is sentient being. (As we will soon see, the combination was an essential element in the era's, and its music's, conception of life.) In Hegel, the bodily equation of music and life that became mental in Condillac and psychological in Reil advanced to become metaphysical.

But although the metaphor equating sentient life and music evolved in this way from the interior of the body to the interior of the self, the music that sustained the metaphor made a point of not leaving the body behind. The big bang of Haydn's "Surprise" Symphony makes that abundantly clear. We will start seeing more of the same before this chapter is over. The organic force in which the force of subjectivity originates was variously conceived from the seventeenth through the early nineteenth centuries: as sheer mechanism, as animal magnetism, as elemental life force, as electrical energy—the last, of course, being the most accurate. The means of representing the same force is, more often than one might think, musical, and music, in return, begins at the same time to assume the character of the force it helps to represent. The harmonious charm of music invoked by Cheyne and Reil gives way to an irresistible energy.

Initially this exchange is a product of musical experimentation, but it quickly, perhaps as early as the first decade of the nineteenth century, becomes assimilated to the concept of music itself. Hegel epitomizes this change when he claims that instrumental music is self-sufficient *(selbständig)* because it is independent of meanings preestablished by language. Instrumental music is "not compelled to move this way or that, but rather in untrammeled freedom grounded in itself alone."[6] And because "subjective inwardness constitutes the principle of music," the freedom of instrumental music coincides with the freedom that subjective inner consciousness takes for itself. The one is the acoustic mirror of the other.

These developments align with the gradual rise of another concept based in the life sciences: the concept of drive. This is the idea, hardly thinkable before the eighteenth century, of an impersonal force impelling the person, the human subject, to irrational acts and attachments. The untrammeled freedom that Hegel finds in instrumental music is the dialectical opposite of drive, which it is therefore in constant danger of becoming. Instrumental music runs the exemplary risk of becoming more manic than unfettered, ruled by "subjective arbitrariness with its inspirations, caprices, interruptions, witty teasing, deceptive tensions, sudden turns, leaps and lightning flashes, oddities and unheard-of effects."[7] Drive is the active and often negative embodiment of subjective interiority, its logical counterpart and—to invoke another trope invented a few years after Haydn's symphony was composed—its inevitable evil twin: the alter ego, the double that exposes the inherent division of modern subjectivity against itself.

The history of drive begins with the philosophical psychology of the eighteenth century, with landmarks in the work of Kant, Herder, and Schelling. Its emblematic point of origin may be David Hume's argument, in *A Treatise of Human Nature* (1739), that only "passion" is capable of motivating human action. Passions for Hume are impervious to reason and capable of annexing thought to shape the direction of desire. Passions are motivating *forces*.[8]

An early musical touchstone comes from Herder, for whom "sensual impressions, forces, drives, are the strongest things we have."[9] As early as 1769 Herder recast the metaphor of sensation as music *in* the body to describe the workings of music *on* the body—and on the soul. Music sets a multitude of feelings in vibration by acting as an "energetic force," as does Herder's text with its resounding emphasis on the key terms *Music, tone,* and *tones*:

> *Music* resounds.
> Here a new sense opens, a new portal to the soul, and feels *tone*. *Tones, tones,* which in every ordinary moment draw the ear voluptuously into itself; *tones,* which touch the soul in a thousand new ways in every ordinary moment and give out new, different, but intimate, immediate sensations: *tones,* which are the most immediate instrument on the soul. So whereas the expression of visual art was nothing but surface, here there is intimate being, that is, the energetic force, the pathos—what should I call it?—the deeply penetrating into the soul: the world of a new feeling. All our sensations here become a play of strings *[Saitenspiel]*, of which what is called tone takes hold in all the strength of individual moments and beautiful alternations and recurring sensibilities *[Empfindsamkeiten]*.[10]

Taking Hume and Herder as exemplary, suffice it here to say that the spread of this conception brought new value and new legitimacy to sheer strength of feeling. Particularly after the turn of the nineteenth century, intensity becomes a mark of value and even an object of desire in both music and life. One reason why the music of Beethoven gained and held a uniquely iconic position in the musical culture of the era was the perception of drive and intensity as among its basic elements. The perception was far-flung; here is Ralph Waldo Emerson on the subject in 1838: "In Music, Beethoven, and whosoever like him grandly renounces all forms, societies, & laws as impediments & lives in, on, & for his genius & guiding Idea. How great the influence of such! How it rebukes, how it invites & raises me!"[11] There is less than a world of difference between Goethe's identification of blessed yearning, *seelige Sehnsucht,* with the self-immolating desire of the moth for the flame,[12] Emerson's passion to emulate the unconditional drive in (Beethoven's) music, and Walter Pater's urging of a "hard gemlike flame" on his readers as the condition to which they should self-immolatingly aspire. It was Pater, of course, who also regrettably said that all art aspires to the condition of music.[13] But if subjective intensity is the criterion, perhaps it does.

Music thus emerges from eighteenth-century thought about life as one of the chief models of drive. Although drive was certainly thinkable apart from music, music is what made it available as an object of experience, as something to be lived and enjoyed, not just suffered or hypothesized. It is time to return to the musical side of its history and its essential entanglement with sensibility. Both develop right alongside our train of metaphors, which will now continue.

FROM VIBRATING STRINGS TO SENTIENT CLOCKWORK

In the course of formulating the protoconcept of drive, Hume framed his own version of the comparison of nervous excitation to the musical vibration of strings: "If we consider the human mind, we shall find that with regard to the passions, it is not of the nature of a wind instrument of music, which, in running over all the notes, immediately loses the sound after the breath ceases; but rather resembles a string instrument, where, after each stroke, the vibrations still retain some sound, which gradually and insensibly decays."[14] Similar figures turn up in the writings of scientists. This is from Jean-Jacques Menuret de Chambord's article "Pulse" in the *Encyclopedie* of Denis Diderot and Jean Rond D'Alembert: "If one wishes to form an idea of the way in which the organs contribute to the movements and contractions of the arteries.... [i]magine strings radiating out from each organ.... [T]he uniform tension of these strings will produce a combined effort.... Such are the varieties of the pulse which an able observer strives to grasp."[15]

In 1769 Diderot wrote a trio of dialogues on the question of life and collected them under the title *D'Alembert's Dream.* Drawing liberally on the work of his friend Theophile Bordeu, a physician, researcher, and leading theorist of the life force who appears as a fictionalized character in two of the dialogues, Diderot described the human subject as a sentient musical instrument, in particular a sentient harpsichord *(clavecin):* "Suppose there is a keyboard with sense and a memory. Tell me if it won't know and repeat on its own the melodies which you have executed on its keys. We are instruments endowed with sensibility and memory. Our senses are so many keys which are struck by nature surrounding us and which often strike themselves. And there we have, in my judgment, everything which goes on in an organic keyboard like you and me."[16]

I should mention that Diderot's sentient harpsichord remained unknown in its own time, since *D'Alembert's Dream* was not published until 1830. The importance of this instrument for us, however, depends not on when it was made public but on when it was conceived, and conceived in relation to a widely circulating body of similar tropes, including Hume's. In a work that did see the light of day in Diderot's lifetime, the *Letter on the Deaf and Dumb* of 1751, a similar analogy appears, this one based on the vibrations of a bell—although strings are still attached:

> If I had to explain [the] system of the human understanding... I should say, "Consider man as a walking clock; the heart as its mainspring, the contents of the thorax as the principal parts of the works; look on the head as a bell furnished with little hammers attached to an infinite number of threads which are carried to all corners of the clock-case. Fix upon the bell one of those little figures with which we ornament the top of our clocks, and let it listen, like a musician who listens to see if his instrument is in tune: this little figure is the soul.... I could pursue my analogy still further, and add that the sounds produced by the bell do not die away at once, but have some duration; that they produce chords with the sounds that follow, and the little figure that listens compares them, and pronounces them harmonious or dissonant; that memory, which we need to form opinions and to speak, is the resonance of the bell; the judgment, the formation of chords; and speech, a succession of chords.[17]

The passage is notable for not being content simply to indicate an analogy between music and the life force. The analogy demands detailed elaboration, a verbal blueprint for the construction of the musical soul. The demand points to the features that distinguish eighteenth-century formulations of what is actually an ancient trope: their emphasis, first, on the materiality of the instrument on both sides of the metaphor, and, second, on the instrument's capacity to vary in levels of intensity. The quantitative factor depends on the workings of a mode of memory associated with sympathetic vibration, a process assigned to the sentient harpsichord in *D'Alembert's Dream* but here given to the bell. The duration of the sounds is sustained by the relationship between one vibration and another. Diderot takes pains to indicate that the results vary in intensity depending on the number of strings that are struck: "If many of these little threads are pulled at once, the bell will be struck several times, and the little figure will hear several notes simultaneously. Imagine that there are some of these threads that are always being pulled."

Like a clockwork, however, the analogy winds down, and Diderot ends it by rebuking himself for indulging in metaphors rather than thinking philosophically. But neither here nor in *D'Alembert's Dream* does he ever surrender his metaphors, or even try very hard to replace them. In that respect he is acting in harmony with his friend Bordeu. In his own magnum opus of 1751, Bordeu explains the scientific necessity of metaphors with specific question to sensibility, his candidate for the vehicle of life force:

> [Sensibility] is one of these metaphors I must be allowed. Those who examine these questions closely know how difficult it is to explain oneself when speaking of the force that directs with such precision a thousand singular motions in the human body and its parts. One does not even know what terms would serve to express certain movements in plants or even certain properties of minerals.... [Georg] Stahl claimed that the soul directed everything in the animal body. However that may be, one can state that all living parts are directed by a self-preserving and ever-vigilant force. Does this [force] in certain respects belong to the essence of a portion of matter or is it a necessary attribute of its matter's combinations? Once more we cannot claim to give more here than a way to conceive these things, metaphorical expressions, comparisons.[18]

Much later, the necessity of such verbal invention was not lost on Freud, who called drives "mythological entities, magnificent in their indefiniteness," and held that without figurative language "we could not describe [depth-psychological] processes ... at all, and indeed we could not have become aware of them."[19] One might remark in passing that Bordeu might just as well be talking about how to describe music, a point worth keeping in mind when we eventually turn back to Haydn and move ahead to Beethoven.

Diderot's little figure of the soul-musician is introduced as one of those metaphors the thinker must be allowed, in part because of the figure's other resonances. The image of the little musical homunculus is consistent with "evolutionary" explanations of life in the eighteenth-century sense of "evolution," meaning that life forms germinate from a condition of "pre-formation" that contains all their properties in miniature. But the image is even more closely connected to another contemporary representation of the life force: the moving, if not walking, humanoid machines that Vaucanson called "moving anatomies."

THE MUSICAL ANDROIDS

These automata, or androids as they were called even at the time, were widely known and admired. Five of them became especially famous, and of these three were musicians. The other two were a writer and a draftsman. This distribution of roles suggests that for an automaton to simulate human life in the eighteenth century it was necessary for the figure to replicate a process of signification or expression. The fact that music took pride of place among these processes suggests that the figure's behavior had to demonstrate both nervous and muscular energy, in other words, both sensibility and irritability. That demand, in turn, meant that the musical androids were required not merely to reproduce music in the manner of a music box, but actually to perform the music as a human player would.

The first of the musical androids met all of these criteria. Vaucanson's flute player created a sensation when it was put on public view in 1738 after first being presented to the French academy. The Academy was no less impressed by Vaucanson's artificial life forms than the public. So was Voltaire, who, anticipating Mary Shelley's description of Victor Frankenstein, called Vaucanson "a rival to Prometheus [who] seemed to steal the heavenly fire to animate bodies."[20] The source of this admiration was a life-sized figure dressed in pastoral costume, his flute held to his lips, and seated on a large pedestal concealing the clockwork mechanism inside. It—he?—could actually play the flute. The spectator could see the figure's fingers move, watch him as he breathed into the instrument, and hear him perform any of twelve different melodies. If the flute player was not actually alive, his demonstration of both sensibility and irritability showed him to be the next best thing.

The other celebrated musical automata were an organ player and a dulcimer player, both female figures in courtly dress, and built on a smaller scale than the flute player, although the organist was still in a sense life-sized, since she is a girl rather than a woman.[21] Unlike Vaucanson's, these automata still exist, and they still work. The organist was built between 1768 and 1774 by members of the Jacquet-Droz family, Swiss jewelers whose firm is still in business; the writer and draftsman are also Jacquet-Droz automata. The dulcimer player was constructed by the clockmaker Peter Kintzing and the cabinet-maker David Roentgen in 1784; it was bought by Marie Antoinette in 1785 and presented shortly afterward to the Academy of Sciences. Like Vaucanson's flute player, the dulcimer player had a repertoire; she could play eight melodies. But what was most important about her in relation to the simulation of life is that while she played her head turned and her eyes moved, so that the motion of her arms, simulating muscular action, was accompanied by evidence of sensibility. The Jacquet-Droz organist was similarly designed, and was more lifelike than the dulcimer player in one respect: like Vaucanson's flute player, the Jacquet-Droz organist breathes.

The combination of sensibility and irritability in these androids gave them a status somewhere between a machine and a life form, something for which the era had no effective vocabulary. The same combination carried over to music when music coupled subjectivity, universally understood at the time as the expression of feeling, with the projection of imaginary bodies. The possibility of this coupling depends above all on quantity, the variation of intensity that has acted as a leitmotif in this chapter. We will shortly sample the operation of shifting intensities in Haydn and Beethoven, but before doing so we need to say a little more about the scientific basis of the process.

The primary question driving eighteenth-century theories of life was whether life could be explained as the product of purely physical mechanism or whether an additional factor, some identifiable version of the ancient idea of a life force, was necessary. In general, the trend favored the vitalists over the mechanists, but by the end of the century the argument was effectively made obsolete by the discovery that nerve impulses were carried by electricity. The distinction between sensibility and irritability nonetheless survived this change, and the association of the primary vital powers with electricity even enhanced the metaphorical identity between the life force and power in its most naked form. The ebb and flow of intensity could stand as both a synonym and a symbol of life.

The interplay of sensibility and irritability gave this fluctuation its specific form. For vitalists such as Bordeu, sensibility was primary; the power to feel was vested in the nerves and formed a controlling center for the other vital functions, each of which had its own independent life. But among those functions irritability stood out, and for Bordeu's chief rival, Albrecht von Haller, the principles of sensibility and irritability were equally primary and life emerged as the functional product of their combination, or, in other words, of the interplay of feeling and action. As Haller developed his model, however, he gradually came to the conclusion that the distinction between sensibility and irritability was porous—a conclusion driven in part by his own discovery that only organs supplied with nerves were capable of feeling.[22] Feeling and action could not be disjoined. The muscles and nerves together were both the vehicles and the objects of the general flow of force that constituted life. The emergence of drive in relation to the composition of life is thus implicit throughout the era—and the same thing applies to the composition of music.

Nonscientists were quick to take up the ideas of Haller and others and to apply them to other areas of concern, music included. Gottfried von Herder was a notable example. He had a strong interest in physiological science and frequently applied its findings to his own subjective life. He had studied Haller's *Physiological Elements of the Human Body* (1757–1766), and in *Kalligone,* an essay on aesthetics published in 1800, Herder showed it. The passage is a Diderot-like dialogue between A and B:

A. A blow disturbs a body; what message does that body's sound communicate?
B. "I have been disturbed; my members are consequently vibrating and eventually coming to rest."
A. Is that what they say to us?
B. Every fiber of our being is capable of responding; our ear, the hearing-chamber of the soul, is ... an echo-chamber of the finest kind. ...
A. What about sounds that get louder or softer, faster or slower, sounds that rise and fall, are increasingly or decreasingly intense? ...
B. As every involuntary reaction to music proves, these all produce similar responses. The tide of our passions ebbs and flows. ... At one moment the passions are intensified, at another they are aroused now gently, now powerfully. ... [T]he way they move varies in response to every melodic nuance, and every forceful accent. ... Music performs on the clavichord within us that is our inmost being.[23]

Herder begins with irritability and passes smoothly to sensibility through the medium of music—not just sound, but music, performed in the concert hall of the ear and on the keyboard of the self. (Herder could not have known Diderot's similar image, which makes this appearance of the sentient keyboard all the more, well, striking.) The blow with which Herder's account begins is the conceptual equivalent of Haydn's "surprise" chord. The element of violence that the blow introduces stems from the discourse on irritability, and the link may be one reason why some of the most prominent musical experiments with life processes come in agitated, minor-key movements. That is the case with the two examples to which we will now turn.

EXCITATION AT THE KEYBOARD: HAYDN

Haydn's Keyboard Sonata in C Minor (Hob. XVI: 20), published in 1780 but probably composed around 1772, is the first of Haydn's sonatas to call for frequent sharp contrasts between *forte* and *piano,* an indication that the

EXAMPLE 2. Haydn, Piano Sonata no. 33 in C Minor, mm. 9–14.

instrument it was conceived for was, precisely, the fortepiano, not the harpsichord, and that the kind of shifting intensity celebrated by Herder thirty years later was the order of the day. (See example 2.) Such shifting is close to the music's only law. It drives everything from *forte* and *piano* attacks on alternating single notes to large-scale scrambling of the order of events as one section follows another. But three of the music's features seem especially close to the play of irritability and sensibility: its percussive opening; a subsequent exchange of right- and left-hand triplets broken by a written-out cadenza; and a later outbreak of triplets combined with percussive jolts.

The movement begins with a pungent melodic figure in dotted rhythm set against off-beat broken octaves in the bass. If muscular irritation gives rise to movement, as Haller showed that it does, this combination would be a good candidate for how that process might sound if it were audible. At this point, though, the combination is primarily a point of departure; it is only one measure long and we hear it only twice, at the head of the opening two phrases. But it will be back.

Meanwhile the exposition goes its impulsive way.[24] At about its midpoint, the movement settles on the dominant of its secondary key, E flat. For the first two of three measures, the right hand sounds a long note followed by a flurry of rapid triplets. The left hand responds in the last two of the three measures by putting its own triplet flurries under the right hand's long note and its own long note under the right hand's triplets. The first time in the right hand alone, and then passing from hand to hand, the animating succession repeats: a blow followed by motion. The process begins *forte* but falls to *piano* with the left-hand triplets in the third measure. At that point Haydn gives the right hand a brief cadenza where its triplets should have been: an unmeasured Adagio written out in small notes, with no accompaniment except for a ghost of one tied over in the left hand. (There is no real bass here, except in a purely formal sense; the whole passage takes place in the middle and upper registers.) The music goes from loud to soft, from fast to slow, and from agitation to a pathos marked by wide melodic leaps. Like Herder, Haydn moves from irritability to sensibility, though with urgency rather than latent violence.

The recapitulation brings this succession back, but most of the movement once past the exposition is a rain of blows, an exercise in unremitting drive. The end of the exposition concedes as much. With the left hand playing a continuous stream of triplets, the right plays a series of rapid little descending figures ending with heavy staccato jolts. The first few jolting figures sound *piano,* separated by rests, but with a turn to *forte* they become continuous, so that the jolts occur on each successive beat. This rise in intensity sets its stamp on the whole movement. The spaced form of the jolts and triplets, now played *forte,* figures prominently in the development.

Intensity rises further when the development begins with the movement's opening figure and its clashing octaves. The figure almost immediately appears upside down, with the octaves in the right hand, and then, flipping itself upright, quickly returns to reassert itself—octaves included—at more than double its original length.

But the combination is not done. When it returns again to begin the recapitulation there is no return to its original one-measure sequel. Instead the figure and its octaves intensify still further. Again they more than double in length, this time in inverted form with the octaves rising in the right hand to magnify their effect. But then, their effect just *is* a magnification. There is little qualitative change here but the quantitative change is decisive. Sensibility may yet return, the Adagio sound again—these things will happen—but the music will be driven onward until, as if exhausted by a final bout of jolting figures with triplets, it suddenly dies away.

EXCITATION AT THE KEYBOARD: BEETHOVEN

Beethoven follows a similar trajectory in the first movement of his Piano Sonata no. 5, op. 10, no. 1, composed in 1796 and, like Haydn's, written in

EXAMPLE 3. Beethoven, Piano Sonata no. 5 in C Minor, op. 10, no. 1, opening.

C Minor. But Beethoven incorporates the violence that Haydn avoids, or, if you prefer, makes explicit the violence that Haydn leaves latent. But this is not so much a dramatic violence as it is the acknowledgment of a physiological principle—though of course these categories do not exclude each other. The music begins with a loud, solitary chord, the kind of noisy shock that Haydn reserved to demolish his pretty little tune in the "Surprise" Symphony. (See example 3.) After this things go from bad to worse, but they do so in a certain determined way. The music sounds as if—and keep this *as if* in mind—it were making a demonstration of the first exchange between A and B in the dialogue from *Kalligone:* "A. A blow disturbs a body; what message does that body's sound communicate? B. I have been disturbed; my members are consequently vibrating and eventually coming to rest." For vibrate the members do, then come to rest—but the blow strikes again; the vibrations resume, they take on new forms and come to rest more slowly, they almost settle down, and then comes another blow, and another, and then another. It seems as if every decrease in intensity were simply creating the potential for an increase, and a sharp one. Drive wants to go into overdrive; a surplus of life force threatens to turn destructive. And only thirty measures have gone by.

At this point Beethoven writes out a grand pause, which I will take advantage of to reflect for a moment on what has just been said.

We do not yet have an effective common language to describe the kind of relationship that this music, as understood here, has to the habits of mind, experience, and observation that surround it. It is easier to say what that relationship is *not;* and the same holds for Haydn. The music does not depict life processes in Enlightenment terms, nor does it signify them, nor does it imitate them. Instead it acts like the era's androids, only with an imaginary rather than a material body: the music makes a demonstration by acting as if it were alive, or, more exactly, as if it were a distillation or sensory realization of the life force as the era understood it. This *as if* is neither exhaustive nor exclusive, but once set into motion it is, or should be, hard to ignore. It should have the force of what I have elsewhere called a constructive description, a statement that alters and expands the possibility of perception by attaching itself firmly to the thing it describes.[25] As we know from the language of Herder, Diderot, Hume, and others, actual descriptions of the sort circulated regularly. The era's understanding of life affected music in part because the era's music affected its understanding of life.

But back to Beethoven. After the pause comes a long period of lyrical rest leading by slow degrees to the secondary key of E flat, and with it a broad, flowing, confident theme. It is as if the music were trying to settle into a normal rhythm of excitation and repose; the new theme is exactly the kind that ought to have appeared first in a normal sonata movement, assuming there is such a thing, rather than turning up displaced in both position and key. The theme offers us the opportunity to hear it against the backdrop of its physiological basis, and more especially against the potential collapse of that basis. Just past the threshold of audibility lies an abyss of pure drive. The conditions for this or any music to present itself as an untroubled source of pleasure and well-being are not easy to maintain, and we can literally hear as much even while enjoying the vigor and sweep of the melody. It should come as no surprise when more blows rain down near the end of the exposition in quick succession.

Like Haydn, Beethoven begins the development section by recalling and extending the fraught opening measures; unlike Haydn, he begins the recapitulation by lowering the level of intensity. He allows the initial vibrations to come to rest, omitting the long series of blows and vibrations that precede the grand pause. If a kind of everyday normality has been the goal, we can plausibly entertain the idea that the music has reached it here. But Beethoven puts that conclusion in doubt by rewriting the rapid series of blows that returns just before the end of the movement. These blows are separated by very brief "vibrations," agitated rising figures in dotted rhythm lasting just one beat. In the exposition, the vibrations find no rest between blows but at least they find a common level of unrest. The first three of them land on the same *sforzando* note, itself another blow, before the fourth thrusts up by a third (mm. 86–90). In the recapitulation the equivalent series does more than just fail to settle down; it intensifies (mm. 263–267). The common level vanishes. The vibrations land on a series of *sforzando* blows that rise by degrees before recoiling: F#-G-A♮-G. In the exposition, the notes involved belong to the tonic triad; in the recapitulation the first and third notes are dissonant outliers. Like Haydn, though not in the same place, Beethoven adds nothing substantial but intensity. Qualitative change is minimal; quantitative change takes over. The intensity may subside in the subsequent closing passage, but it still seethes, as we learn soon enough when a sudden *fortissimo* cadence ends the movement—almost. The actual end is a prolonged silence.

The subject of modernity typically encounters the force of drive in forbidden but desired extremes of pleasure and pain, set at equal removes from the disciplines of everyday life. "Everyday life" is itself a concept of modernity; in traditional society the only difference between "life" and "everyday life" was the cycle of rituals and festivities that organized the year. The modern everyday world is a space from which drive has been, or ought to have been, excluded. The everyday thus becomes both a safe haven and a boring trap, normal and inauthentic at the same time. The modern entertainment industry developed in part to provide fantasies of escape from what Wallace Stevens called "the malady of the quotidian," to which, however, the satisfied customer returns with strict punctuality.[26] What Adorno called the culture industry is based on the impossible domestication of drive—a fantasy in its own right, but a timid one.

This modern tension between drive and the everyday, a tension that helps define the condition of modernity itself, has had difficult consequences. Consider the distinctly modern history of self-affirmation by self-destructiveness, something unique to the post-Enlightenment era. If Michel Foucault is right that social regulation in this era manifests itself through "bio-power," the management of life rather than the punishment of death, then to be healthy, wise, and good is to become something less than an individual.[27] The only way to resist the power exerted on one, to find identity beyond ideology (though that is of course impossible), is to invent what Freud would call the death drive, to make oneself sick, foolish, and wicked. Better death, in Gilles Deleuze's words, than the health one is given.[28]

Beethoven's Sonata no. 10 anticipates a drive toward that conclusion that runs through a pair of more famous sonatas and rings out in the hammer-blow climaxes of their finales. The "Moonlight" and "Appassionata" Sonatas mark epochs in the aesthetic presentation of drive, the first in its release of unfettered vehemence, the second in its rush to an unfettered tragic denouement, perhaps already to Deleuze's version of the death drive. The "Moonlight" finale especially draws its still-undiminished power from a simulation of life in its raw state, life as if on the threshold of its human embodiment. The movement turns the slow, absorbing bass arpeggios of the first movement (an ebb and flow of sensibility that becomes articulate in the upper voice, but barely so) into a swift, pervasive vibration. This virtual nervous excitation reaches into every register and at times produces a cacophonous jangle that pushes the fortepiano for which the music was written past the limit of sound into felt vibration; even a modern concert grand succumbs a little. The movement's main theme wrestles the flood of impulse into articulation, but never for very long, leaving its resounding hammer blows, like their later counterparts in the "Appassionata," to assert the sheer force of action against the sheer force of suffering (in both senses of the term, receptive sensation and the sensation of pain). At the moments of peak intensity the fortepiano itself acts—cries out—like a living creature shaking with the force of its own sensations.

The music thus becomes a sustained simulation of the two fundamental elements of the life force as its own era had come to understand it over the course of the preceding century. And it is perhaps no accident that the music involved is for solo piano: music in which the instrument becomes an acoustic mirror of the performer's individual—mortal—life.

"A BLOW DISTURBS A BODY"

The piano decidedly plays that role in Michael Haneke's film *Amour* (2012), which I mention here to suggest that the problems of sensibility and irritability first posed musically at the close of the eighteenth century are still pertinent today, not least because they are still unresolved. The narrative begins in a concert hall, shot from the point of view of the stage. We see only the audience as it assembles and we do not know what kind of performance is about to start. Then we hear a sudden loud octave on the piano—a musical blow like the one in Beethoven's sonata, another Haydn-like surprise displaced to the point of departure. The music is Schubert's Impromptu no. 1 in C Minor, op. 90, which confronts its initiating moment of raw life force with a contrary expression of sensibility in the form of a funeral march. In so doing, the music provides, in advance, a condensed version of the film's narrative. The narrative traces the consequences of a blow to the body, a paralytic stroke, which destroys the body it irritates and leads inexorably to an act—perhaps euthanasia, perhaps murder; it is impossible to tell—that might well take Deleuze's maxim as its own: better death than the health one is given. At the same time the film associates this music with the intuition of a persistent substrate of vital force, an unextinguished and perhaps inextinguishable sensibility, in Bordeu's sense of the term, which the narrative of paralysis cannot quite overcome. The first thing we see in the film, before the title sequence, is a violent breakthrough into a closed apartment, the narrative equivalent of the forceful octave. The film, like the music, begins with a blow that breaks a seal.

A lot is at stake in that blow. One might argue that modernity has often sought to realign the human subject with the presymbolic substrate of things—a now secular substrate that in premodern culture was uniquely controlled and regulated by the categories of the sacred. The world of the subject has an underlying pulse, a Great Beneath as opaque as the subject itself but nonetheless, to echo Menuret, something that the able observer strives to grasp—above all, perhaps, to hear.

In the later eighteenth century music became the chief way to hear it. It did so in part by making a demonstration of life. Music helped establish intensity of feeling as an aesthetic good. It did so by making intensification a compositional principle—a principle still in effect, though no longer as universal as it once was. The spirit of defiant life is already perceptible, literally audible, in our C-minor sonata movements by Haydn and Beethoven, and so, especially in the Beethoven, is the temptation to let drive go to its unknown limit. The aesthetic of this music, and much of the music to follow, incorporates the ever-present possibility of *inflicting* pleasure as a sign of life.

TWO

From Clockwork to Pulsation II

ACTION AND FEELING

NEARLY ALL OF THE METAPHORS we have been following depend on making a musical instrument the visible equivalent to an invisible bodily process. Eighteenth-century medicine had no way other than listening for Menuret's "varieties of the pulse" to make such a process directly observable. The first real step in that direction came early in the nineteenth century with the invention of the stethoscope, which made internal processes audible with startling clarity.[1] The imaginary music of the body turned out to have real sonorities.

But how did it get them? The transition between inanimate and animate bodies remained mysterious, spurring the debates between vitalists and mechanists touched on in chapter 1. The simulated life of androids represented one way to address the question; simulated life in music represented another. In a narrow sense, the musical simulations have a limited presence in the canonical repertoire of the period. There are several celebrated examples; we will consider them. But the attitude supporting this handful of explicit musical experiments has wider reverberations, and we will consider those too.

THE MUSICAL BODY

Musical thought has been much concerned with the body in recent years.[2] There has been a growing realization that for much of the past two centuries, the conception of music as art went hand in hand with a denial of its corporeality, despite the fact that until the advent of digital technology all musical sounds originated in the movement of the hands, feet, arms, torso, mouth, throat, and lungs.³ But it is not enough simply to assert the body's rights and dignities while de-idealizing the abstract musical artwork, valuable though these things are. As so often with music, its relation to embodiment rests on fundamental ambiguities that can never be more than temporarily and uncertainly resolved. The most fundamental of these, testified to repeatedly throughout history, is the contradiction between music's call to release social constraints on the body's motion, sensation, and desire, and its call to limit that release by submitting it to the constraints of form.

Music and the body have commonly been linked by a sensation of life independent of any sublimating idea. The sensation is both a bodily state and a trope. In *Interpreting Music* I discuss at some length a particularly striking example from the neurologist, author, and music-lover Oliver Sacks. Sacks first observed the alliance of music and the sensation of life in the partial recovery of the encephalitis victims whose history he recounts in *Awakenings*. But the issue became personal in his own recovery from a mountainside accident that had "extinguished" one of his legs. The injury he suffered wiped out all feeling in the leg except for the impression, a kind of antisensation, that the leg was dead, a carrion appendage. In *A Leg to Stand On,* Sacks says that when feeling finally broke through the deadness, the "decisive" factor in its emergence was the Mendelssohn Violin Concerto: "I felt, with the first bars of the music, . . . as if the animating and creative principle of the whole world was revealed, that life itself was music, or consubstantial with music; that our living moving flesh, itself, was 'solid' music."⁴

Sacks does not go into musical detail (he seems to have a purely emotive view of music), but the connection between the revival of his leg and the Mendelssohn concerto becomes quite literal at the crucial moment of his recovery: "an abrupt and absolute leap from . . . awkward, artificial, mechanical walking . . . to an unconscious, natural-graceful musical movement." The "unconscious rhythm and melody" of walking came back to him only when it was "attuned" to the rhythm and melody of the Mendelssohn in his mind's ear.⁵

Sacks's account eloquently records a common experience more often expressed with epithets, gestures, and nonverbal vocalizations, an experience known to everyone who has ever shimmied along or tapped a finger or toe to the sound of music: something comes alive when you hear it. Music is disembodied life continually reembodied in whoever hears it fully. This is a matter not of signification or semiotics but of ontology. It is not a matter of what music means (and it means plenty) but of what music *is*. A visual parallel develops with the moving image if it is right to say, with Gertrud Koch, that cinema's primary "reality effect" is to "make life and ban death."[6] The moving images of cinema come almost to life by overcoming the deathly effect of the still photograph and, more broadly, of the still image that not only stands motionless but also arrests motion when it captures the gaze. But the parallel with music is imperfect in a way that will concern us in chapter 6. Although music without moving images seems naturally animate, moving images need sound, especially music, to avoid seeming uncanny or mechanical. Music *and music alone* is disembodied life continually reembodied in whoever hears it fully.

In some cases, this principle takes hold not only in what music is but also in what it "says" it is. Some music reflects on its own condition as a source of animation. Some music embodies its own relationship to embodiment. In what follows I would like to look further into this practice in the genre—classical instrumental music—that gave birth to it in the later eighteenth century. How does this music give itself a body? How does it come to inhabit and sense that body? What problems does its embodiment pose, what limits does it confront, and what possibilities does it open—or close?

To date there has been no generally accepted procedure to ask these questions, let alone to answer them. There is no theory of the musical body. In lieu of one, I will concentrate here on the implicit body images projected by the performance of instrumental music.

For virtually no musical event can avoid projecting an imaginary body. The wide variety of such images may perhaps be most readily conceived along a continuum between the two modalities of embodiment identified by Mikhail Bakhtin as the "classical" and the "grotesque."[7] The classical body, associated with social order and top-down authority, is a closed, smooth, idealized whole. The grotesque body, the body of popular disorder and European carnival, is an open, rough, visceral jumble of parts. The classical body is sculptural; the grotesque is vital. For working principles, I will assume that all such body images are historically bounded, that they are inevitably figurative, and that they find expression in concrete musical events. Before going forward, however, two cautions are necessary: two points of method.

First, the elements involved in constructing the musical body image have at best a limited semiotic value. They do not need to be invoked overtly, they do not all work at the same time with the same import, they may not always be distinct from each other, and they do not come close to determining what the body image they support may mean.

Second, the effect of music's bodily immediacy can never escape mediation. One might make the same claim of bodily immediacy in general, but that is for another day. Whatever an eventual theory of musical embodiment may propose, it cannot depend on an opposition between embodiment and meaning or on any notion that the corporeal and material are noncognitive and nonfigurative. Such oppositions may occur or not in any given case. They do *not* occur in principle.

To confirm the point, and take it as a point of departure, consider once again the slow movement of Haydn's "Surprise" Symphony. As in the last chapter, the discussion in this one will start with Daniel Chua's recognition that the movement's famous surprise—which is still effective, something we should not take for granted—turns on its era's concern with the relationship between mechanism and animation.[8]

Chua traces what he takes to be a reversal of the relationship between instrumental music and the body across the span of the eighteenth century. The starting point is the vexed Cartesian opposition between mind and body, which for Chua translates musically into a common perception that music unauthorized by the voice is mechanical and soulless. The midpoint is occupied by the slow development of organic conceptions of the mind-body relationship. These conceptions derive from the beginnings of biological science and they deny the sufficiency of mechanical explanations for bodily life. That denial leads to the endpoint, which affirms the animation of body by spirit and, as Chua argues, translates musically into the establishment of instrumental music as the sign or vehicle of the very soul it was initially thought to lack. Chua's account leads him to some interesting further remarks about the surprise:

> By the late eighteenth century instrumental music had developed the ability to distinguish between the living and the dead.... It managed to have the last laugh at an old ideology that had brandished it as a "mechanical doll." It depicted such tick-tocking machines as something to be tinkered with [and] ... sometimes it even smashed the mechanism to pieces, as with the unexpected hammer-blows in Haydn's "Surprise" Symphony. The surprise ... is in the human hand that comes to tamper with the self-wound motions that the music signifies with its clockwork tune. Conscious life had seeped into the score, and the mechanical was merely a play of signs for the organic.[9]

Just so; but Chua stops there. He does not comment on what happens after the big surprise, nor does he mention that the surprise comes, not at the end of the theme, but at the end of the theme's first half. We need to go further, though we are certainly off to a good start.

The surprise in the "Surprise" Symphony announces the claims of animation with a bang. As noted in chapter 1, Haydn himself simply said that he wanted to do something new, but the categories of mechanism and vitalism may help to explain both his sense of novelty and the particular form that the novelty could plausibly take. To carry this thought further—and to see it as the thought *of* the music, not just our thought *about* the music—we need to go into more detail than we did before.

As we know, the "surprise" movement is a set of variations in which, typically for Haydn, the theme reappears in each segment; the variation comes from changes in orchestration, articulation, and ornamentation. But the theme in this case is distinctive, and doubly so. First, it resembles the French folk tune "Ah, vous dirai-je maman," on which Mozart wrote a set of variations for piano and which is almost universally known in English by its nursery-rhyme title, "Twinkle, Twinkle, Little Star." That would perhaps not be very remarkable in itself, but it becomes so here because, second, the theme is presented with ostentatious simplicity.[10] The texture is tissue-thin and there is virtually no accompaniment; the violins play the melody in a light staccato, eventually supplemented by pizzicato, while the other strings add light punctuation on the downbeats. The rest of the orchestra is silent. Clockwork indeed; the melody says in all but words, "I am a music box." Or rather, that is what the first half says; the second half says something different—we will come to that.

Meanwhile, what does the loud chord say? The first time I ever heard it, the chord came as a relief. The occasion was a high school class, back in the days when high schools in America, at least in New York City, still taught classical music. I remember thinking that the opening tune was mincing and insipid, so it was gratifying when the orchestra pounced. I said to myself something like, "Ah, he doesn't really mean it!" The moment sounded like a rejection of social complacency, and it still does. But it sounds like something more if we ask exactly what we hear when the orchestra pounces. For one thing, we hear the weight of the orchestral mass, solidly grounded by the brass and timpani; we hear the bodily dimension of the sound, which elicits a sympathetic resonance in our own bodies. But more particularly we hear two kinds of sound production linked to the vital functions of the body. The instruments that enter with the surprise chord are the full complement of woodwinds plus horns and trumpets on the one hand, and the timpani on the other. This impromptu band makes its big noise by blowing and striking. It forces air through an open body cavity and causes an enclosed body cavity to resonate. The music jolts violently to life like a subject in a galvanic experiment.

This might as well be music by Breughel. It sounds something like the way Breughel's *The Kermess* looks, with its squealing bagpipes and thumping dance steps, memorably evoked by William Carlos Williams:

> the dancers go round, they go round and
> around, the squeal and the blare and the
> tweedle of bagpipes, a bugle and fiddles
> tipping their bellies . . . Kicking and rolling
> about the Fair Grounds, swinging their butts, those
> shanks must be sound to bear up under such
> rollicking measures.[11]

One body part involves another. The music, like the painting (and later the poem), affirms the crude grandeur of the grotesque body. Haydn's lack of transition even resembles Williams's lack of syntax. But the antagonist of the musical outburst is not primarily the static and rounded classical body and the social hierarchy associated with it. The antagonist is the lifelessness of mere mechanism. Not that the mechanism is other than social; it is even a metaphor of the social. But it is also a phenomenon in its own right that the orchestra blows out and pounds down.

Or so it seems at first; the full import of conjoining the clockwork and the uproar is yet to come. But at this point we can surely hear, or rather we can't help hearing, that life has entered the scene. This life is not so much conscious—the conscious irony lies *behind* the scene—as it is merely sentient. The awareness it suggests is the awareness of its own being alive, which it marks, as so many living bodies do, by making a sound. And in this case the sound should be ugly, raucous; it is best realized on natural trumpets and timpani with skins, the instruments for which it was written, and which give the sound a rawness that modern instruments refine away.

The remainder of the movement aims to sublimate the outburst of life and to reconceive its relationship to mechanism. Before we consider that effort, however, we need to examine further the parallel, introduced in chapter 1, between music of this kind and the era's premier android. As we know, in 1738, the French inventor Jacques de Vaucanson exhibited his life-sized flute player to the French Academy. The figure was modeled on a statue that then stood at the entrance to the Tuileries gardens: a seated musician costumed as a satyr and known as *Shepherd Playing the Flute*. The choice of model is evocative. The shepherd connotes closeness to nature and innocent vitality; the satyr adds a rough touch of the grotesque body. Music serves as a measure of both.

But Vaucanson's "statue" was half-alive. The impulse to build such animated figures stemmed in part from the tradition of musical clocks and mechanical birds, but in part from our train of metaphors and the widespread perception of an intimate connection between music and the body. The android virtually had to be a musician, but it could not be just a mechanical imitation of one. The artificial man was not simply the cover for a music box; it was, to anticipate Victor Frankenstein's dream, the first member of a new species of "happy and excellent nature" Its genuine ability to play the flute, to play more than just one tune, and to move its lips and tongue while doing it, was necessary if the machine was to exceed its mechanism without ceasing to be mechanical. Simulation had to approach emulation. As one contemporary explained, "The infinity of wires and steel chains [inside] ... form the movement of the fingers, in the same way as in a living man, by the dilations and contraction of the muscles."[12]

In this connection it was essential not to disguise the relationship between mechanism and life but to emphasize their conjunction. Vaucanson himself did just that in the elaborate technical report he submitted to the Academy in 1738 along with the flute player. The aim of creating the android was to make the boundary between life and mechanism waver, so as to investigate where, if anywhere, mechanism crossed over into life and what happened if it did.

THE MECHANICS OF MUSIC: SPACED TEXTURE

Later in 1738, Vaucanson won further acclaim when he exhibited the flute player publicly, this time together with two other automata: a second life-sized android that played a tabor and a duck that simulated the process of digestion. The duck, which will return in the next chapter, actually became the most famous of the three artificial life forms, but for the present it is the human figures that command our attention. One blew, the other struck. The evidences of artificial life were precisely those that Haydn, at the end of the century, built into his raucous "surprise" chord, and with the same kinds of instrument: wind and percussion, extensions of lungs and the hand. Breathe; beat; live.

A broader affinity lies in the principle that life and mechanism should appear together, as if superimposed on each other. During the second part of the century, European composers devised a way to make such a superimposition possible musically. I propose to call this device *spaced texture*. It consists of a pattern of rhythmically regular attacks in moderate tempo, usually in simple time, usually but not always staccato, with a clear separation between one attack and another.

The opening of Haydn's "Surprise" movement is a prime example. It soon demonstrates that spaced texture can both stand on its own and form an accompaniment for flowing legato melody—for Haydn's movement will use it that way too. The device is not, of course, confined to any single meaning, and in diffuse forms it has great metaphorical flexibility, but it did provide a very effective means to raise the question of mechanism and organism in music. The essential thing about it is the spacing itself, the regular pattern of silences that it brings to the fore.

Spaced texture gives the space between its notes the status of a virtual extra note—a silent thirteenth tone that allows the music to give audible form to the interaction of mechanism and animation. A change in musical alphabet produces a change in the character of experience, musical and otherwise. The metaphor of alphabetic change is not causal here. The space of spaced texture is analogous to the mute twenty-seventh letter of the English alphabet hypothesized—or, according to Lydia Liu, discovered—by Claude Shannon in the part of information theory that grounds the possibility of digital processing.[13] Here too a silent extra becomes an essential component in a previously unknown, even unimaginable, mode of experience. And nothing could be simpler.

To return to the course of the variations: the process of sublimation and integration begins with the second half of the theme. In other words it begins right after the surprise. As heard initially, the second half returns to the string band and incorporates touches of flowing melody over the spaced texture. Upon restatement, it adds winds and horn, with the melody carried on the lyrical voice of a single flute with support from the oboe.

The first variation takes the next step. It begins with another loud chord over a timpani stroke, continues with the combination of spaced texture and flowing melody, and again—this time during the first half of the theme—transfers the melody to a single flute, this time playing solo. The music thus follows the protocol of the eighteenth-century android as set by Vaucanson's flute player. It conjoins life and mechanism rather than separating them and it draws on the flute, resonant with pastoral connotations, to signal the awakening of life.

The succeeding variations create a higher-order pendulum swing or pulsation between mechanism and organism, which grow further apart in order to draw closer together. The first half of variation 2 is all spaced texture. The string mechanism that started the movement goes haywire here. First it shifts to the minor mode and hammers out the theme in loud octaves. Then it turns to the relative major and quietly runs three different clockworks simultaneously before reining them in. Mechanism reaches its apex in this segment, which is the last one in the movement to be repeated literally. The second half of the variation leaps to the opposite extreme. It is all resurgent life: life at a roar, sounded by the full orchestra with rough trumpet-and-drum strokes fully incorporated.

This segment is extended rather than restated. It ends with yet another loud chord, supported by timpani, and segues into a quiet transitional passage for unaccompanied violin. The violin traces a descending line, in the course of which it turns back from legato melody to spaced texture. What follows is a process of transformation that allows us to hear life emerging from the chrysalis of mechanism. Initially, the first half of variation 3 transfers the melodic mechanism to a solo oboe, which sounds the theme in diminution against a backdrop of ticking strings. The texture suggests both uncertainty and potentiality; the oboe both conforms to the mechanism and stirs it up.

The uncertainty is resolved as the potentiality is realized. Both the restatement of this first half and the initial statement of the second half restore the spaced texture to the violins under melodic elaborations on the winds, now once more under the auspices of the flute. The lower strings remain silent during these passages, so that the spaced texture now sounds delicate. The melody grows increasingly florid, a process that continues throughout the restatement of the second half. Mechanical regularity has seamlessly become enhanced continuity, both within this variation and across the span of the movement so far. And with these transformations there comes another, as the grotesque body of the initial surprise is elevated into a classical smoothness, or at least into the quasi-Arcadian vigor of Vaucanson's flute player.

The final variation celebrates this outcome by triumphantly bringing all of its elements together. But the variation ends on a dominant-leaning chord prolonged under a fermata, which in normal classical practice—though not in a symphony!—would signal a cadenza. And a cadenza, being improvised, would be a strong sign that life was fully informing this music: machines do not improvise. But there is, of course, no cadenza, and the ensuing coda is touched by ambiguity. The theme now sounds softly on the lower winds against sustained, faintly mysterious harmonies on the strings and horns. The reversal of texture is transformative. The effect is as if the principle of mechanism itself had briefly come alive, if only to mark its departure. One of the flutes detaches itself to drop off-beat notes into the texture like little gasps from above while the timpani sustain a soft pulsation below. But the last few measures are all spaced texture and nothing more. The end is not a period, but a question mark.

The question derives from the spaced texture, or rather from the tradition of thought that makes it possible. At this point we need to turn for a while from classical music to classical deconstruction. In *Of Grammatology* Jacques Derrida identifies what he takes to be a bias in previous Western thought in favor of unbroken presence and continuity, whether in meaning, consciousness, or the subject, and whether in the world of phenomena or in its transcendental envelopes.[14] In part because the tradition often identifies presence with the immediacy of spoken language, Derrida identifies the breaching of such presence with writing, sometimes with literal writing in mind, and sometimes with a general movement of breaching and externality that he calls, among other things, arche-writing. The two modes of writing can be neither distinguished firmly nor securely equated to each other.

One of the chief properties of writing in both senses is what Derrida calls "spacing," referring to the gaps and absences necessary to make articulation possible: think of the white spaces between letters, the larger spaces between words, the spaces at the end of paragraphs, and the marginal spaces that frame the page. Implicit in such spacing, and always ready to widen the breach, is the working of something inanimate. Derrida simply calls it death, but nonlife might be a better term; spacing belongs to the mechanism of writing. Either way, Derrida writes that "Spacing is always the unperceived, the nonpresent, and the nonconscious. . . . It marks the *dead time* within the presence of the living present, within the general form of all presence." A little later he adds that "Spacing as writing is the becoming-absent . . . of the subject. . . . As the subject's relationship with its own death, this becoming is the constitution of subjectivity. On all levels of life's organization, that is to say, *of the economy of death*."[15]

Depending on how it is used, the spaced texture of classical, that is, Enlightenment, music forms a potent simulation of that economy. Before the mid-eighteenth century, music in general abhorred a vacuum. If it learned to do otherwise thereafter, the era's preoccupation with the basis of life, together with the vexed relationship between mechanism and organism, was probably one reason why. Especially as the connections between music, feeling, and subjective inwardness grew ever closer and more complex, the threat of the subject's becoming absent in the very medium that was supposed to make it more present constituted a frontier that the more experimental of the composers confronted by it felt compelled to explore.

PULSE: BORDEU AND MOZART

One way to counter the "economy of death" latent in spaced texture was to oppose spacing, not with the continuity of melody, but with the regularity of pulse—a regularity that not only showed life but also required its presence. Both spacing and pulse are measured, but spacing is mechanical whereas pulse is vital. (That does not mean it is always possible to tell the difference between them.) The term "pulse" in this context had a much wider reference than the same term does today. Its chief theorist was Diderot's friend Theophile Bordeu, whose work was the basis of Menuret's article on "Pulse" in the *Encyclopedia*. For Bordeu the human body was nothing less than a resonating space of pulses, with each organ contributing its own rhythm through the excitation of the nerves. The source of this excitation was sensibility, the capacity to feel that was widely taken as the principal criterion of human and animal life. Sensibility in general consisted in the ensemble of the organs' sensibilities, and pulsation, in its multiplicity, was the sign of sensible life. Every site of sensibility had its own pulse; life and pulsation were coextensive. As Bordeu explained:

> The movements of the pulse depend undoubtedly on the *sensibility* of the nerves in the heart and arteries ... Every organ being sensible in its own way, and unable to perform its functions—particularly the most forceful—without making an impression on the entire nervous system, it is evident that each organ must make a particular impression upon the *pulse*.[16]

For Bordeu, moreover, the pulse must be heard to be interpreted, so that, as Anne Vila observes, "The pulse allows the medical observer ... to 'hear' the body's inner language directly."[17] Or, as Menuret put it, "The pulse is an essential object... linked to the very constitution of the machine.... When the pulse's traits are skillfully grasped and developed, it reveals the entire interior of Man."[18]

This emphasis on the auditory guides Diderot's account in *D'Alembert's Dream,* where Bordeu appears as a fictionalized character. Diderot dwells on the metaphorical equivalence of nervous excitation and music, which, as we've seen repeatedly, was not entirely metaphorical. The difficulties of the concept of life, Diderot tells D'Alembert, has sometimes led him to compare our "organic fibers" with sensitive vibrating strings, especially with the phenomenon of sympathetic vibration in mind. For Diderot, as for Cheyne, Condillac, and others, this comparison was one of the necessary metaphors that Bordeu had defended in his scientific work (chapter 1). It formed the basis of Diderot's conception of the human subject as a sentient keyboard instrument and the provocative rhetorical question to which the conception led: "Is a lark, a nightingale, a musician, or a man anything else [than such an instrument]? And what other difference do you find between a canary and a canary-organ?"[19] One might, with spacing in mind, say that the only difference is that the canary-organ cannot die.

Diderot will not go quite that far. His fictionalized self is exaggerating, ironically commenting on the extravagance of a speculative language that nonetheless enchants him. (He subsequently brings in Bordeu to talk scientific sense.) But the thrust of the hyperbole is revealing. Speculatively, at least, music is not merely *capable* of simulating life. It *is* a simulation of life. Like Vaucanson's flute player, music simulates life by chiming with the mechanism of life.

At this point we can turn from Diderot and an imaginary keyboard to Mozart and a real one. The turn will show us spaced texture in opposition to pulsation but not without ambivalence. Sensibility bespeaks vitality but also susceptibility to pain. As Bordeu pointed out, pulse is most evident when most disturbed. The economy of death works most forcefully where life is felt most intensely.

Mozart composed his Fantasy for Piano in D Minor, K. 397, in 1782. Like most fantasies from the later eighteenth century, this one jumps abruptly from mood to mood, genre to genre, without pretext or apology. But like Haydn's variations in the "Surprise" Symphony, Mozart's fantasy is distinctive in the way it observes its protocol. Between a nocturne-like opening in moody arpeggios—Mozart channeling Chopin—and a mindlessly cheerful conclusion, each of which we hear only once, the piece sets a series of three agitated

EXAMPLE 4. Mozart, Fantasy in D Minor, K. 397, mm. 12–13, 20–21, 23–24.

episodes with silent spaces between them. Each episode has its own distinctive pulse and each pulse has its own distinctive place: the middle voice in the first episode, the upper voice in the second, and the bass in the third. Pulsation reaches everywhere. (See example 4.) The full series appears twice in succession, but it is interrupted at a pivotal point by an outburst of keyboard-spanning scales. A third round begins after another such outburst but breaks off after the first episode. If we hear the opening as the least mechanical segment in the piece and the conclusion as the most, what is going on in between?

To answer, we literally need to take the music's pulse, or rather its pulses. These pulses consist of repeated attacks on single notes or chords within the measure. They enable whoever plays and/or listens to them to assume the position of Bordeu's medical observer and hear directly the inner language of the musical body. In the first and third episodes the pulsed texture spans several measures and changes pitch level from measure to measure. In the brief second episode the pulsations take the place of the melody and remain on the same pitch. The melody in the first and third episodes is subject to spaced repetition of short phrases and a tendency to break up into detached single attacks descending by semitones. The pulse in these passages breaks off as spacing intensifies and sensibility winces. But every episode begins with a resumption of pulse. The music throbs.

The series of episodes is increasingly hectic. Sensibility intensifies within each episode and intensifies further as we pass from one episode to the next; the second full series is more intense than the first. The tempo of all three episodes is Adagio, but the melodic motion becomes faster as one episode follows another. The pulsations are in eighth notes throughout.

The first episode spins a plaintive melody out of a long initial note in the right hand and sets it over the pulsating accompaniment in a closely knit left-hand texture; the bass rarely descends below middle C. In the brief second episode the pulsation in the upper voice combines with a chromatically descending bass in octaves. The third episode repeats the pattern of the first at a higher level of agitation and intensity. Its first half remembers an isolated phrase from the earlier melody and scatters it over the pulsation in twitches, twinges, and splinters of tone. Its abbreviated second half goes even further, breaking up into isolated staccato notes while the underlying pulsation drops away. At this point the expected silence is extended with a fermata, as if sensibility had been pushed to its limit. The slightest sensation would be painful. Vitality pauses in the dead time of the living present.

And then the whole process starts over with the return of the first episode. This time, however, there are interruptions. The sweeping scale passages I mentioned earlier burst out after the first episode in the second cycle and again, more extravagantly, after the third episode. The scales are presto in tempo and *forte* in volume; they plunge from high to low and surge back from low to high. In light of the continuously increasing agitation *within* the sequence of episodes, these noisy flourishes may seem like efforts at recovery, as if to say "Get hold of yourself!" in a loud tone of voice—with exactly as much success as you might expect. The effect is particularly strong in the extended second Presto, which erupts after the return of the third episode ratchets up its agitation with an extra measure of syncopated staccato twinges.

The pulsations in the Adagio episodes consistently act in opposition to spacing; where spaces open, pulse hastens to fill them. But in so doing pulse also seems to precipitate the spacing it cannot tolerate, as the third episode shows in the series of gaps that breaks up its right-hand line and stipples it with off-beat attacks. Pulsation here seems to turn against itself. Besides, nothing can be done about the spaces *between* the episodes; the economy of death can be absorbed but not abolished. A similar imbalance attaches to the higher-order pulsation created by the full and curtailed returns of the sequence of episodes between the fluid opening of the Fantasy and its rigid close. Pulse will not be quelled but spacing will not be denied. And the spacing prevails.

Or does it? However curtailed, however pained, the pulses in this music are what the pianist primarily plays and the listener primarily hears. The spacing only makes them more audible. The cyclical repetition of the Adagio episodes acts in the same spirit as the retrieval of melody on Diderot's imaginary keyboard—a keyboard whose strings remember their own vibrations:

> The philosophical [i.e., human] instrument is sentient—it is at the same time the musician and the instrument. As something sentient it has the momentary consciousness of the sound it is making; as an animal, it has the memory of that. This organic faculty, by linking the sounds in itself, produces and keeps the melody there. Suppose there is a keyboard with sense and a memory. Tell me if it won't know and repeat on its own the melodies which you have executed on its keys.[20]

Only when its embodied memory grows too intense to sustain does the music retreat from animation to the comforting mechanism of the close. By stopping with the first episode, where the underlying pulsation is at its most sustained, the Adagio forestalls the disturbances of pulse that would otherwise have come. Nothing in this music suggests the grotesque body (Mozart avoids it in general), but the music does take pains to protect that classical body on which it cannot quite rely.

In this context the ensuing Allegretto sounds less like music than like the simulation of music. It acts—how credibly in its own time it is hard to say; with little credibility in ours—like a cancelation of the vibratory memory. This music is an exercise in willed amnesia, an effort that it seems to acknowledge, and perhaps to question, by making room for an intrusive unmeasured scale passage of its own, although one that might also pass for a miniature cadenza.

If Haydn's "Surprise" movement has affinities with Vaucanson's flute player, this fantasy of Mozart's might be said to have its own affinities with another musical automaton of the time, the organist built by the Jacquet-Droz family of jewelers around 1768, which is, unlike Vaucanson's androids, still extant—and in working order. As noted in chapter 1, the organist, a young girl, accompanies her actions with marks of exquisite sensation and awareness. She breathes, turns her head, and moves her eyes as she plays her instrument, accompanying her external simulation of life with expressions of sensibility. In her case, however, the sensibility appears in a state of refinement and control, precisely the social and physical ideal that Mozart's Fantasy puts in jeopardy.

PULSE AND SPACED TEXTURE: BEETHOVEN

Both the pulsed texture of the Fantasy and the spaced texture of Haydn's "Surprise" movement occur in the second movement of Beethoven's Piano Sonata no. 10 in G Major, op. 14, no. 2. Only a few years separate this sonata, composed in 1798 or '99, from Haydn's "Surprise" Symphony, and Beethoven's movement, like Haydn's, is a set of variations. But something has changed. The logic of simulation has started to get tangled.

The theme tells us as much right away. Unlike Haydn's, its spaced texture is not delicate but ponderous; the music drags its feet. This heavy spaced texture occupies the theme's first half, occasionally destabilized by syncopated accents. In the second half, spaced passages alternate with moderately lyrical legato writing until the theme rounds back to the texture of the opening. The movement as a whole seeks to transform this adjacency of spaced and smooth textures into their simultaneity, and in so doing to accomplish a passage from mechanism to organism. In this case that passage also involves passing through both a pulsed texture and the kind of saturated syncopation that Mozart uses as the mark of acute sensibility. The pulsed texture anchors variation 1; the syncopation pervades variation 2. The process culminates in the third and last variation, which presents the simulation of life as an ongoing event—or would do so except for the way the piece ends.

Variation 3 presents spaced texture in inverted form—the theme below, higher-order spacing above. (See example 5.) The inversion is also a hyperbole that pushes the limits of credibility. The theme in the bass is so smooth and tranquil that it seems half asleep; the melodic embellishment in the treble is so excitable it can barely contain itself. The agitation here is not vibratory; it is galvanic. Haydn's single jolt has become a fusillade of shocks. The effect is as if—though *as if* is all one can say—the music were aligning itself with Luigi Galvani's discovery that nerve impulses are, in fact, electrical.

EXAMPLE 5. Beethoven, Piano Sonata no. 10 in G Major, op. 14, no. 2, opening.

Speculation aside, the treble figures are all legato, but almost all of them occur off the beat with rests in between. If they allude to mechanism, it is not mechanism as opposed to organism, but mechanism in the process of becoming organism. The process is one that has to be renewed continuously. It is marked in the music by moments in which the treble forgets the rests between its figures and emits a longer spurt of continuity. Meanwhile the theme in the bass continues on its way as if nothing could possibly disturb it, as if its capacity to absorb the energy that envelops it were unlimited. But it turns out to be wrong.

It is wrong because the end of the movement returns to the raw material of spaced texture. Everything happens very quickly; six measures and we're done. First the opening measures, all spaced texture, return, transposed up an octave. Then the space between attacks widens and the dynamic level falls from *piano* to *pianissimo;* the machine seems to be winding down. And then, in both hands, widely spanned—where have we heard this before?—there is a sudden *fortissimo* chord. The movement is over.

One can just hear this ending saying, with a shrug, "What else did you expect?" All of the elements of simulation are in play in this movement, but they do not quite come together in the right way at any point. Beethoven's music has long been associated with Romantic irony, the self-exposure of aesthetic illusion in the act of producing it; the effect may playful, serious, or, as here, an unstable mixture of both.[21] The elements of ambiguity and ironic distance that inform Haydn's movement but are subsumed by it become, in Beethoven's movement, the wider frame that subsumes the rest. This difference may be a sign of the times. Was Michel Foucault right to suggest that by the turn of the century the fundamental protocols of Western knowledge were undergoing a tectonic shift? Foucault says that knowledge in general, exemplified by knowledge of work, life, and language, withdrew from the sphere of direct observation in which it had flourished for the previous century and a half and reoriented itself toward underlying processes.[22] Beethoven's set of variations shares that orientation. His sonata movement concerns itself less with integration, as Haydn's symphonic movement does, than with transformation, less with progress than with process. The music is more rather than less exemplary because it is not a major statement but rather a jeux d'esprit. It does not proclaim big changes but models changes already in place.

As for the ending, we have to wonder: Did Beethoven know Haydn's "Surprise" Symphony? Is he alluding to it here? Whatever the answer, the gesture is the same. But by placing his surprise at the end rather than near the beginning, Beethoven makes its integration impossible. The loud chord becomes an indigestible lump of sound, and no one can say for sure whether it is a clunk protesting on behalf of mechanism or a grunt protesting against it. How are we supposed to tell the difference?

As we will see in the next chapter, musical experiments in the simulation of life regularly posed that question. Sometimes they even offered answers.

THREE

From Clockwork to Pulsation III

METABOLISM

> But now I see with eye serene
> The very pulse of the machine.
>
> —WILLIAM WORDSWORTH

SPACING, PULSATION, INTENSITY, DRIVE—we seem to have covered a great deal of ground on the subject of artificial life in music. But there is still more to the story, which has so far not asked about the nature of the life being simulated as the eighteenth century conceived of life. What makes bodies, especially human bodies, into sentient machines? Machines with pulses? What did it mean to ask that question during the Enlightenment? What, if anything, do simulations of life, including musical simulations, have to contribute to the answer? And what—this is not a frivolous addition—does a duck have to do with it?

To broach the question, consider a sequence of four examples.

LIFE AT BOTH ENDS: FROM SONG TO DIGESTION

I. Vaucanson's Flute Player

The simulation of life in this first of the automata was divided between mind and body. The flute player breathed and his fingers moved individually on his instrument, but these simulations of self-motion (the criterion of life from Aristotle to Descartes) operated in tandem with an invisible mental activity. The mark of mind was music-making, a cultural attainment widely regarded as a primary expression of sentience. To some degree what was invisible about the flute player took priority over what was visible. Another way to say this in eighteenth-century terms was that the simulation of life in the flute player was not physiological. Recalling that Vaucanson thought of his automata as "moving anatomies," we might say that in the flute player there is more moving than anatomy.

It was probably the combination of physical and mental simulations that made the automaton so popular. The same combination may also have been what led Voltaire to compare Vaucanson to Prometheus in 1740 and Julien De la Mettrie to follow up in his materialist treatise of 1748, *Man a Machine*, by remarking that a "talking man" would have been harder for Vaucanson to construct than the flute player but that "[such a] mechanism [is] no longer to be regarded as impossible, especially in the hands of another Prometheus."[1] Voltaire and De la Mettrie were thinking of the version of the story in which Prometheus gives human beings the gift of fire—symbolically the arts and sciences—because he had also given them life. Human beings, to borrow the title of the ballet on the subject that Beethoven composed in 1801, were the creatures of Prometheus. But astonishing as it was, this creature of Vaucanson-Prometheus was not a simulation of physiological life.

II. Vaucanson's Second Automaton, the Digesting Duck

This sequel to the flute player made good the omission of its predecessor. The virtual duck is as close to a real moving anatomy as Vaucanson could invent, and it was correspondingly his most famous invention. The duck proposed no theory of mind; it was designed as a transparent simulation of the process of digestion from eating to defecation. Although it sat, like the flute player, on a pedestal concealing the mechanism that operated it, the duck made visible the organic mechanism it simulated. And as Michel Foucault has argued, visibility was the basic criterion of understanding in the life sciences of the eighteenth century.[2]

But there is something more to the story. The duck also forms a playful reversal or inversion of the flute player. The one engages in respiration and emits music, the other engages in digestion and emits, not to be too delicate about it, duck poop. So why, visibility aside, this passage from flute to duck, mouth to anus, music to digestion? Let's keep that question in reserve while we complete our series of examples, the second half of which will repeat the same passage in musical terms.

III. The "Lark" Quartet

The duck did not have a voice. It could only make what Vaucanson described as "gurgling sound, like a real duck," as it swallowed. But plenty of other birds sang. Mechanical birds sang on clocks and other automata, and imitations of birdsong on flute or violin were nothing new. But the bird song that, as we know, opens Haydn's String Quartet op. 64, no. 5, is something different. It does not mimic the singing of a natural bird but simulates the singing of a mechanical bird. The lark in "The Lark" is an automaton.

The "Lark" nickname (which did not originate with Haydn but quickly stuck) suggests that the quartet's listeners were hearing a literary image in this artifice. The European lark sings from so high in the air that its song seems to come from an invisible source; the best-known allusion in English is by Shakespeare ("Hark! hark! the lark / At heaven's gate sings"); eighteenth-century German poetry includes similar allusions by Friedrich von Hagedorn ("Nun springet die steigende Lerche" [Now springs the soaring lark]), Friedrich von Klopstock ("Vernehm' ich nicht süsse / Töne, wenn zu der Wolke du steigst?" [Do I not hear sweet tones / When you soar to the clouds?]) and Goethe ("So lieb die Lerche / Gesang und Luft" [So does the lark love / Song and the air]).[3] Listeners apparently heard Haydn's soaring violin as a musical metaphor for the lark's simultaneously piercing and distant song, which is itself a metaphor for transcendental aspirations soaring up from their earthly points of origin (the lark sings at dawn and is a harbinger of spring). Certainly this hearing took hold once the name had stuck, regardless of Haydn's unknown intentions—which would hardly have mattered in any case. What is at stake here is an underlying logic, a shared habit or discourse or representation, common conditions of possibility. The singing, soaring lark is a product of what Foucault calls archeology.[4] Once the name is given, once the lark becomes audible, a certain discourse comes into play.

Nor is imitation directly at issue here, though it may inflect the music. The real issue is the simulation of an underlying process, which in this case is the production of artificial life. The opening of the quartet enters Vaucanson's arena by invention, not by imitation. The duck digests visibly; the lark soars audibly. So Haydn does audibly to the lark what Vaucanson did visibly to the duck: he sets it on top of its mechanism.

He does so by employing the spaced texture described in the preceding chapter: the sound of mechanical motion as the later eighteenth century came to imagine it. Of course spaced texture does not register as mechanism

EXAMPLE 6. Haydn, String Quartet no. 53 in D Major, op. 64, no. 5, "The Lark," opening.

every time it is used; everything depends on just *how* it is used. But it has proven to be surprisingly durable even in later eras replete with less noisy machines. The bond between the sensation of mechanism and regular, rhythmically rigid punctuation has become second nature.

The opening of the "Lark" is the locus classicus of spaced texture, which sounds alone on the lower strings like a clockwork mechanism. What follows is equally exemplary: the first violin soars high above the clockwork with florid melody. (See example 6.) Haydn's lark thus sings, and sings eloquently.

But it sings, not like a "real" bird, but like a mechanical one. Or does it? Mechanical birds are supposed to sound exactly like real ones, and that is just the point: it is hard to tell the difference. We cannot always discern where the creature ends and automatism begins, and vice versa. And in its positive form that indeterminacy becomes an occasion for wonderment.

Writing in 1769, Denis Diderot caught both the point and the tone while developing his comparison—more than metaphor, less than identity—between sentient life and the vibration of "sensitive" strings. To recall it from chapter 2: "Is a lark, a nightingale, a musician, or a man anything else [than a keyboard of such strings]? And what other difference do you find between a canary and a canary-organ?"[5] Haydn's combination of continuous melody and spaced texture supplies the sensitive strings, and in the process it questions even the difference between the canary and the canary organ.

One sign of organic life, however, is a certain imperfection, and Haydn's lark offers that too. Most of its song is entirely melodious, free of any dissonance, but some of the music around it is dissonant indeed. As we will see in more detail later on, the dissonances involved form a kind of byproduct. They are not virtual or mimetic and they do not represent anything; they are extrusions of sound; they operate by a parallel logic to the digestion of Vaucanson's duck but they do not amount to signification, at least in any obvious or unimpeachable way. The weight of their presence serves to mark the difference between imitation and simulation.

IV. *The Ninety-Third Symphony*

Another feature of the organic byproduct comes into view when we think of Vaucanson's duck not in opposition to the flute player but in balance with it. As we know, the flute player breathes into his flute and touches its stops with soft fingers. Breath, it could be argued, is the counterpart of feces in another register as the sign of the organic. The two substances occupy equal and opposite bodily orifices, both are distinct to living creatures, and both involve processes of intake and release. The scale of respectability that separates them is a cultural form that was less robust in earlier eras than it is today.

The slow movement of Haydn's Symphony no. 93, composed in 1791, contains a graphic demonstration of that fact. The movement culminates in an unexpected and very physical dissonance, much more rude than its counterpart in the "Surprise" Symphony. The sound is the work of renegade bassoons playing down and dirty in their lowest register. It has sometimes been called a raspberry or Bronx cheer, but it is not a vocal sound. Nor, despite its origin, is it a breath sound. It stands as the exact opposite of the sound produced by Vaucanson's flute player. Haydn has composed an artificial fart.

This indelicate moment, the production of wind music in the lowest possible sense, acts as a reminder that there is more to life than Voltaire's Promethean fire. At one level, the sound is a social indelicacy, aimed to provoke the very sort of unease reflected in the euphemisms still often used to describe it. Although most more recent descriptions are perfectly frank, the discomfort level can still produce language like this, from Daniel Heartz: "In polite society this kind of noise, emitted willy-nilly, is called an eructation or breaking wind—more vulgarly a belch or fart."[6]

The belch in this statement is itself a kind of euphemism. Its presence as a less drastic alternative misses the point of Haydn's ultra-low pitch and ultra-dark tone color, sounds that defiantly come from the bottom up. Haydn's own comfort with such social and physical discomfort draws on the traditional association of high and low, mind and body, with the ups and downs of social hierarchy. The low sound reminds the respectable audience of what links them to the kind of people not present at the concert, including their servants. It intrudes a reminder of the ritual reversal of high and low in carnival festivity, the licensed anarchy of the world upside down. It may even serve notice that the famous composer spent most of his life in livery and hadn't forgotten about it. That may be one reason why this social gaffe formed part of the series of public concerts that decisively validated Haydn's hard-won independence. At another level, and by no means an unrelated one, the flatulence of the bassoons is an outburst of surplus life, a messy splotch that resists assimilation into the musical and social orders.[7] Its presence links the expression of sensibility that dominates the movement to the underbelly of Life as such, and it does so neither as organism nor mechanism, but as an undecidable mixture between the two.

The whole thing is very carefully calculated—calculated, one might say, with mechanical precision. The movement begins with a solo string quartet quietly playing a semipastoral melody. In the orchestral context, the quartet texture sounds strangely ethereal, a little unreal or phantasmal. This impalpability can hardly last long, and it doesn't. The texture and theme are repeated immediately, but with a resonance that feels more corporeal as the full body of orchestral strings supports the theme on solo bassoon with the rest of the orchestra silent. Then everything changes at a stroke—literally at a drum stroke under a loud chord followed by full-bodied agitation.

Excitation arrives as dream departs. If the pastoral passages reflect the sensibility of Bakhtin's classical body, this outburst shows the grotesque body springing to life. The interplay of the two types determines the course of the movement, but not quite on equal terms. The classical body takes pride of place, filling in the spaces in the texture in which it first appeared and restoring equilibrium after each earthy outburst. The antagonists almost find common ground in a heavily pulsed passage following a return of the pastoral theme in the strings (without bassoon—as if to say, "Just wait"), but the classical body again prevails as the strings lead smoothly back to another return of their pastorale. Thus when the bassoons make their rude intrusion in the coda, their blast challenges the aesthetic premise of the whole movement by subordinating a refined form of the body's vitality to one much earthier.

In the same study of European carnival that introduces the opposition of classical and grotesque bodies, Bakhtin located the source of that earthiness in the body's orifices. He found it especially in the nether regions, which he called the lower-bodily stratum and identified with resistance to all forms of top-down authority.[8] The ill-mannered intrusion of the lower-bodily stratum in Haydn's coda makes a similar connection. The coda begins after a resurgence of the earthy music interrupts a lyrical passage for solo oboe and strings. But the outburst breaks off short; something is awry. Scattered fragments of phrases follow in an increasingly spaced texture. Isolated strokes by the timpani act as lower-bodily pulses, falling queasily on weak beats. The fart on the bassoons thus does not come from nowhere, but from a buildup of physical discomfort that demands release. When release comes, thanks to those bassoons, the first thing we hear is the roar of the grotesque body, robust once more. The whole passage shows viscerally the visceral truth that the classical body denies. The return to the pastorale that follows by way of conclusion is hard to take at face value, and confesses as much by quickly petering out. The aesthetic premise of the movement has been reversed.

But isn't this bassoon business just a joke, and a dumb one at that? Of course it is; that is precisely Haydn's point. But the joke throws the whole movement out of alignment and mocks the any attempt to equate sensibility with refinement, whether sensory or social. Mozart's D-minor Fantasy is far more polite but it makes the same point. The bassoon joke is one of those highly overdetermined moments—music has a lot of them—that have an impact all out of proportion to their brevity. Haydn's joke connects sensibility with physical mechanism in terms that threaten, almost literally, to deflate sensibility. It converts the pastoral to the animal. It replaces the distance of fantasy with the closeness of digestion—but in the manner of Vaucanson's duck. This is a joke, all right, a real canard, but it's a Freudian joke—not only in the sense that it calls attention to something commonly repressed but also in the sense that it does so by means of a mental short-circuit that replaces anxious effort with a laugh.

It is also a very eighteenth-century joke, though we still get it, and probably always will. Leonard Bernstein's marked up score gives evidence of that.[9] In the measure preceding the bassoons' low C, Bernstein marks down the wind dynamic to *pianissimo* and the strings to triple *piano*. This measure happens to end a right-hand page, and in the margin Bernstein anticipates what comes just after the page turn by writing "fg FF!" with the FF in extral-arge letters ("fg": *fagotti*, bassoons). Then, just to make sure no one misses the point, he circles the bassoons' note at the start of the next page. Clearly changing times make no difference with this prank. Bernstein seems to have liked it as much as Haydn did. But if we imagine hearing the bassoons' visceral blast with eighteenth-century ears, we will hear it not only as a protest on behalf of the body, and the body of the people, but also as an experiment in artificial life. If Vaucanson, why not Haydn?

FROM MECHANISM TO ORGANISM: TWO LOGICS

Like the era's automata, eighteenth-century musical simulations sought to blur the boundaries between organism and mechanism just enough to make the difference between them count for less than the pleasure of animation its own right. Whether they aim to simulate the life in mechanism or the mechanism in life, pieces like Haydn's "Lark" Quartet and Symphony no. 93 tend to draw on two relatively straightforward logics to make their demonstrations. These logics, moreover, extend beyond their original uses to ripple through music in general.

The first logic is that of hard (mechanism) versus soft (organism), well illustrated in the Jacquet-Droz organist: the lifelikeness of the effigy is created by the pliability of feature and the suppleness of worked leather, the artifice by the elaborate metal mechanism under the skin. It remains ambiguous whether the soft skin is a covering for the hard metal skeleton, and thus an illusion only, or whether the skin is a natural quickening or intensification of the interior mechanism. The music of Viennese classicism typically embodies this hard-soft logic in the combination of spaced texture and emergent melody, sometimes together and sometimes apart. The legato lines emerge, as if by quickening, in—or from—their mechanical surroundings. Haydn's simulated lark is the paradigm case.

The second logic is that of emission, illustrated by the supposed waste products of Vaucanson's defecating duck. The sign of the duck's artificial life is a byproduct that a lifeless mechanism could not produce; a machine cannot defecate. The pellets that came out of the duck were different from the kernels of grain that went in. The excremental thus takes on a new, oddly aesthetic value. The pellets dropped by the duck become desirable rather than repellent because they carried the presence of the organic along with them. But of course they do remain in ambivalent proximity to the viscous, ugly, detestable side of organism, and so pose the necessity of being somehow integrated into the symbolic order once they have been produced. Real or simulated, life requires metabolism.

This necessity is fully at work in the first movement of the "Lark" Quartet. The movement's soaring melody demonstrates its virtual life not only by being what it is, but also by acting like the lowly duck. High and low go together. Once fully aloft, the melody is repeatedly brought down to earth by outbursts of descending scales in triplets. The triplets emerge only briefly in the exposition but they dominate the development. At first the music tries to strike a balance with them, though on unequal terms; low descents by the cello and viola together are answered by high ascending triplets on solo violin. But the triplets prove indigestible. They end the development by erupting in *forte* octaves played by all four instruments. The octaves extend over six consecutive measures, the last two of which are conspicuously clotted. The six measures are an excrescence unlike anything else in the movement.

When they return in the recapitulation, however, the triplets behave better. They pass from one instrument to another in combination with smooth, more slowly moving melodic lines that assimilate them thoroughly. This process turns out to be the preparation for an extra return of the "lark" melody in its pristine form. The melody sounds over another extra, a second clockwork pattern superimposed on its spaced texture. This time around, the triplets have been metabolized—metaphorically speaking.

Other metaphors would certainly be possible, but I am not suggesting that the music in any way *depicts* metabolism, only that it acts in ways consistent with Vaucanson's conception. That action includes a second musical parallel to the duck's pellets. The dissonances I referred to earlier belong to an extended chordal passage that is also notable for rhythmic irregularity underlined by climactic *sforzandi* on weak beats. This unmelodious mass comes fairly late in the exposition, but in the recapitulation it comes, without transition, directly after that extra return of the "lark" theme. High and low form a pair. The chordal passage is not particularly dramatic, and it is certainly not disturbing; it's just very *corporeal*. Its dissonances now sound like—as—ejected matter. Of course the dissonances "resolve," but that does not make them less pungent.

What follows is quite brief, almost an afterthought. The unaccompanied first violin picks up a last pair of descending triplet scales and turns them into the prelude to a final rising arc, though not the full-throated one we have heard before. The lark gets the last word, but the force of its artificial life resides in the fact that it almost didn't.

Sounds like the octaves and dissonant chords in the "Lark" Quartet, the flatulent outburst in the Ninety-Third Symphony, and, as we'll see, visceral rumblings in the Allegretto of Beethoven's Eighth Symphony form the musical bridge between mechanism and life. They do so by challenging their era's aesthetic view of disgust, that most physical form of judgment. The argument ran that the expression of pain had aesthetic value but that the eliciting of disgust did not. In *Laocoon,* Gotthold Ephraim Lessing connects disgust primarily to "physical deformity" and bodily discharges. He worries that even a little disgust might be more than aesthetic pleasure can handle. He does allow just a little to poetry but warns painting to stay away.[10] In the *Critique of Judgment* Kant goes further: "There is only one kind of ugliness that cannot be represented naturalistically without all aesthetic pleasure ... being destroyed [literally sent to the ground, *zu Grunde zu richten*], namely the kind that awakens *disgust.*" He goes on to identify the source of disgust in terms that fit our musical instances; disgust awakens when it seems as if the imaginary object is "forcing a pleasure on us that we forcibly resist."[11] Things have obviously changed since Kant and Lessing wrote. But for Haydn and Beethoven they had changed already. The raw vitality of music could break the decorum prescribed to the other arts.

The organic byproduct shows that the mechanism producing it also produces animation—that the mechanism is virtual organism: neither living nor nonliving but somewhere in between. The appearance of the byproduct, which is paradoxically both extraneous and necessary, endows the simulation with the status of virtual life. Vaucanson's duck did not have to waddle but it did have to excrete. The byproduct distinguishes life as a substantial entity from the classical property of being alive. It carries the definition of life beyond the ancient criterion of self-impelled movement. Such movement must be still present, but to simulate life it must incorporate some form of metabolism, a movement of passage that is also a change in substance.

This criterion forms the link between the duck and the musical automata. The passage from mechanism to music is a kind of higher digestion; the music is the high form of byproduct of which the fecal pellet is the low. It is thus no accident that three of the eighteenth century's most famous automata were musicians: Vaucanson's flute player, the Jacquet-Droz organist, and the Roentgen-Kintzing dulcimer player. The Jacquet-Droz androids illustrate the process of artificial metabolism in its less earthy form, especially the organist, with the movement of her eyes and the rise and fall of her breath. Animation requires sound, even if only the scratching of the writer's pen or the plop of the duck's excretion. Music gives that sound its superlative degree.

When sound fails in some way, the apparently animate form is revealed to be an effigy: not a simulation but a simulacrum. In E. T. A. Hoffmann's tale "The Sandman" (1817), the fictional android Olympia is programmed to play the harpsichord well and even to sing a "bravura aria." But she sings in "the almost cutting voice of a glass bell," and she cannot speak at all, only sigh a toneless "Ach ach." Everyone but the hapless protagonist recognizes that she is a puppet, not a person. Real-life efforts in the late eighteenth and early nineteenth centuries to build machines that could speak ran into the same obstacle. Life demands tone. Mechanism is incapable of inflection.[12]

The Olympia in Jacques Offenbach's opera *Tales of Hoffmann* (1880) carries these features to their logical extreme. This Olympia can speak but her vocabulary consists of only one word, "Oui." When she sings, she can only repeat the same verses twice. Her song is a showstopper, but with an ironic edge that threatens to expose not only Olympia but also the soprano who sings her as a singing machine. After an episode of spaced texture for voice that splits up words and syllables, the "Doll Song" becomes absorbed in increasingly extravagant coloratura. The vocal line is replete with notes above the treble staff, at times reaching the high E but crowned by a series of seven consecutive high Bs—not to mention a trill elsewhere on that same note, preceded by a trill on the high G a third below. The tessitura throughout is punishingly high. The aria comes as close as possible to making the singer sound like the almost cutting voice of a glass bell. It places sufficient stress on the mechanism that Olympia's voice breaks down from time to time and has to be revived by the audible release of a spring.

The logic of musical metabolism is the basis on which the musical simulation of life becomes a general phenomenon, exemplified by its explicit instances but not confined to them. The generalizing impulse is also audible in the "Lark" Quartet. As noted earlier, the music does not have a simple relationship to mechanical birds. It does not signify them; we would have known long since it if did. Nor does it imitate their song; we would have known that too. Any signification or mimesis refers to the lark of literature and folklore and the invisible movement choreographed by its acousmatic sound. So what, again, is that relationship?

The music reembodies the birds' principle of operation. In doing so it echoes the mechanical birds' simulation of a life form and thus of their becoming a form of artificial life. The music, in other words, simulates the process of simulation, to which it thus becomes assimilated; to simulate simulation is simply to continue it. At the same time the music gives the activity of simulation a sensory form and, therefore, insofar as the process gives pleasure, an aesthetic form. The music thus puts the logics of quality (hard versus soft) and process (metabolism and emission) on audible display and makes them available for new uses. The movement is just a single act of simulation, but the logics it embodies have a strong ripple effect.

LIFE FORMS

Michael Thompson's account of the logic of life-form concepts offers a means to describe the movement from life form to life.[13] Thompson argues that without a framing concept, observations of organic process remain mechanical. Only the presupposition that something is alive, that it exemplifies a particular life form, allows us to perceive a phenomenon such as bird song. Without the concept of the living creature, there is only a high-pitched warble; there is no song. Such perceptions are mediated by experience and empirical knowledge, and, though Thompson's concerns lie elsewhere, by narrative and metaphor. The mediations give all life forms the particularity by which they are recognized.

Unless, that is, the life form is human, and thus also mediated by the unique human capacity to say "I." What Thompson calls "the life form I bear," which we might rewrite as "the life form 'I' bears," may have little or no particularity as we bear it and only a speculative particularity when we reflect on it. The human life form is full of indeterminacy. We each inhabit it with a combination of blindness and invention. There is no other way for us to inhabit it. The "I" is first among equals as a linguistic "shifter," a word whose meaning is determined entirely by its immediate circumstances; virtually anyone can say it, and virtually everyone does. The "I" of the life I bear is always borrowed. (One narrator in Yoko Tanada's novel *Studies in Snow*—a polar bear—puzzles over the human habit: "What a strange phenomenon! [What] did Matthias call himself? 'I.' What was even stranger is that Christian too referred to himself as 'I.' Why didn't they get confused if they all kept using the same name?")[14] But this unsettled condition may take positive form as a principle of vitality: we live by moving among particulars that touch but do not determine us. What if the music that simulates life is the aesthetic realization of that principle? Another form of the constantly shifting "I"?

The "Lark" movement again can illustrate. In its most immediate dimension the movement is a demonstration that music can embody the animation of a particular life form. The demonstration models the attitude of the observer, the experimenter, who finds in an automaton a means of conceptualizing life. But this same demonstration also raises the question of whether the musical simulation of life needs to refer to a particular form. What if music, or rather a certain music, the highly changeable and increasingly individualized music of the late Enlightenment, could also simulate the life of the "I" and engage, not with the life form we observe, but with the life form we bear? What if the music's aesthetic power comes from this source and draws on the same sensation of wonder that made automata so popular and fascinating during the same era?

The era's discourse makes this a real likelihood, with the additional proviso that this enveloping form would be less our life form than simply life, or, to double up again, the life form of life as such. As Michel Foucault observed, it was the eighteenth century that first conceived of life as an observable phenomenon and devised the concept of a single life shared in by all living creatures. Prior to the modern episteme, "Life did not exist. All that existed were living beings."[15] Foucault dated the "existence" of life to the end of the eighteenth century, but its elements were already in place at the beginning. As early as 1689, John Locke referred to the phenomenon in which living creatures share as "one common Life," a principle of vital continuity joining the parts of an organism and preserving their unity: "constantly fleeting particles of matter are . . . successively vitally united to the same organized body" by "participation in the same continued life."[16] Living creatures persist because life does. What if a movement like the one from the "Lark" Quartet is an early attempt to express just this life—a particular demonstration of a general power?

I would like to suggest that that is exactly what it is. Music acquired the ability to simulate life as soon as it absorbed the expressive vocabulary of organism and mechanism. All that remained was to put the elements of both into play, or even just to have them in reserve. The outcome was never predetermined, although there is a historical tendency for the reciprocity found in the "Lark" Quartet to become an opposition. We can begin to trace this process through, and beyond, a new series of examples by that canonical trio, Haydn, Mozart, and Beethoven. In each case, the issue of life will turn on the vicissitudes of spaced texture and pulsation.

ON THE LIFE OF CLOCKS: HAYDN

The slow movement of Haydn's "Clock" Symphony, marked Andante, can be said to create an idyll of artificial life, almost to realize the pastoral dream implied by Vaucanson's flute player. It does so by evoking a pair of differences that it proceeds to ignore whenever it pleases: the difference between organism and mechanism and the difference between real and artificial life.

The soft tick-tock figure that gives the symphony its nickname opens the movement on its own, and with notable gentleness; if this is a clock, it is not a big one, but something that might fit on a table. The gentle feeling combines with a sense of acting on the fringes of perception, even though for the moment the figure is all we hear. In part this is because what we are hearing is obviously an accompaniment with nothing as yet to accompany, but in greater part it is because of the delicate timbre: two bassoons in thirds playing staccato, backed by pizzicato violins and cellos. The figure sounds like a mechanism of a particular cast: something underlying, something that measures and regulates. So if this is a clock, it is a clock that has animal or human figures on it that move with its gears and perhaps add chiming sounds over its ticking.

But we never learn what those figures might be. Unlike the "Lark" Quartet, the "Clock" symphony does not simulate the animation of a particular life form. Instead it simulates animation per se. It combines melody with the clock figure, lyricism with spaced texture, hard (but not very hard) and soft (but not always soft) sounds so as to create an alternation between two contrary but not incompatible effects. On one side there is the display of the music as an ingenious mechanical device, but an altogether charming device that needs no organic dimension. On the other side there is the simulation of the same music suddenly coming to life, as if it were waking up to leap the gap between mechanism and organism. In his account of the continuity of life, Locke compares the living organism to a watch, saying that the only difference is that the motion of the watch has an external source.[17] Haydn's clock demurs; it moves its own hands. The tick-tock figure permeates the entire movement, which is a set of variations; the melody responds, at different times, with docility, impulsiveness, belligerence, and lyrical disregard.

The belligerence comes in the first variation, which trades the light, transparent texture of the theme for the full orchestra and erupts in the minor key. Most classical variations feature such a *minore* section but rarely as a first installment. This variation forms the moment of "Surprise"-Symphony-like protest against the rule of mechanism, but its position suggests that the idea here is to get the thing over with as expeditiously as possible. The protest is understandable, but it is not definitive. Accordingly the variation tries, and fails, to cut out the tick-tock figure; the figure simply dispatches its rocking rhythm to the bass, where cellos and double basses keep it going. That clears the air for the second variation, which completely transforms the scenario.

This *pianissimo* variation is an episode of chamber music; we hear only the first violins, solo flute, solo bassoon, and, except for a brief moment *a due,* solo oboe. The bassoon carries the tick-tock in the lightest possible way while the violins and especially the flute unfurl spans of florid, lyrical melody with a quasi-improvised feel. Especially the flute: and we are once again back in Vaucanson's version of pastoral, but with no hint of the satyr in the piping. But it is not just the lyricism of the flute that counts here. At the start of the variation, and intermittently thereafter, the flute plays the tick-tock together with the bassoons, though with wide registral separation. The registral space proves to be the site of potential life. When the flute shifts from tick-tock to melody, it enacts the awakening to life that is the heart of this movement; we hear it cross the space between mechanism and organism, regular motion and impulsive sensibility. The flute turns out to be one of the creatures of Prometheus. This process culminates twice: first in two consecutive measures of fluttering thirty-second notes, and then, to conclude the variation, a dialogue in thirty-seconds with the violins, which coincides with a gradual crescendo that briefly brings the dynamic level to *forte.* Motion by thirty-seconds is the quickest to be found in this movement. When it occurs here, at the apex of the melodic line, it constitutes a figurative quickening of the organism, a quickening of sensibility.

From one perspective, though, that quickening is more than figurative, even more than simulated. Or at least its first half is: those two measures of rapid fluttering on the flute give the sound a material density matched almost nowhere else in the movement and one that makes breath audible. Breath, as we know, was a fundamental mark of animation in both Vaucanson's flute player and the Jacquet-Droz organist. When it comes into its own here, however, its origin is not mechanical but organic. It is a real person's breath that becomes part of the sonority; a real life mingles with the simulated life assumed by the flute. Of course in a sense this happens whenever a person plays the flute or any other wind instrument, but the point here is not simply that it happens, but that it is presented as happening, marked as happening, addressed to the sensibility of the listener.

This moment resonates with several others that, taken together with it, establish the logic of animation in this music. Early during the second half of the theme, while the violins take the melody in a docile mood, a solo oboe holds a single note for four measures, executing a crescendo on the last of the four. Like the continuous thirty-seconds on the flute, this gesture is like nothing else in the movement. It once again marks itself as a musical exhalation of breath, and, moreover, the most sustained act of breath the music has to offer. In a sense close to literal, the oboe breathes life into the body of the music. Later, during the *minore* variation, the moment of organic protest supports itself on other acts of breath, and loud ones: measure-long blasts on pairs of horns and trumpets. A few of these brass shouts get support from the timpani, but Haydn uses them very sparingly here. Only in the last variation, which is loud and celebratory, do they get to cut loose. And because they have been held in reserve, to erupt only at the close, they introduce into the music the other logic of simulation, the one that has gone underemphasized: the logic of emission. Not that their role here is scatological, like that of the bassoons in Symphony no. 93. But they represent, and also enact, outbursts of physical, palpably material vitality that the music has come to produce.

The moments of animation in the "Clock" symphony partake of the ripple effect I spoke of earlier. Because the texture that juxtaposes melodic utterance with mechanical motion does not suggest a specific simulation of artificial life on the model of the "Lark," the music is able to pose indirectly the same question that preoccupied the era's experimenters with the new concept of life: To what extent is life the product of, or to what extent can it be produced from, mechanism? The musical answer is usually left in suspense in favor of the pleasure of the ambiguity, which brings the music into the arena of wonderment, the attitude typical of the public responses to the automata of Vaucanson and Jacquet-Droz and, for that matter, to the later symphonies of Haydn.

PULSATION EVERYWHERE: MOZART

The slow movement of Mozart's Symphony no. 39, marked Andante con Moto, is another prime example of that ripple effect. Its perspective, however, is the reverse of the one we have focused on so far. The era's automata are based on a simulation of function and the logic of musical simulation has the same tendency. But as noted in chapter 2, for many at the time the key element in life was not function but feeling: nervous excitement, sensitivity, sensibility. Was it possible, then, for music not only to show the marks of sensibility, as Haydn's flute does in the "Clock," but also to simulate sensibility itself? Could music materialize the ability to feel?

That question was most often a question of pulse. Pulsation was a primary mark of feeling in part because it is observable both in and by the human subject: be it the heart- or pulse beat or the throb of nervous excitement. The automata themselves did not leave such things out. The breathing of the flute player, the eye movements and breathing of the Jacquet-Droz organist, even the gulping of the duck—all intimated life as both something to be felt and something to be observed.

This seems to be the aspect of virtual life that interested Mozart, as we saw in the previous chapter in the Fantasy in D Minor. The Rondo in A Minor, K. 511, comes alive in a similar way by giving its plaintive recurring melody a throbbing pulse—unexceptional at first but more urgent with each repetition. The recurrence of the minor mode situates sensibility near the threshold of pain, which the melody approaches but is too delicate and restrained to cross. The underlying pulse appears where the melody does but nowhere else. The anticipation of its return diffuses the pulse's presence throughout the piece for both the pianist and the listener. Like the Fantasy, the Rondo is piano music composed as if for Diderot's keyboard of sensitive strings—a keyboard with a memory, or what Gottfried Herder independently called "the clavichord within us that is our inmost being."[18] A performance of either piece can be thought of as validating Bordeu's precept, noted in chapter 2, that pulsation must be heard to be understood. The music that makes it heard on a material keyboard is music that simulates the workings of sensibility.

The element of virtual life in the symphonic Andante likewise depends on the vicissitudes of pulsation, specifically on the interplay between two different types: the continuous pulsation found in the Fantasy and Rondo, and spaced pulsation, a series of detached short figures sounded at regular intervals. All of these pulsating figures do more than simply simulate organic pulsation. Both here and in the piano pieces they are also actual pulsations in themselves, rhythmically marked, and they invite the listener who hears the music with sympathy to match them body for body. The result is more lifelike in its intensity than anything Haydn was seeking. In the "Lark" Quartet, as we've seen, the sequence of spaced texture alone and spaced texture under soaring melody supports the simulation of an artificial life form—Haydn's lyrical version of Vaucanson's duck. The Andante uses spacing as a disclosure of mechanism where life wants to be. Its spaced pulsation is shadowed by the void of "spacing" in Derrida's sense (chapter 2): the imposition of dead space in the living present.

The movement aims to bridge the resulting gap. Its music first releases and then progressively heightens an upsurge of life in the form—the person?—of continuous pulsation steadily throbbing under the melodic surface. This beating pulse soon appears as a surplus of excitation. Sensibility once again wells up near the threshold of pain. This time, however, it does not stay there.

The Andante begins with a simple lyrical melody for strings only, both halves of which are repeated. The distinctive feature of the melody is a rising series of continuous dotted-note figures, most of them also rising. The second half introduces a light continuous pulsation in the violas, but after five measures the pulsation stops and the melodic spell breaks. Spaced pulsation arrives in the form of a largely descending series of separate two-note figures formed by cutting out gaps in the dotted-note pattern. (See example 7.) The first violins play the descending passage over a very sparse spaced texture—pinpoints—in the other strings. At first the pulsating two-note figures rise as the pattern that they form descends, but eventually they also descend as the figures pass from unaccompanied violins to unaccompanied lower strings.

The remainder of the movement answers the discomfiture of spacing with constantly increasing fullness and continuity in melody, texture, sonority, and rhythm. The process is an almost uninterrupted burgeoning supported by abundant continuous pulsation. The feeling is so pervasive that the movement's sectional repetitions assume a feeling of pulsation too.

EXAMPLE 7. Mozart, Symphony no. 39 in E flat Major, K. 543, Andante con Moto, opening.

The "pinpoints" underlying the initial spaced pulsation return twice in the same texture: under the first violins in a passage for strings alone. In the first instance the spaced pulsation returns along with them. But in the second, near the end of the movement, the pinpoints combine not with the rise and fall of the cutout pulsation but instead with an extended form of the continuous dotted-note melody. The melody rises, reaches a plateau to linger on, and briefly descends. We know this sound: it is the "Lark" texture, now taken not as a given but as a goal. (We also realize that it has been anticipated by a stray three-measure fragment earlier in the movement.) The rising melody culminates high in the first violins with three pulses of its top note, the first and third of them attacked off the beat and tied over the bar line. The passage almost literally brings sensibility to a peak.

Another extended return involves the music heard immediately after the opening: an agitated minor-mode passage for strings under sustained wind sonorities. (See example 8.) The second instance is more intense than the first

EXAMPLE 8. Mozart, Symphony no. 39, Andante con Moto, mm. 30–34.

(which might have been thought intense enough) not only because it is longer but also because its melodic line, in the first violins, is higher—the highest sustained line in the movement. Continuous pulsation is at its strongest in these passages. The cellos and basses pulse on the beat; at the same time the violas and second violins pulse off the beat. But the surrounding music absorbs the surplus intensity of these passages without succumbing to it. Both melody and pulsation glide steadily and easily from one register, one instrumental color, to another, from low strings to high winds and back. The flow continues unbroken, its ripples encompassing the whole movement. There are no more gaps anywhere. If there is a musical equivalent to participation in Locke's "one common life," this is it.

Of course there is no guarantee that these felicitous links between life and mechanism will hold up in the ear of the listener or be realized in any given performance; the links may break or just fail to catch. But the presence of the question is more important than its answer on any given day.

The Andante may thus be heard to make a demonstration that music can simulate life in general. In so doing, it raises the question of pulsation as an organic transposition of mechanical regularity, especially in relation to breath, the beating heart, and the vibrating nerves. This general possibility of simulation licenses the listener to refer any particular texture or event to a life process that in turn refers to the general form of life and conveys—this being a key source of the music's aesthetic power—the feeling of abundant, sometimes superabundant, vitality. The Andante con Moto is all about the creative incorporation of superabundance by abundance.

That does, however, leave open the question of what to do about superabundance in its own right. One answer is simply to affirm it unconditionally. For that affirmation, we can turn to Beethoven.

MECHANISM UNWINDING: BEETHOVEN AND OTHERS

Superabundant vitality is the signal feature of the Allegretto second movement of Beethoven's Eighth symphony. Earlier I mentioned an element of protest on behalf of organism in the slow movement of Haydn's "Clock" Symphony. A similar protest helps propel Beethoven's movement. But it is important to note the difference between Haydn's rude vitality and the visceral-organic outburst to which the Allegretto is climactically directed.

The movement broadly follows the model of the "Lark." It sets up a persistent tick-tock mechanism, according to legend an imitation of the newly invented metronome, amid which melody assembles itself and flourishes. But as the movement proceeds it pushes against the limits of the model. At intervals the cellos and basses emit an abrupt rumbling sound, distinctly visceral in character. The result, which happens twice, is to break up the mechanism and replace it with pulsation: tiny two-note squibs of sound spaced off the beat at regular intervals and gradually merging (after a melodic interlude) with a continuous pulsation, also off the beat, in horn octaves. The first time this happens it leads to a resumption of the mechanism—but not the second time. At that point pulsation takes over, first in spasms and then, to conclude, with a surge that spreads out over the full orchestra in multiple rhythms and drives, crescendo, to a final eruption of the visceral rumble: *piano* to *fortissimo* in just the three last measures. And thus ends the movement: splat!

The sheer visceral force of Beethoven's conclusion, pulsation speeded up to become a raw upsurge of corporeal energy, almost expulsive, awakens mechanism into the grotesque body described by Bakhtin and, more *Kermess*-like than anything in Haydn, impudently celebrates the lower-bodily counterpart to pulsation, namely excretion. This byproduct of musical digestion, of "passage," is at one level the culmination of the virtual life that pulses throughout the music as the clockwork mechanism joins with melodic flowering. At another level the same passage is a protest on behalf of "real" life, an effect of the real organism seeking to break out, though it can do so, paradoxically, only from within the virtuality from which it is trying to escape. The sound both ends the movement and recoils from it. This rumble is not a signifier, nor is it an imitation; it is visceral agitation in musical form, as the duck's digestion is organic process in mechanical form; it is a low sonorous mass in motion, a fragment of bodily life split off from the body. Here already the strands of organism and mechanism are beginning to separate more widely. In a few years they will simply pull—and fall—apart. Haydn's clock can no longer tell the time.

Another measure of the historical shift that occurred between Haydn's "Clock" Andante and Beethoven's Allegretto is that Haydn's movement presents itself as a *mise en abyme*. The circular motion and circular returns of the clockwork motive suggest that the movement as a whole, even the symphony as a whole, is an artifice of the sort that the motive represents. The music is poised between organism and mechanism at every level. But Beethoven's movement is linear, designed to suggest the bursting out of real, "natural" life from and against the charm of its simulations. The prevailing opposition of on- and off-beat rhythms articulates the same antagonism. Beethoven begins to break with the eighteenth-century project of trying to reconcile mechanism and organism and to anticipate the nineteenth-century project of maintaining their opposition.

Even so, Haydn and Beethoven share a body image that briefly replaced mutual exclusion between the classical and the grotesque types with alternation. The two types could and did inhere in the same body. It is not always possible to distinguish one from the other. (When the melody in Beethoven's Allegretto is at its height, the mechanism sounds like a pulsation. Haydn's clock has a life of its own.) This was a body defined less by its boundaries or the lack of them than by its juggling of the elements of life known to its era: drive, intensity, irritation, sensibility, pulse, metabolism.

In its dual character, the body made audible in this music stood uneasily between departing and arriving epistemes. According to Foucault, the end of the eighteenth century witnessed an epochal shift in the conceptual basis of thinking about life. The fluid opposition between mechanism and organism, categories that could mix or overlap, gave way to a rigid opposition between the organic and the inorganic, categories that marked an absolute difference.

Foucault quotes Felix Vicq d'Azyr, the founder of comparative anatomy, writing as early as 1786: "There are only two kingdoms in nature. One enjoys life and the other is deprived of it."[19] If so, the inorganic becomes as much the threat as it is the place of that deprivation, which would give anyone at risk, that is, everyone, a powerful reason to keep it at bay. One consequence is that artificial life loses its credibility; simulation becomes a matter less of virtuality than of trickery.

One sign of this change involves nothing other than Vaucanson's duck. The French magician Robert-Houdin (whose name was later borrowed by one Harry Houdini) took an interest in automata, but as mechanisms, not simulations. In 1844 Robert-Houdin examined the still-extant duck and discovered that its digestive process rested on an illusion; a secret compartment in the duck's viscera contained the "digested" form of the duck's grain, which it released as the duck's feces. But the point was not to debunk the trick but to admire it. By the time Robert-Houdin made his discovery, the turn from the simulation of life to the simulation of live action was already a fait accompli, supported in part by large-scale theatrical illusions—something that will come up in the next chapter. For Robert-Houdin the duck was not a moving anatomy but a magician's prop.[20]

Nineteenth-century advances in theatrical technology shifted interest in virtual life away from automata, which had come to seem too mechanical, and toward protocinematic spectacle, the technology of the moving image. The object of simulation shifted from life and life forms to continuous motion: live action. The turning point can be symbolically dated to the invention, late in 1832, of small cardboard disks that produced the illusion of motion when rotated rapidly. Marketed under many names (the umbrella term is "phenakistiscope") the disks immediately became very popular; by the end of 1833 more than a dozen publishers were marketing them internationally. Whereas in the eighteenth century the capacity to make music was a primary sign of life, the auditory byproduct of embodied sentience, the nineteenth century preferred the visual illusion of continuous motion. Sound was in principle secondary—though it quickly proved irrepressible. We will see as much in the next chapter.

At the same time, music adopted a more diffuse, less precise sense of vitality than those found in the pieces we have been studying. Changes in Foucauldian episteme aside, the era had embarked on a concerted effort to separate music from the body and give it an immaterial life of its own. Composers like Berlioz and Liszt, who emphasized the bodily and material aspects of music, were often lampooned for it. As the concepts of life and mechanism drew ever further apart, music offered an escape from mechanism, including its own. As Emily Dolan has observed, the sensory dimension of music represented by orchestration was steadily deprecated over the course of the century (one result of which was the decline in the reputation of Haydn).[21] Similarly, some of the era's commentators on its paramount instrument proposed that the piano's inability to sustain melody fully renders it the "ideal instrument" because the listener must imagine the sound it intends.[22] For A. B. Marx in 1859, the piano "prompts mental fulfillment and completion and points to the realm of the ideal."[23] The most striking trend to the contrary, the rise of virtuoso performers, particularly at the piano, ended mainly in producing a high-minded split between contemplative reserve and empty display—art and entertainment.[24]

The retreat of nineteenth-century music from the element of mechanism might be said to have taken the form of a kind of exaggerated legato principle by which motivic density and the erasure of formal boundaries produce an image of pure organism indifferent to its barely acknowledged mechanical basis. The technical correlatives are familiar: the rise of continuous composition and the decline of literal repetition; the rise of cyclical construction and the decline of clear segmentation. Discrete bits of music increasingly flowed together like the images in an optical device.

After around 1830, the conjunction of hard and soft inherited from the eighteenth century became a separation. The separation was one-sided. It consisted of disavowal of the hard, which left the next century with little else to do but disavow the soft. Once music had to live on its own, without, so to speak, mechanical life support, a paradox ensued. Music as art became more idealized (into abstract "organic" form) the more material resources it had at its disposal (grander pianos, bigger orchestras). One mark of the modernism that started to emerge in the early twentieth century was an effort to make music not only a product of this paradox but a reflection of it—and on it. Once the association of music with interiority and subjectivity became questionable, eighteenth-century tropes for organism and mechanism returned to question it—a kind of haunting that will claim its share of attention in chapters 5 and 6.

Meanwhile, every so often a composition would come along to challenge the legato principle in the very act of adhering to it. Pulsation, for example, plays a decisive role in the first movement of Brahms's Piano Quintet of 1865 and the entirety of César Franck's Piano Quintet of 1879. In the first, pulsation repeatedly breaks out in the space of melody; in the second, it acts as an intensifier of melody, primarily on the piano but eventually migrating to the strings. It is hard to imagine watching a performance of either piece without becoming acutely aware of the sheer physicality involved. The act of performance fuses its real bodily impetus with the music's imaginary impetus. That, however, is how these exceptions prove the rule: by demonstrating, not assuming, the life inherent in music.

The conversion to the organic ideal in nineteenth-century music was swift, largely accomplished between the turn of the century and its third decade. A symbolic turning point comes in 1807 with the publication of Beethoven's "Appassionata" Sonata, which he had composed between 1804 and 1806. The sonata is all the more revealing in this context because the question of mechanism is not its primary concern. The harmonic volatility and unremitting intensity of the first movement clearly point to a crisis of subjectivity. No one ever quarreled with the piece's nickname. But mechanism does become a metaphor for one piece of the crisis. The slow movement, a set of variations, ascends step by step to the threshold between organism and mechanism. The last variation is either the ultimate form of the overlay of hard and soft, spacing and continuity, or a travesty of it—and the ambiguity causes the music to collapse. The finale crosses the threshold decisively, plunging into a relentless mechanism of texture and form that ends only after being broken off twice, as if by alternative endings: first by more mechanism, driven haywire to the point of self-destruction, then by transformation into psychological catharsis.

The variations follow the "Lark" model in reverse. Instead of beginning with spaced texture and superimposing melody on it, the movement takes the combination—an extreme version of it—as its goal. As in Mozart's Andante con Moto, the interplay of animation and mechanism becomes something revealed rather than something assumed. But what is revealed here is discomfiting.

Following a traditional scheme much favored by Beethoven, the successive segments combine melodic variation with figuration in progressively smaller note values. In this case the theme is chordal, resonant and richly voiced. The variations gradually disassemble it into its components, as if to expose its underlying mechanism. The first variation makes the theme itself an instance of spaced texture, cutting out spaces in it in the manner of the spaced descents in Mozart's Andante. The second variation hesitates a little. Its first half strips away the theme's chords, sounding the varied melody in the bass one note at a time; the second half gradually brings the chords back. The third and last variation makes no such concessions. It reduces the theme further to its bare attack pattern amid swirls of continuous thirty-second-note figuration.

At that point the theme becomes the stuff of higher-order spacing. It breaks up into a chain of detached phrases marked by off-beat *sforzando*s and repetitive attacks. As the phrases move up and down the keyboard, they lose substance and coherence, in the end breaking up inwardly. At the height of the process, the phrases reduce to consecutive attacks on a single note, a bare minimum heard twice in succession. The result is to reverse polarities: the theme no longer sounds like a melody but the soaring figuration does. Animation passes into the unbroken flow of sound. But if the superimposed layers thus seem to have achieved an exquisite if precarious balance, the music to follow will soon put that in doubt.

The finale is essentially a turbulent expansion of the texture of the third variation, dominated by repetitions both large and small. On the large scale, both halves of the movement are repeated. On the small scale, melodic repercussion is pervasive. It climaxes with returns of the consecutive attacks of the slow movement's third variation, rapidly spanning the entire keyboard. The question is whether all this activity is pulsation or mechanism, and the answer is that it is impossible to decide. The issue comes to a head in the transitional passage linking the second half of the movement to the coda: an episode of thumping foursquare pounding of the keys, both halves of which—what else?—are repeated: a parody of the movement as a whole. The subsequent closing passage returns to the voracious subjectivity that pervades the first movement, now bent on forming a tragic catharsis that regains, but discharges, its seething animation. But does it? Has the large mechanical rotation of the finale really revealed itself as the measure of a passion (grounded in the body) or a compulsion (grounded in the mind) or both? Or is the vehement conclusion a deus ex machina that sweeps aside a mechanical energy it is incapable of transforming? The question is the point. And the ending does not so much answer it as seek to so overwhelm its listeners that they forget to ask it.

Twenty years later, Schubert makes an almost complete transition to passion and compulsion with the pulsation-laden finales to his late C-Minor Piano Sonata and his two last string quartets, in D Minor ("Death and Maiden") and G Major. It is hard to resist the idea that these tarantella-like movements model Schubert's struggle with the knowledge of his fatal illness, especially given the explicit presence of mortality in the D-minor quartet, where the music denies what the song it alludes to affirms: that death comes bringing comfort. In any case the music would fit the bill. But the key word in my initial description is *almost*. The pulsations of these pieces, articulated at multiple levels—note, phrase, passage—go on so relentlessly, and for so long, that they threaten to recede from animation to mechanism. That may be one reason that the nineteenth century had little patience for them, with the partial exception of the D-minor quartet. What the "Appassionata" poses as a question, however fraught, becomes in these Schubert finales an unambiguous threat. This was not a threat to be enjoyed, although, as we will see in the next chapter, other threats, associated with projection, were enjoyed very much.

FOUR

1812 Overtures

WELLINGTON'S VICTORY AND LIVE ACTION

WELLINGTON'S VICTORY? BEETHOVEN'S ONLY VENTURE into battle music has long been something of an embarrassment. Beethoven reception has been happy enough (too happy, if you ask me) to find metaphorical battle in Beethoven's music, but literal battle has been, well, just too literal. But *Wellington's Victory* is more than just a curio, in part because it is as much a work of technology as it is of music. It forms an early contribution to the project that would span the nineteenth century and culminate in the invention of cinema: the project, literally, of projection, the simulation of life not as form or process but as action. Another signal feature of this music is that it places its live action in close proximity to death. Death, the inanimate, and its companion, the spectral, become the grounds against which living emerges as a figure—quite literally a figure, or a parade of figures: human forms in (musical) motion.

The music celebrates the Duke of Wellington's victory over Napoleon's forces in Spain in the Battle of Vitoria. The battle was fought in 1813, but its story really begins a year earlier. 1812 was a good year for war. The British made the mistake of invading their former American colonies (neither side won; the fighting dragged on for three years; the biggest battle, a British defeat, took place after the war was over); the French under Napoleon made the far worse mistake of invading Russia (their Pyrrhic victory ended in a catastrophic withdrawal—a death march through the Russian winter); and the Spanish, with help from the British and Portuguese, revolted against the rule Napoleon had imposed on them under his brother Joseph Bonaparte.

Each of these wars produced an indirect but notable musical legacy. The American War of 1812 yielded lyrics that, set to an old British drinking song, would become "The Star Spangled Banner"; the French invasion of Russia provided the retrospective occasion for Tchaikovsky's *1812 Overture;* and the Spanish War of Independence prompted Beethoven to write the piece that forms the fulcrum of this chapter, a piece famous for being no good: *Wellington's Victory.*

THE HISTORY OF A PUZZLE

The dates almost work out. In 1808 Napoleon engineers the coup d'etat in Spain; in 1812 Spain produces its Liberal Constitution as an act of defiance. The constitution is announced on March 19 and war against the French for control of the Iberian Peninsula breaks out on May 2. For a little over a year the French army and an allied force led by the Duke of Wellington face and chase each other with no clear result. Then on June 21, 1813, Wellington's forces win a decisive victory at the Battle of Vitoria and break the power of French rule in Spain. Spanish rule resumes in March 1814—which leads, ironically, to the abolition of the constitution only six weeks later.

The chief musical outcome of these events was an equally short-lived triumph. The scene now shifts to Vienna and the date moves to 1813. Beethoven composes a symphonic extravaganza titled *Wellingtons Sieg oder die Schlacht bei Vittoria (Wellington's Victory, or, the Battle of Vitoria)* op. 91. The work is an immediate success and earns Beethoven a lot of money. But very quickly a reaction sets in; the work is judged to be unworthy of its famous composer and for almost two centuries it is regarded as a curiosity, even a monstrosity, and in any case something that should not be taken seriously. Not until 2003 did a contrary view develop, thanks to an important article by Nicholas Cook titled "The Other Beethoven."[1] Cook argues convincingly that the music Beethoven wrote during the late years of the Napoleonic wars has a rational aesthetic that should not be lightly dismissed, even if the music is not to our taste. One of Cook's insights will become important to us later; at this early point, however, I want to concentrate on the question of why *Wellington's Victory* in particular *could* be lightly dismissed after its initial success.

One reason is simply the music's genre. Battle pieces had been composed, of course, long before Beethoven, but they carried little prestige. They were regarded as a lesser genre, partly because history painting and the classical epic had a stranglehold on the representation of battles, and partly because, almost by definition, a battle piece was a specimen of tone painting. The rise in the value placed on "self-sufficient" instrumental music after the 1790s seemed to demand a corresponding decline in the value of pictorial music; it is as if the very possibility of tone painting compromised the integrity of music that did without it. This trend intensified during Beethoven's lifetime, partly as a result of Beethoven's career, and it has had a long tail. If pictorial music, and later "program music," could not be suppressed, at least it could be deprecated. Yet people kept on writing it. Certainly battle symphonies still found an audience.[2] The genre refused to die until the movies took over and killed it off—but even then, not without music.

Beethoven could not have said about *Wellington's Victory* what he said about his *Pastoral* Symphony, that it was more an expression of feeling than painting. *Wellington's Victory* is almost entirely painting—or at least its first movement is. But it is painting of a peculiar kind; it has more in common with a technology that largely postdates it, the projection of moving images, than with the motionless grandeur of history painting. And with this observation we come to a puzzle that will turn out to have surprising implications for the history of simulated life in music. *Wellington's Victory* marks a shift in that history. It exemplifies a turn from simulation by invention to simulation by projection, from "moving anatomies" like Vaucanson's flute player to animated figures of life in motion.

The puzzle stems from the fact that the two movements of *Wellington's Victory* belong to different genres. Their titles make that perfectly clear: the first movement is called *The Battle;* the second is the *Symphony of Victory.* The first movement seems to be programmatic battle music of the traditional type; in other words it seems to be pictorial in technique and narrative in design. I say "seems to be" because we will soon need to understand that this description is wrong in crucial respects. But the description corresponds to the way the music has always been classified; for the time being we can let the classification stand as a useful fiction.

The second movement is quite different. This movement is a concert overture. In style and sentiment it sounds like an expanded form of the miniature *Symphony of Victory*—the names are the same—that Beethoven had written in 1810 to conclude his incidental music for Goethe's play *Egmont.* The same music ends the famous *Egmont* Overture that quickly became a concert standard. Like its model, the expanded *Symphony of Victory* is not programmatic. If the first movement of *Wellington's Victory* is more painting than the expression of feeling, the second movement is the reverse. We can describe the difference by saying that as we go from the first to the second movement we change our primary focus from the immediate force of the music to its general significance.

That change is the puzzle. If the first movement of *Wellington's Victory* depicts—well—Wellington's victory, why do we need the *Symphony of Victory*? Why does Beethoven's Wellington have to win twice? And what does the motive for this change, if we can identify it, have to do with the musical simulation of live action?

FORCE AND SIGNIFICANCE

The answers I propose will turn on the terms "force" and "significance" and on the condition that the philosopher Giorgio Agamben describes as "being in force without significance."[3] Agamben's phrase is a little mysterious, but even before we begin to clarify it we can note the latent antagonism that it expresses between what is binding on us and what is meaningful to us. The condition arises when the dictates of law, language, or custom remain binding, that is, are in force, despite a perceptible lack of foundation. In his formulation of the moral law in *Critique of Practical Reason* (1788), Kant raises this possibility and rejects it. In the funeral marches of his Piano Sonata no. 12 and the *Eroica* Symphony, Beethoven can be said to raise the same possibility—and let it stand.

Kant famously argues that our relationship to the moral law is based on form, not content. Insofar as the law applies universally to rational beings, we must choose to obey it. The moral law is a categorical imperative. We obey the law because it is the law. This principle, however, assumes that the law is meaningful, that its force has significance, because the force of law depends on reason. But what if it doesn't?

Skip forward a century and a half. For Gershom Scholem in 1934, the answer to that question had been supplied by Kafka. For Scholem, Kafka's world is characterized by "a state in which revelation appears to be without meaning, in which it still asserts itself, in which it has *validity* but no *significance [gilt, aber nicht bedeutet]*. . . . a state in which the wealth of meaning is lost and . . . [what appears] is reduced to the zero point of its own content, so to speak."[4] For Scholem, this state is or should be exceptional. Skip forward again to our own day, and Agamben compresses Scholem's wording to "being in force without significance" *(vigenza senza significato)* with a new end in view. He claims that this state is not an exception but the universal rule.

Agamben thus makes an ironic, inverted return to the Kantian starting point. The force of law depends no longer on reason but on the absence of reason. We may not be willing to go quite that far, but we can perhaps position ourselves between Scholem and Agamben and describe being in force without significance as a condition in which a symbol, a ritual, or a concept stands exposed as hollow but does not, for that reason, lose its coercive force, or at least not all of it.

But what condition is that? Eric Santner describes it as the condition of "undeadness," figuratively the condition of something that should be dead but acts as if alive, and literally the condition of something that has forfeited a claim on life but makes the claim anyway.[5] More is at stake in this claim than the persistence of "zombie" ideas; undeadness is an existential burden. The burden is not lack of meaning but empty meaning. The force that persists despite the emptiness is antithetical to the sensation of life. It has, as Santner says, "a peculiar form of vitality and *yet belongs to no form of life.*"[6] It reduces the subject, the person, to a de facto automaton.

What, then, does being in force without significance have to do with *Wellington's Victory*—a work of music that might well be classified as undead?

The answer lies in the relationship between *The Battle* and the *Symphony of Victory*. *The Battle* seeks to produce an impression of violent, antiheroic chaos—lifelike to a fault—in which force erases significance almost completely. The force involved is physical to an unusual degree, physical in the extreme, and it is a force *wielded* by the music rather than merely portrayed by it. Significance doesn't stand a chance. After ceremoniously establishing the order of battle, the music revokes the very idea of such a thing by becoming weaponized noise. The impression it makes is so vivid that it threatens to hollow out in advance any possible celebration of victory, to foredoom any declaration of triumph to fatuity.

Or rather it *threatened* to do that. The threat has become hard to hear because the music's force depends on performance spaces smaller than most modern concert halls. Heard in those spaces, though, *The Battle* was shockingly immediate as a kind of acoustic war correspondence. In that respect it had affinities with the roughly contemporary descriptions of Napoleonic battle in Lord Byron's poem *Childe Harold's Pilgrimage* and with later descriptions in a series of novels that extends from Stendhal to Thackeray to Tolstoy to Zola. Like Byron, Beethoven invokes "[the] deep thunder peal on peal afar; / And near, the beat of the alarming drum" with carnage, not glory, in mind. When "the thunder-clouds close o'er' the field of battle,"

The earth is covered thick with other clay,
Which her own clay shall cover, heaped and pent,
Rider and horse,—friend, foe,—in one red burial blent!⁷

But then there is that *Symphony of Victory*. Like Scholem after him, and quite unlike Stendhal, Beethoven apparently preferred to think of being in force without significance as an exceptional state. The *Symphony of Victory* is an attempt to recover from it. Hearing as much is not at all hard, and doing so is in keeping with the political aims of the music, which were perfectly genuine. Enthusiastic listeners who rejoiced in Napoleon's defeat had no trouble enjoying the *Symphony*. But Beethoven had not always been so accommodating. His earlier essays in the music of war had aimed at a different and more difficult outcome. Written in the first few years of the century, these pieces do not yield musically to a meaning that their music itself has sought to discredit. They work hard to expose the strangely forceful emptiness of such meanings and they take that emptiness as a hard truth that demands to be worked through. The turn to a less rigorous stance in 1813 needs to be understood as much in relation to these pieces as to the events of the Peninsular War.

DIFFERENT GUNS: THE FUNERAL MARCHES

Before going further with *The Battle*, we accordingly need to step back about a decade and shift the focus of attention from battle to its chief byproduct: death. In 1802, after a long string of humiliating defeats, Austria had accepted a peace imposed by the French. In 1802, though already expressing some doubts, Beethoven still regarded Napoleon as a revolutionary hero; he would famously change his mind in 1804 when Napoleon became the Emperor of France and thus lost the dedication of Beethoven's Third Symphony. The symphony became *Eroica* rather than *Bonaparte*, though the change, contrary to legend, did not happen all at once.⁸ The link with the *Eroica* is important because in 1802 Beethoven wrote the Piano Sonata no. 12 in A flat, op. 26, which takes its familiar nickname, "Funeral March Sonata," from its third movement. The march in the sonata clearly served as a model or trial run for the vast, complex funeral march that forms the second movement of the symphony. And because the symphony is explicitly concerned with the experience of Europe in the shadow of Napoleon, it seems plausible to think of the sonata in similar terms. The sonata even begins the way the symphony ends, with a theme and variations movement. So what, we might ask, are these funeral marches telling us about the cost of what Beethoven knew as modern war: that it was widespread, very long, and very bloody?

One thing that the march in the piano sonata tells us straightforwardly is that heroism demands sacrifice; the march is subtitled "On the Death of a Hero." The obvious question then arises: How may such sacrifice be justified? Both the sonata and the symphony suggest that whatever the answer may be—and they give different answers—heroism itself, heroism as a noble virtue, is not enough. Glorious death in the interests of victory is not enough. The tradition of heroic epic is put into question as its inherited literary and iconographic terms break down when confronted with harsh new realities.

In both the sonata and the symphony, the funeral march seeks justification through a depiction of military ceremony. In each case the ceremony fails, and the march presses on to the end without finding the justification it seeks. State ceremony, military ritual, posthumous glory—all stand revealed as being in force without significance. Their justification is not something present but something to come, something that can arise only if the revolutionary energy embodied by Napoleon can be channeled to peaceful ends. The aim is to replace perpetual war with what Kant called perpetual peace.

The finale of the *Eroica* seeks to imagine this outcome. Like the ballet to which its alludes, the movement embraces creative rather than revolutionary Prometheanism, that is, it invokes Prometheus as the elevated spirit who refines humanity with science and art rather than as the thief of fire who defies the will of Zeus. The course of its variations, famously beginning with the piecing together of the theme from its basic elements, embodies the prolific movement of this evolution. The symphony as a whole may be thought of as tracing a long arc from one Promethean mode to the other (as would Percy Shelley's *Prometheus Unbound* in 1819). We know that Beethoven thought of the ballet, and thus presumably of the theme he took from it, in these terms, from his insistence on printing the ballet's playbill in the score of the ballet music and even, uncharacteristically, offering to pay for it. The *Eroica* contains no *Symphony of Victory*.

The finale of the piano sonata—a rushing, seemingly oblivious moto perpetuo—makes no parallel effort. Whether this finale constitutes a retreat or a refusal is not clear. What *is* clear is that the sonata's funeral march imagines the need for something more than the sonata itself can provide. The answer to the sonata's question becomes possible only in the symphony. For that reason, and also because the fascinations of the sonata's funeral march have led me to write about it elsewhere in some detail, my comments on it here will be brief and functional, oriented strictly around its relationship to its successor.[9]

The outline of the movement is almost painfully clear. There is a self-contained statement of the funeral march, a middle section in which the march is suspended, a repeat of the march, and a coda. The march proper is dissonant, insistent, and harmonically volatile, a study in restless gloom; the coda is a descent into darkness. But the middle section, an imitation trumpet-and-drum salute, is rigid and symmetrical to the point of parody. The harmony is all primitive tonic-and-dominant in A-flat major, the parallel key to the march's A-flat minor, a key burdened with seven flats. In every dimension the contrast with the march is shocking—shocking enough that one can hear the military ritual emptying itself of significance while remaining in force. The more it asserts itself, the more vacuous it becomes. Heard after this hollow ceremony, the recapitulation of the march becomes a confession of defeat.

The march thus passes into a sphere of alienation and unreality. This is a sphere in which death occupies a tonal crypt that defies the understanding of the living, and yet at the same time dwells in a world of its own like the classical underworld, the world of shades, oddly resembling the world of the living but insubstantial. The characteristic dotted figure that forms the melodic nucleus of the march assumes the aspect of the obolus, the burial coin that gives passage to the underworld. The march, indeed, may have been partly inspired by the funeral march for the Greek hero Patroclus in Ferdinando Paer's opera *Achilles*. Beethoven expressed a wish to "compose" Paer's march himself; the sense of remoteness carried by the harmony of the march in op. 26 may be linked with a feeling of exclusion from the simplicity and grandeur commonly linked at the time with the vanished ancient world.

It is ironic that an orchestrated version of this march was played at Beethoven's own funeral. Beethoven had composed the orchestration in 1815 as incidental music for a play, *Leonora Prohaska*. This later version has three interesting features. First, it involves a key change to B minor, a pragmatic change to be sure but also an expressive one given Beethoven's known identification of B minor as a "black key." Second, the *Prohaska* version limits the negativity of its close. B minor may be gloomy but it is not almost unthinkable. Hence this version cuts the coda in half and omits the extended descent of the theme's dotted rhythm into the far depths of the bass. Last, the wind band consists of flutes, clarinets, bassoons, and horns: no oboes, no trumpets. The omission is audible, especially in the central fanfare section. Is it supposed to remind us of something?

Does it, perhaps, echo the funeral march of the *Eroica*? From the beginning, the symphonic funeral march has a more complex agenda than the march for piano. The assignment of the melody to the solo oboe after the opening rumble on the contrabasses is like a joining, but not a union, of two worlds. Pastoral meets epic; there is no realism here, no leaning in the direction of *Wellington's Victory*.

Like the sonata, however, the symphony does embody the relationship of force and significance in a ceremonial military salute. The salute is very much a matter of force—really a matter of violence. When a *piano* passage based on a consoling C-major melody begins to intensify with a crescendo, the salute rushes in as a blaring *fortissimo* fanfare. This turn of events happens twice, the second time with a rise in both the intensity of the consoling passage and the violence of the fanfare that cancels it. But unlike the sonata, the symphony makes no room for this intrusion. The ceremonial gesture collapses almost as soon as it can be recognized. It does not happen, it does not even *arrive* except as a mistake. It is something to be repelled.

To register this, the symphony makes the strange instrumental choice of leaving the clarinets out of the first tutti fanfare. This omission is completely inaudible; it is addressed not to the ear but to the eye as a symbolic mark, or more exactly as the symbolic erasure that designates the hollowness at the core of the military ceremony. This absence establishes itself only gradually. It persists throughout the entire *maggiore* section framed by the fanfares. On first hearing, the consoling melody passes from oboe to flute to bassoon—but not to clarinet. The same thing happens later in varied form. Only with the second fanfare do the clarinets return—again an event to be seen more than heard, because the change in sonority and tone weight is subliminal at best. The result is to turn the disappearance of the clarinets, observed in retrospect ("ah—now I hear, it's been missing since..."), into a manifestation of sheer meaninglessness, for which no amount of force can compensate.

This strange rift looks forward to the ultimate negativity of the whole movement, which brings neither catharsis nor reconciliation but only the recognition of work yet to be done. The music that follows this episode is a long march through the ruined symbolic landscape of death. Every advance in its expressive force is a further decline in significance. With the movement's catastrophic fugues, the musical medium of choral celebration and intellectual depth falls headlong into the abyss of history. Any possible resolution lies on the other side of a zero point that the music must take as its end. In light of what the two preceding chapters have said about spacing and the economy of death, the tick-tock memento mori played pizzicato by the cellos and basses at the very end makes that zero into a void.

Strange though it may seem to compare them, the *Battle* of *Wellington's Victory* proposes the same critique of sovereign but empty significance as does the funeral march of the *Eroica*. Both contest the power of heroic symbolism to count the cost of heroic action. But as I have already suggested, the sting of this critique is blunted in 1813 by the *Symphony of Victory*, which embraces the very condition of being in force without significance that *The Battle* strips down to its elemental form.

MUSIC AS BOMBARDMENT

As I noted earlier, *The Battle* only seems to be battle music of the traditional type. It is actually spatial music, probably the first modern example of music that makes the location of sound in space an element of composition. Unlike traditional forms of antiphony, *The Battle* does not seek to redefine musical space as acoustically symmetrical, that is, as stereophonic, although it begins by doing just that, separating the orchestra into British and French sides. Once the sides begin to clash, the performance space becomes saturated with sounds that seem to come from everywhere at once, so that the audience is enveloped in a 360-degree acoustic panorama—or rather diorama. We will come back to those terms.

The music's calls to arms are untimed. We first hear offstage trumpets and drums "on the English side" reiterating their fanfares; according to Beethoven's instructions, they begin very softly and stay at that level "for a while," and then grow gradually to *fortissimo*, approaching the orchestra from the greatest distance the performance space allows. The result is to bring the battle from far to near, from rumor to reality—and in particular to do so by reversing naturalistic movement: it is not we who approach the battle but the battle that approaches us. Once this marshaling of forces has occurred it is repeated from "the French side" in the same indefinite zone of time. The antagonistic sounds of "Rule, Britannia" and the French "Marlbrough" are to be imagined as sounded on the field, where they lay claim to significance via statements of national identity.

The fighting breaks out as trumpets from either side play the same fanfare against each other; from this initial clash of sounds the battle rapidly descends into chaos. Beethoven uses an expanded percussion battery to re-create the booming of cannonades and the hail of small-arms fire. The pounding of the cannons persists throughout. It is notated in the score by large white and black circles—little visual explosions—that alternate sides in asymmetrical, unpredictable, and never repeated sequences. Overlaid on this barrage is the sound of continuous musket fire produced by multiple rattles. As Cook observes, the music is planned to be random; its randomness is what testifies to its realism.[10] That, plus the sensory impact of all the noise, overwhelmed Beethoven's audiences in 1813. Until the end, the dynamic level never falls below *fortissimo*. The score to the first edition asks for a pair of the largest possible bass drums and instructs that the orchestra also be as large (*stark,* "strong") as possible: "The bigger the room, the larger the ensemble."[11] Modern research into the acoustics of Beethoven's performance spaces suggests that the sound produced by his symphonies when they were new "would seem more appropriate today to a heavy metal concert in a sports arena than [to] a classical music concert in a symphony hall."[12] With *The Battle,* you take the heavy metal effect and double it.

The musical battle of Vitoria reaches a point of maximum violence in a long passage in which the English drums break through those of the French by overpowering them in volume. The music mounts to a triple *forte* climax followed by a long series of *sforzandos*, and then trails away to near silence. This series of aftershocks and the subsequent fadeout form an important moment, though a transient one. Although the French have lost and the British and their allies have won, and although the *Symphony of Victory* will go on to celebrate that outcome, there is nonetheless a stunned winding down, at two points reduced to nothing but the *pianissimo* murmur of tremolo strings in octaves. Sporadic cannon fire persists to the very end. This is a moment in which neither side, but only violence, has been victorious. Friend and foe are in one red burial blent.

Audiences at the time did not quite have the vocabulary to describe what was happening in this music, but they clearly perceived it. Admirers of *The Battle* praised the extraordinary "illusion" the music produced, while a hostile critic faulted the music for exactly the same thing, that is, for producing sounds of battle too realistically. Cook cites a favorable review from the *Allgemeine musikalische Zeitung:* "As for the *Battle,* if one were to attempt to describe it in musical notes, one would have to do it just as it is done here.... The effect, even the illusion, is quite extraordinary, and leads one to conclude without hesitation that there is no work equal to it in the whole realm of tone-painting."[13]

But if the music is unique in the realm of tone painting, perhaps it no longer belongs to that realm. Anton Schindler's account of a performance in Vienna's Grosse Redoutensaal, also cited by Cook, comes close to saying so: "From the long corridors and opposed rooms one could hear the enemy armies advance towards each other, creating a stunning illusion of the battle."[14] The poet Clemens Brentano waxed more rhapsodic: "With this work . . . all were one; there were no more artists, even no more Beethoven. . . . The work was alive; it was created and lived through."[15] Brentano later incorporated his response in a poem in which the battle and the music, Wellington and Beethoven, merge seamlessly with each other, in this case triumphantly. The poem makes it impossible to say whether it is describing the music or the battle:

> Who has pounded out the battle,
> Who has made the battle sound.
> Who in harmony so borne
> The scythed chariot
> Menacing the field of blood
> That pain grows reconciled . . .
> Wellington, Victoria!
> Beethoven, Gloria![16]

The music thus seemed to its early listeners to make a breakthrough from reference to reenactment. Representation and reality became confused, producing an illusion that could be described only in the superlative degree: stunning, quite extraordinary, created, and lived through. What Beethoven's contemporaries were struggling to say is that the music projected the auditory equivalent of images in continuous motion. The effect was more lifelike than any visual equivalent available in 1813. *The Battle* did more than just depict the sounds of battle realistically; its extra-large orchestra, added percussion, and composition of space produced the chaotic uproar as a virtual reality.

It would be nice to take as the last word on this subject a backhanded compliment by none other than the Duke of Wellington himself. Wellington missed the performance of *Wellington's Victory* at the Congress of Vienna. He is said, however, to have heard a later performance there. Asked afterward if the music was anything like the real thing, his reply, the story goes, was "By God, no. If it had been like that I would have run away myself."[17] The anecdote may be apocryphal but it does sound like the Duke.

FROM AUTOMATONS TO MOVING IMAGES

By the early nineteenth century, efforts to project virtual experience were well under way and very popular. Perhaps the forms most compatible with *Wellington's Victory* were the panorama and the diorama, which created a visual spectacle that, like Beethoven's acoustic equivalent, seemed to surround and envelop an audience.[18] The term "diorama" today means a three-dimensional scale model, but the original Diorama was a light-based theatrical medium. It was invented in 1822 by Louis Daguerre, who is most familiar today as the inventor of the photograph image that bears his name, the daguerreotype. One can think of the Diorama as an animated daguerreotype on a large scale. It "featured two immense paintings lit from the front and through the back inside an otherwise pitch-black, rotating auditorium";[19] the manipulation of light via shutters, skylights, and screens created an impression of being present at a changing scene—a landscape or the interior of a cathedral observed at sunrise or sunset or in changing weather—that audiences found more lifelike than illusory. The technology of the Panorama was somewhat older. Panoramas were huge paintings of an extended view displayed in a semicircular or circular pattern around a room; battle scenes were popular. Later panoramas used a scrolling mechanism to make the painted images move, and both panoramas and dioramas often added sound effects or music.

As I observed in chapter 3, this fascination with the creation of technology-based virtual reality developed alongside a decline of serious interest in humanoid automatons. As projection advanced, automatons tended to become sources of amusement rather than wonder, though they also became sources of anxiety over lifeless mechanism.[20] The era's best-known example was a holdover from the previous century. It was also a game-playing fake. The Automated Chess Player, invented by Wolfgang von Kempelen in 1770 and popularly known as the Turk, consisted of a mechanical dummy dressed in Turkish costume that could defeat most human opponents; the real chess player was a person cleverly concealed within the mechanism. Von Kempelen's invention toured throughout Europe and the Americas from 1779 until its destruction by fire in 1854. (Walter Benjamin brought it back to life in the celebrated opening paragraph of his "On the Concept of History" [1940], where its "philosophical counterpart" is the hidden theology directing "the puppet called 'historical materialism,' [which] is always supposed to win.")[21] The Turk was suspected of being a hoax for much of its colorful career; it prompted several important exposes, including one from Edgar Allan Poe. But the Turk's success, along with its implausibility, derived in part from what the device was simulating. No one thought the Turk was alive (which, ironically, is exactly what it was). It was supposed to be an intelligent machine. The Turk was simulating an android.

In 1809 a match took place in Vienna between the Turk and none other than Napoleon Bonaparte. Napoleon lost. The match was arranged by Johann Nepomuk Mälzel, who had bought the Turk in 1804. Mälzel, the inventor of the Mälzel Metronome, was a friend of Beethoven's and the originator of the idea of *Wellington's Victory*.

The music was originally supposed to be performed by a mechanical orchestra, the Panharmonicon, that Mälzel had invented. Things did not work out that way. The version of *Wellington's Victory* composed for the Panharmonicon consisted only of the introduction and the *Symphony of Victory*. It is not clear whether Beethoven already had *The Battle* in mind, but its music was certainly far more than the machine could handle. Beethoven added *The Battle* only when he prepared the work for live performance. The result was a kind of auditory diorama in which music crossed the barrier separating the representation of narrative action from the simulation of action in real time. For a little while, at least, this music was an acoustic movie projector. It had the visceral realism of early cinema, not merely the amusing flutter of a zoetrope.

Beethoven's decision to "go live" when the opportunity arose suggests that the "shocking illusion" of life could not (yet) be created for an action sequence by mechanical means. An android could simulate organism, but some marriage of mechanism and live operator was needed to project dynamism. Simulation had yet to make a full transition from life in motion to life in action. Music, as the androids suggest, could be proof of the former, but the proof of the latter had to be set before the eye before sound could enliven it. Faced with this visual obstacle, Beethoven literally overcame it with a bang.

That he did so was long an embarrassment to mainstream Beethoven reception, which could not stomach the popular appeal and supposed crudity of *Wellington's Victory* as measured against the high seriousness of the greater Beethoven. Like Cook and Nicholas Mathew, I find this attitude misguided in its emphasis and questionable in its assumptions.[22] This is not to say, foolishly, that we are wrong to admire extraordinary works like the *Eroica,* but it *is* to deny that we can isolate even the most extraordinary works from the full and messy complexity of the world, or worlds, around them. I no longer feel that it is unusual to say so, though it does at times still need to be said.

FROM SIMULATION TO SYMBOLIZATION: *THE SYMPHONY OF VICTORY*

Wellington's Victory reverses the values of Beethoven's funeral marches for several reasons. The most obvious is the topical character of the piece, which was responding to a specific event rather than to general circumstances. Doing so more or less committed it to a symbolic affirmation. Something of this disposition survives today in the "battle proms" held at stately homes in Britain during the summer; the proms typically culminate with full-bore performances of *Wellington's Victory,* muskets and cannons included. Another factor was surely that the Battle of Vitoria, following closely on the disastrous French invasion of Russia, really seemed to herald Napoleon's downfall. Waterloo was just two years away. But a more revealing reason derives from the difference between simulation and symbolization.

The failures of significance deliberately staged in the funeral marches are symbolic events, based on the imitation of music proper to military ceremonies. The funeral marches question the claims of the symbolic from within. But *The Battle* is a virtual event, based on the immersive lifelikeness of its music. *The Battle* is not simply *about* violence; it *is* violent, with an impact that no recording can capture—not by a long shot. That its violence is virtual does not make it any less real; as Gilles Deleuze's famous definition says, the virtual is what is real but not yet actual.[23] But because of this virtuality, because *The Battle* simulates instead of imitating, its own force limits its critical significance. The chaos of virtual battle exposes as hollow the epic-heroic symbolization of war by precluding it, not by subverting it. Simulation has succeeded, not where symbolization has failed, but where it has not been attempted. *The Battle* leaves symbolization intact, ready if called upon to reaffirm what has been questioned. The *Symphony of Victory* promptly does just that, ignoring the possibility (and thus guaranteeing) that its triumphal military rhetoric may be in force without significance. It acts as if listeners to *The Battle* were not required to believe the evidence of their own senses. The trouble with *Wellington's Victory* is neither some intrinsic defect in the music nor its topical character but its misunderstanding of itself.

But something about this music still needs explaining. One of the most remarkable things about the success of *Wellington's Victory* was the unambiguous pleasure given by the music's virtual violence. This pleasure seems to have been independent of the *Symphony of Victory*, which, as noted earlier, drew less attention than *The Battle*. The violence seemed to need no rationale, even if its implications were disturbing. The main immediate response to *The Battle* was amazement. Its source was the combined perception of simulated experience and the experience of simulation: the music's "stunning illusion." Violence, even lethal violence, becomes the measure of vitality; it even becomes strangely reassuring. As with the big chord in Haydn's "Surprise" Symphony with which chapter 1 began, a blow makes things come to life. Its action recalls the passage from Herder's *Kalligone* also considered in that chapter:

A. A blow disturbs a body; what message does that body's sound communicate?

B. "I have been disturbed; my members are consequently vibrating and eventually coming to rest."

Wellington's Victory was not alone in using simulation to correlate violence and vitality. One of the most popular panorama exhibits of the nineteenth century—one also involving Beethoven—was a simulation of the Great Lisbon Earthquake of 1755. The quake, joined by a tsunami, virtually destroyed the city and killed as many as one hundred thousand people. Voltaire's Candide famously used the event to chastise belief in benevolent providence and to satirize Leibniz's principle that ours is the best of all possible worlds.[24] The exhibit, complete with moving scenery and a musical underscore played on a grand organ, ran four times a day in London between 1848 and 1851. Beethoven's *Pastoral* Symphony was displaced from the countryside to depict the cityscape as an innocent idyll before the disaster, prefacing a natural violence from which, unlike the subsequent storm in the symphony, there was no recovery. According to *The Illustrated London News*, a "subterranean roar" accompanied the onset of the quake, followed by an "appalling crash" and a plunge of the exhibit space into total darkness.[25]

Half a century further on, in 1903, *The Great Train Robbery* (1903), the first movie to employ crosscutting in its narrative, littered the screen with bodies in ten minutes of Wild West banditry and gunplay. The closing "shot" (or opening; the director, Edwin Porter, left the choice open) was literal: the outlaw leader points his gun at the audience and fires point-blank.

LATER DISPATCHES: FROM LISZT TO TCHAIKOVSKY

The tension between simulation and symbolization in *Wellington's Victory* has a close literary parallel in Stendhal's novel *The Charterhouse of Parma* (1839). Stendhal's protagonist Fabrizio stumbles his way through Wellington's other and more famous victory at the Battle of Waterloo without understanding anything that happens. His movements are in a sense impossible to narrate because they, like the battle, lack all coherence and direction. The actions traced by the chapter "The Guns of Waterloo" and by Beethoven's *Battle* are essentially the same: the production of a confusion that reduces narrative to random metonymy and exposes the narrative form as a system of signs in force without significance. Stendhal even seems to impart a certain virtuality to the experience of battle conceived along the same lines as Beethoven's, that is, of battle as an acoustic envelope filled with a monstrous music, a counterpoint of booming cannons and rattling guns: "The noise of the guns grew twice as loud and seemed to be coming nearer. The explosions were beginning to form a kind of figured bass; there was no interval between one explosion and the next, and above this figured bass, which resembled the roar of a torrent in the distance, the sound of musketry firing could be clearly distinguished."[26]

Stendhal's account of Waterloo contains graphic details that intrude abruptly on the narrative and arrest its movement. The text simulates the blockage it describes. Readers accustomed to epic heroism encounter only a bloody mess—a disemboweled horse, a battlefield amputation, and this:

> Fabrizio had not gone five hundred yards when his nag stopped short: it was a corpse, lying across the path, which terrified horse and rider alike.... A bullet, entering on one side of the nose, had gone out at the opposite temple, and disfigured the corpse in a hideous fashion. It lay with one eye still open.[27]

A more radical and more literal simulation comes about via the chapter's quasi-random shifts among multiple and inconsistent points of view and types of narrative: from dialogue (in which the characters almost invariably mistake what's going on), to narration through Fabrizio's eyes, to detached authorial reports on his movements. The reports are typically marked by an ironic tone—Fabrizio's adventures achieve nothing but continual irony—and sardonic references to Fabrizio as "our hero." The references extend the irony from the character to the narrator, who is compelled to repeat at the level of narration the anarchy that overwhelms Fabrizio at the level of narrative. The chaotic polyphony of the battle repeats itself in the chaotic polyphony that describes the battle. That unseeing eye (which "horrified [Fabrizio] more than anything") has the truest point of view; it is in force without significance.

The difference between Stendhal and Beethoven is Stendhal's irony. Unlike *Wellington's Victory, The Charterhouse of Parma* has no interest in restoring meaning to the signifiers from which it has emptied meaning. Perhaps this is because for Stendhal the outcome of the great battle is less the defeat of Napoleon than the defeat of reason. He is already writing about history whereas Beethoven was responding to current events. But another, perhaps even stronger factor is that Stendhal's irony is irreversible. Any attempt, for example, to make Waterloo a part of Fabrizio's education would have been an obvious fabrication, an almost cynical indulgence in signifiers in force without significance. Beethoven's *Battle* is not at all ironic, and there is even a case to be made that its reduction of glorious battle to inglorious noise went further than it was meant to. In any case, as we've seen, Beethoven's technological means left the door open for the *Symphony of Victory*, and the *Symphony of Victory* crashed right through it.

Later essays in battle music did the same thing without taking the risks that Beethoven did. A good example is Liszt's *Battle of the Huns,* composed in 1857 after a monumental painting from 1837 of the same name (also known as "Spectre Battle") by Wilhelm Kaulbach. The battle involved was fought in 451 CE between the armies of Attila the Hun and Christian Rome. The conflict was said to be so fierce that the spirits of the dead continued fighting as they rose over the battlefield; Kaulbach's painting is a still image of their motion. Freud later adopted the image as a metaphor for the conflict between the ego and superego: "The struggle which once raged in the deepest strata of the mind . . . is now continued in a higher region, like the Battle of the Huns in Kaulbach's painting."[28]

Liszt follows tradition in treating the outcome as a major victory for Christianity. Like Beethoven, he deploys new instrumental resources, including muted strings playing *fortissimo* and the climatic participation of an organ. But the musical narrative remans firmly within the limits of symbolization. The work does not seek to simulate the battle, and its aim is the very reverse of showing signifiers in force without significance.

Liszt planned his proportions accordingly. The depiction of the battle takes up less than a third of the work's running time. The music is very sonorous but there is nothing chaotic about it. It deploys a series of clear-cut melodic figures and elaborates them sequentially; clashing trumpet blasts inject the main note of drama. Where Beethoven attacks the possibility of observation, Liszt enlarges it. Unlike Beethoven's, Liszt's battle music uses percussion as expressive commentary, not as simulation. The emphasis is on cymbals, not drums—until the end, that is, when the bass drum appears to wield ecclesiastical force in alliance with the organ (an instrument, as Liszt noted in a letter, that had not been invented at the time of the battle). Finally, Liszt employs a plainchant melody, *Crux Fidelis,* as a signifier immune to critique. He asks us to accept the premise that the law behind this chant can never lose the significance that keeps it in force.

The chant first rises above the sounds of battle on massed trombones, and subsequently joins with the organ and offstage brass in a majestic conclusion. The only complication is the matter of reference. Unlike Beethoven's *Battle,* Liszt's refers not to an event but to the painting of an event. The plainchant as master signifier is as much a device of ekphrasis as it is a declaration of faith. It deals with art as much as it does with war. This ambiguity opens up a certain possibility of critical distance. But it does little to impede the music's investment in a significance that it does everything in its power to uphold.

The complication is revealing. Liszt symbolizes instead of simulating, but *what* he symbolizes comes close to the phenomenon of projection. The music's novel sonorities and its use of plainchant combine to suggest, even to form, sensory traces of moving images. The images are those of Kaulbach's painting, which is itself an image of motion, even of images in motion. The music's sonorities repeatedly afford the listener the chance to see those images move in their being heard.

The most famous source of this affordance is the use of muted strings throughout the battle music, in which, Liszt says in the score, "all the instruments must sound like ghosts." The battle goes on behind an auditory veil. In turn, the battle music subsequently becomes a veil for the ghostly sound of the brass quietly intoning a chorale under the turmoil. But perhaps even more telling is what appears when the veils are lifted. After the victory arrives at top volume, the soft recurring sound of the *Crux Fidelis,* played unaccompanied on a harmonium or organ placed behind the orchestra, seems to come from long ago and far away. A later episode of lightly scored, almost pastoral tranquility has a similar quality. And as the music drives hectically to its conclusion, it is interrupted by a brief, similarly tranquil passage for winds alone that carries the intimation further, only to be absorbed by the final symbolic tumult.

In this one respect, although their moods could not be more different, the spectral forms in Liszt look forward to waltzing specters in Mahler and Ravel—apparitions to be encountered in chapter 6. But this spectral condition is not merely ghostly or fantastic. Instead it is an approximation to the condition of the moving image, a form that is *almost* materially present, a thickened spirit or thinned matter, or what Daniel Tiffany has termed "lyric substance."[29] In keeping with a principle famously put forth by Walter Benjamin, the moving image is an imaginary form before it is a technical effect.[30] At each phase of its development it is virtual before it is actual. In the early phases of precinematic technology, the effect of projection involves a perceptible transition from "statics" to "dynamics,"[31] an effect that would later recede to the threshold of perception as the hypnotic flicker of film in darkened theaters. Liszt's imaginary forms are precursors. They are much like the seven old men in Baudelaire's contemporaneous poem of that name:

> Suddenly an old man whose yellow rags
> Resembled the color of a rainy sky ...
> Appeared to me ...
>
> His likeness followed: beard, eye, back, stick, rags,
> No trait to tell them apart, come from the same hell,
> This centenarian twin and these baroque specters
> Walking with the same steps toward an unknown goal.[32]

The spectral figures move in flickering repetitions like the images in a zoetrope or what Baudelaire and Liszt would (or could) have known in its earlier form as a magic disk or phenakistoscope, or, if we look ahead rather than behind, the devices capable of projecting moving images in color that by the last third of the century could be bought in French department stores.[33]

The nineteenth century found battle music in the parlor as well as in the concert hall. Piano pieces depicting particular battles were popular during the American Civil War, for example, many of them played or composed by women, and most drawing their narrative techniques from Frantisek Kotzwara's *Battle of Prague,* a piano piece composed in 1788 that remained popular well into the middle of the nineteenth century.[34] Beethoven and Liszt were both likely to have known it. But these piano works remain firmly in the space of representation. For simulation, the full power of a large orchestra was required. None took this requirement further than the century's most famous battle piece, Tchaikovsky's *1812 Overture*, the only musical work examined here that has a solid place in the standard repertoire.

The similarities with *Wellington's Victory* are obvious. Tchaikovsky too commemorates a major defeat for Napoleon, his retreat from Moscow after apparent victory at the Battle of Borodino. Tchaikovsky's interest in simulation extends to calling for a carillon and a real cannon, plus an extra brass band using whatever instruments are available, as parts of his orchestra. But Tchaikovsky too reverses Beethoven's priorities, and more radically than Liszt does. Simulation in the *1812 Overture* belongs less to the depiction of the battle than to the equivalent of the *Symphony of Victory*.

Tchaikovsky follows Beethoven by using thematic motifs for the opposing armies but unlike Beethoven he does not give these motifs separate locations in space. He simply opposes them dramatically. The battle is not simulated at all except for the placement of five cannon shots aimed at a fragment of the "Marseillaise." The cannon fire returns in the triumphant conclusion, now with eleven shots to accompany the anthem "God Save the Tsar!" The musical narrative—and it is important to note that the music *has* a narrative—is clear in outline and rich in melody, which probably helps account for the work's popularity. The music integrates its triumphant cannon shots and other effects of virtuality into a firmly articulated order, rather than setting them loose as agents of disorder. Tchaikovsky treats the heroic signifier as if nothing had ever lost or emptied it. Like Liszt's, his music elaborates on an anthem to reinforce an institution thought to be under threat, there the Catholic Church, here the Czarist state.

This ardent nationalism has had a surprising consequence. It has allowed listeners to adapt the music to whatever nationalism they prefer; the Russian details are examples, not essentials. Non-Russian listeners, even French ones, can universalize the heroic, military, and nationalistic signifiers that the overture employs and at the same time enjoy the "colorful" and "exotic" qualities stereotypically used to characterize Russian music. It is tempting to ascribe half the overture's success to its anachronistic use of the "Marseillaise" for the French rather than Beethoven's "Marlbrough," which is better known today as "For He's a Jolly Good Fellow" or "The Bear Came over the Mountain." In any event, the *1812 Overture* succeeds by celebrating the signifier's force without worrying about its significance. The music assumes an unblushing naïvety that dares the too-knowing listener to denounce it, to be a killjoy, to crush a butterfly with a sledgehammer. Why spoil the fun?

This attitude has worked to the benefit of *Wellington's Victory*, too, if "likes" on YouTube are any guide.[35] From here it is only a short distance to John Williams's film scores for *Star Wars* and *Superman*—music that inherits from this genealogy of battle pieces a self-conscious blatancy that invites us to enjoy it precisely because it is such a fake. Even, and perhaps especially, because we *know* it is just a fake. In this context the battle movement of *Wellington's Victory* gains cultural, if not exactly musical, stature—and really, why judge it musically by an aesthetic standard it does not aspire to? Like Stendhal's self-fractured narrative of Waterloo, Beethoven's musical diorama of the Battle of Vitoria parts the veils of symbolization to expose a terrifying reality that no symbol can subdue. This music has the courage of its confusions.

FIVE

"Dear Listener" . . .

MUSIC AND THE INVENTION OF SUBJECTIVITY

UNTIL JULY 18, 1877, VOICE WAS LIFE. On that day it became permanently posthumous, because on that day—the day Thomas Edison invented the phonograph in the form of a cylinder wrapped in tinfoil—the dead acquired a voice. Any voice could now outlive its speaker; each living voice was potentially the voice of the dead. The same change overtook music at the same time. On that day music became durable as well as transient. These changes coalesce in some of the earliest surviving recordings. One of them, on Edison wax cylinders, preserved a performance of Sir Arthur Sullivan's "The Lost Chord" on cornet and piano; a recording of Sullivan's speaking voice quickly followed. Earlier still, when Edison introduced the phonograph in London at the Crystal Palace, he used a recording—the earliest surviving recording of music, and perhaps the first—of an extract from Handel's oratorio *Israel in Egypt* sung, so an inscription on the cylinder claims, by a chorus of four thousand voices.[1]

Novel as they seemed, these developments were not unexpected. They had been in preparation since the beginning of the century, when various inventors took up the challenge of la Mettrie's observation that a "talking man" would be harder to create than Vaucanson's flute player, but not impossible. La Mettrie was half right; it did prove possible to synthesize voice in a limited way, but a talking man remained out of reach.[2]

These efforts to capture voice by mechanical means led to the contradiction that gives this chapter its topic. Until well into the twentieth century, recorded voice seemed both uncannily alive and merely mechanical. The same was true for recorded music, with voice or without. Early recording devices were the heirs of the eighteenth-century androids. As Rolf Goebel has observed, the Edison Company in 1906 even marketed the phonograph as a sentient creature while also emphasizing its mechanical perfection.[3] Sound recording, however, did not create this ambiguity. Instead it exposed the mechanical element that had been hiding in voice all along. It had been hiding behind the most vital aspect of voice, its embodiment of subjectivity.

As with living voice, so with live music. As a vehicle of subjectivity, music stood opposed to mechanism; that opposition was what underwrote the train of metaphors we have been following and it is what the music examined in chapters 1 through 3 put at risk when it sought to move from mechanism to life. But the opposition could stand only as long as subjectivity itself was opposed to mechanism. And like voice, like music, subjectivity had been hiding an element of automatism all along.

In music the subjectivity doing the hiding had a virtual voice.[4] Not a singing voice, even when there was singing, but a voice that, as voices do, as voices will, addressed itself to the listener as if from one sentient being to another. That this voice was only a metaphor, that the voice of music was virtual rather than acoustic, counted more for it than against it. The voice of music spoke so compellingly because it seemed to embody a primary act of relationship. In music someone known only in sound enabled whoever heard that sound to feel addressed by it in a direct act of mutual discovery and self-discovery.

This address form constituted the link between music and subjectivity and thus the link between music and the sensation of life. In everyday parlance "subjectivity" refers to the private experience of the individual, particularly with respect to its fallibility. But as used here, in a more philosophical sense, the term denotes the self-awareness of the living person's, or subject's, existence, and the ensemble of feelings and dispositions available at any historical moment that make this self-awareness possible and give it content. A person gains access to that ensemble by addressing others and being addressed by them. Contrary to the experience of Condillac's statue, but in line with that of Frankenstein's creature, life becomes self-aware only in being shared. Once music had come to be heard as addressing its listeners, it became the sensory embodiment of that primary sharing.

Sharing was essential to the invention of musical subjectivity for practical as well as symbolic reasons. The thread of subjective life ran from the work of the composer through the event of performance, the agency of the performer, and the response of the listener. Everywhere within this relay music seemed to reenact the origin and continuation of subjective life in the experience of hearing a call. Especially since the mid-eighteenth century, music and subjectivity could not easily be disentangled.⁵ Always close, they became inseparable in association with two pivotal developments: the invention of the concept of the aesthetic to account for the pursuit of pleasure in perception, and the conception of music as the primary medium for the communication of emotion. Alone among the arts, music gave the ontology of subjective life a sensory form.

A few brief quotations may help capture the fervor that music often aroused when experienced in these terms. From Jean-Jacques Rousseau in 1767: "The musician of genius ... expresses ideas by feelings and feelings by accents, and the passions that he voices move us to the very depth of our hearts.... He experiences in his heart a feeling for life that never leaves him, and which he communicates to those who possess responsive hearts." From J. G. Sulzer in 1771, with a strikingly erotic inflection: "[When we hear] a melodic language whose perfectly-shaped and uninterrupted flow of notes reveals the outpourings of a sensitive heart ... [o]ur soul is borne to rest, undisturbed, on a kind of couch of sound, and can abandon itself to every emotion that is aroused in it by the expressive melody." (Sulzer elsewhere observes that composers can express emotions other than their own by means of imaginative empathy.) From J. G. Herder in 1800: "Music travels with us as our most intimate companion, enlivening and uplifting our existence from childhood on." When G. W. F. Hegel in the 1820s identified music as the means by which the subject's inner life becomes apprehensible to itself, he summed up several generations of experience and set the terms for a good many more.⁶

These accounts assume a concert setting or the equivalent: music taken in as the primary object of attention, not as the accompaniment to something else. The assumption carried over easily to cover the phonograph and later recording media, but it does not extend to background music or music on soundtracks, neither of which will be considered here. The assumption granted, these terms of listening lasted a long time and they persist even today, perhaps more helped than hindered by digital media. Nonetheless, the era in which music and subjectivity were inseparable, what Sander van Maas calls "the grand history of musical subjectivity,"⁷ may now be nearing its end. The reason is not just that music for roughly the past century has been increasingly skeptical about subjectivity. (We will see some of that skepticism in the next chapter.) Subjectivity itself is at a historical crossroads, as is the concept of the human that goes with it. At the very least, subjectivity in the forms familiar since the early modern era is disappearing today and has been doing so for quite a while. To be sure, this disappearance is not absolute. Past subjectivities survive their obsolescence in practice by becoming the possibilities of imagination, narrative, and fantasy on which they had always depended anyway. But the difference between the subjectivity we inhabit and the subjectivity we revisit is a historical reality that cannot be wished or brushed away. Once subjectivity begins to change its form, we have to refocus our understanding of it on the cusp between what is still possible and what is no longer possible.

Or perhaps we need to focus on something stronger, namely the impossible, which brings me to a slightly displaced epigraph. This is from Jacques Derrida, on the "unique situation" of invention:

> The invention of the impossible is impossible.... Certainly. But it is the only possible invention: an invention has to declare itself as the invention of that which did not appear to be possible; otherwise it only makes explicit a program of [established] possibilities.[8]

The phonograph is a case in point, and a pivotal one in the history of subjectivity, which is the history of the invention of subjectivity. Go back a few steps: before the invention of the telegraph, it was impossible to convey thoughts instantaneously across long distances. Not so afterward. But before the invention of the telephone, it was impossible to transmit voices instantaneously across long distances. Not so afterward. But before the invention of the phonograph, those voices were doomed to vanish in the act of transmission. Not so afterward. But the fact that the preserved voices could survive their speakers made that last step treacherous. Like the photograph, which Roland Barthes famously said always conveyed the message "that-has-been," the phonograph drives a wedge between subjectivity and life.[9] It marks a decisive turn in a process of reinvention that links both life and subjectivity to technological apparatuses and storage media.

Does subjectivity in music still exist in alliance with life and address? Does subjectivity itself? Certainly. But it has existed that way only since it was invented, and once invented it has had to be reinvented continually, fixed up, tinkered with, redesigned, made experimental, and eventually confronted with the impossibility, in Derrida's sense, of the existence that it pursues.

This chapter examines a few key moments in the unfinished history of subjectivity, its erosion and transformation, its rises and falls, in Western culture since the Enlightenment. To begin, here are some inventions, three of them.

THREE-PART INVENTIONS

I. Last Words

It is one of the most famous lines in English literature: "Reader, I married him." That is Charlotte Brontë's Jane Eyre speaking at the end of the novel that bears her name. Speaking? No, not speaking: writing, as one writes a letter, as one *addresses* a text to someone. This abrupt shift to direct address, at the head of the last chapter, recalls, perhaps, that the modern English novel began in the form of letters, in the eighteenth-century epistolary novels of Samuel Richardson, *Pamela* and *Clarissa*. Or perhaps, following Derrida, we should speak not of letters but of postcards, since the letters in Richardson have been opened to be read by all and the epistolary break in Brontë is addressed to anyone who happens to see it, just as anyone who picks up a postcard becomes its addressee by virtue of the card's exposure, failing the protection of an envelope, to just anyone's gaze. Letters, Derrida is implying, are veiled postcards.[10] The novel, Brontë is saying, or no, not saying, but letting it go without saying, links the author and reader (a reader, the reader, any reader, every reader) in the address form.

II. First Words

It is one of the most famous moments in musical history: "O friends, not these tones." That is Beethoven's baritone-avatar speaking at the turning point of the symphony so closely linked to his name that there is, though there are many, only one "Ninth Symphony." Speaking? No, not speaking: calling (for this is not yet singing), as one calls to someone across a room or a street, as one *addresses* someone with a call. This abrupt shift to direct address, coming near the head of the last movement, recalls perhaps—but here the parallel breaks down. There is an act of address here, to be sure, but not a recollection. This call is not only a calling out and calling up but also a calling off. In rejecting the music of the symphony's first three movements, the Beethovenian voice is silencing the past: silencing not only its expressive conventions and their formal conveyances but also its practices of listening. Music, this music says, is a call. To hear it is to heed it. Music in the past was something in the air: something to hear. Music from now on, from this very moment on, will be an address, an address to you, whoever you are: something to receive. Music will even be the act of address itself in material form, the vibratory throw issued from one (any one) to another in the expectation of a catch. This music may have voices and it may not; the finale of the Ninth—we should not forget this—has it both ways.

But what kind of address will music be? Beethoven's call (he wrote the words as well as the music) joins an exclamation to a pair of injunctions: "O friends, not these tones! Rather let us . . ." Is "not these tones" a plea or a dismissal? Is "Rather let us . . ." an invitation or a command, a request for consent or an exercise of authority? To what extent do the answers depend on performance? And are the questions supposed to be answered at all, or answered the same way twice?

III. Not a Word

It is one of the most famously unhinged moments in the history of the musical avant-garde. A pianist plays a cramped, meandering, melancholic theme in the bass, with the left hand only, and then repeats it under a loose skein of chords in the right hand. Although the tempo is very slow, the whole process takes only about a minute. Then the pianist does it again. And again. And . . . keeps on doing it until the same music has been heard 840 times.

The piece is "Vexations," by Eric Satie, composed in 1893, never published by its composer, and never heard until John Cage—who else?—organized a performance with a team of eleven pianists in 1963. The concert, if that's what it was, lasted eighteen hours and forty minutes. Apparently only one member of the audience lasted that long.

Whether Satie was serious about the number 840 remains unknown. He was whimsical on principle, and his score does not exactly call for the marathon of repetitions. Instead it explains what the marathon would demand: "To play this motif 840 times in succession, it would be good to prepare oneself in advance, and in the utmost silence, through serious immobilities."[11] By taking Satie at his word, Cage engaged in a kind of higher whimsy that turns "Vexations" into an invention by John Cage. He recasts Satie's "impossible" piece as an exercise in mental, even spiritual discipline, like a mantra in the third person. Satie's "serious immobilities" migrate from preparation to performance, or more exactly cancel the distinction between them. And whereas Cage's best-known inventions involve music incorporating the operations of chance, "Vexations" seems to do the exact opposite: to immunize the music against any and all contingencies. Repetition cancels expression; the music addresses no one and communicates nothing but its own replication.

But that is not what happens, especially when teams of pianists are involved. Since 1963, "Vexations" has seen a good many performances, ranging in duration from fourteen to twenty-four hours. The differences in duration occur because different pianists (including single pianists in different moods) interpret the slow tempo marking differently, with different degrees of strictness, and make their own decisions about dynamics, which the score does not specify.[12] The result is music that cannot help returning to the address form that it means to spurn with its maddening sameness, music that cannot help admitting the force of subjectivity that it means to forestall with its numbing automatism.

No "Reader!" here; no "O friends!" Does that mean that music as call has been revoked except as a failure of discipline? Or, on the contrary, that the call comes regardless of any attempt to revoke it, an outcome that Cage, perhaps, would not have wanted? Does "Vexations" finally negate the possibility of address by its unbearable length? Does it merely evade the questions of address raised by the Ninth Symphony, or does it travesty a coercive excess of address that, by the time this music was "composed," whether in 1893 or 1963, had come to dominate the cultures of both classical and popular music? Does Cage, channeling Satie, propose that music as address is a deceptive fiction masking the reality of music as command?

So many questions. These first three "inventions" open them up; those that follow will seek some answers to them. And to these: Who is addressing what to whom when music becomes an address to a listener? Does the historical invention of that address apply in retrospect? And once music has become an address, can it become something else? What happens when the circuit is broken? What happens when it isn't?

ADDRESSING HISTORY

Well, what *has* happened? Song is an address by definition, but when did musical sound as such become a form of address? (Note that I don't ask when it was *conceived* as a form of address. Invention is not a metaphor but an act; through that act music becomes an address, becomes address, regardless of how it is conceived.) The representation *in* music of music as an address can be traced back at least to the middle of the eighteenth century and no doubt much further. Iconic examples include the slow movement of J. S. Bach's keyboard concerto in D Minor, BWV 1052; a transitional movement in Haydn's Symphony no. 7 in C, "Le Midi" (Noon), Hob. 1:7 (1761); and the slow movement of Mozart's Piano Concerto no. 9 in E flat, K. 271 (1775). All three instances are in a minor key, all invoke tragic sublimity, and all incorporate instrumental recitatives that seem to enter the music from outside and afar. The sense of address might thus seem to represent an exception, and to some extent it does; the combination of features in these pieces is unusual. But the exception makes itself the rule, or reveals that it has always been the rule, virtually as soon as it appears.[13]

Once heard, the recitatives resound, not as symbolic voices intruded into a body of music without voice, but as *other* voices cutting through the symbolic voice that (we now understand) belongs to music in general the moment we hear it as expressive of anything subjective.

Bach frames his slow movement with two exceptionally intense and impetuous fast ones. The level of energy is so high that the more vulnerable middle movement seems to require the protection of a second frame, a prologue and an epilogue forming a buffer zone around the movement proper. This second frame consists of an extended instrumental recitative in octaves that both begins the slow movement and ends it. In between there is a solo "aria" combining elements of vocal expressiveness and keyboard ornamentation. The aria steadily grows more elaborate but remains anchored in the recitative, which persists throughout in the bass. The movement thus explicitly situates instrumental music within the address form. The impassioned circumference speaks, and because it does, because it can, the intimate center sings.

Haydn concentrates his recitatives in one place, an interlude marked "Recitativo," the better to translate their symbolic value into sensory intensity. The recitatives belong to the "accompanied" type in which the voice and the instrumental ensemble each take a share. The voice is represented by an increasingly elaborate and expressive solo violin. The instrument's vocalizing reaches its peak with an unaccompanied warbling at the end of the interlude, which turns out to be an extended introduction to the Adagio that follows. The import of beginning this way soon becomes apparent as the Adagio reveals itself to be a lightly accompanied series of dialogues between the solo violin and solo cello, with interjections from a pair of flutes. As in the Bach, the recitatives have done precisely what recitatives are supposed to do. They have introduced an aria—in this case a duet. Aside from its last two measures, the movement ends with a lengthy cadenza for the solo violin and solo cello, their individual voices addressing each other and the listener alike.

Mozart's slow movement treats the voice as a means of coming to terms with anguish. The movement begins with a pulsing, throbbing, rhythmically disrupted melody low in the strings; the movement asks what to do about it. The instrumental introduction ends with a recitative, the first of four. The recitative introduces the solo piano, which enters over the opening melody with an ornamented cantabile line: a consoling if melancholy aria. The second recitative is for the piano, which returns the orchestra's earlier favor: it introduces a new, full-throated "song" for the orchestra alone. The third recitative follows the return of the piano's aria over the opening melody; the recitative, shared between the soloist and orchestra, releases the piano from the burden of the melody and ushers in an extended aria-like passage for piano alone. The final recitative, primarily for piano, evolves directly out of the cadenza and takes on a higher degree of expressivity than its predecessors. It seems to be reaffirming its freedom from the burden of the opening, but its success is equivocal. This last recitative ends the piece. No aria follows.

In their different ways, Bach's, Haydn's, and Mozart's instrumental recitatives and arias explicitly place the listener in the position of one subject addressed by another. That position is very difficult to relinquish for at least two reasons. First, the sheer fact that voiceless instrumental recitative can be heard as an address implies that the possibility of such hearing is inherent in the musical event. More exactly, it has been *made* inherent by this music's invention of the "impossible," an address without a voice, or with no voice except the one that stands as the music's own. Second, the inherent subjectivity thus recognized is not simply musical or aesthetic but ontological. To be a subject is necessarily to be the subject of address. To be a subject at all, to be any kind of subject, is to be the potential subject of address. Conversely, insofar as the human is constituted by the power and obligation of speech, insofar as we are beings who symbolize, refer, imagine, and represent, to receive and acknowledge an address is necessarily to act as a subject.

This relationship is not metaphorical. As Judith Butler has argued, the basis of subjectivity is literally the condition of being spoken to. More particularly, for her, it is the condition of being addressed by a call to give an account of oneself—an account that is impossible to give.[14] We invent such accounts because the call is hard to refuse and because the impossibility of the task only increases our desire to accomplish it. The recitatives in our trio of examples, and the arias in two of them, are inventions that show their music trying to give an account of itself. Bach's concerto grasps that address begins at a place of vulnerability, Mozart's concerto that pain may press us to more calls than one, and Haydn's symphony that the essential need of the subject is finding a counterpart to converse with. These accounts necessarily fail before the subjective force of the music that invents them (just as my very short descriptions do), but their failure is nonetheless meant to be pleasurable and moving.

The music acts this way in part because it belongs to the era that discovered the possibility of the aesthetic—here again meaning simply the enjoyment of perception for its own sake, a kind of higher hedonism. From the beginning, aesthetic pleasure arose in relation to both works of nature and works of art (that is, of fine art, a category newly separated from other practices of making). This distinction in the object of enjoyment brought another in its wake. To enjoy objects in nature, one simply had to find them, but objects of art had to be *given*. The "work of art" as a vehicle of pleasurable perception is necessarily a medium of address.

Implicitly recognizing as much, the musical aesthetics of the time raised the stakes of musical expression to endow aesthetic pleasure with ethical value. As J. G. Sulzer wrote in his widely read *General Theory of Fine Art*, "The principal, if not indeed the sole function of a perfect musical composition is the accurate expression of emotions and passions.... Without [expression], music is just a pleasant toy; with it, music becomes an overwhelmingly powerful language which engulfs the heart. It compels us in turn to tenderness, resolution, and courage."[15] Sulzer's linguistic metaphor does more here than simply provide a customary excuse for affirming without explaining the intelligibility of music. It endows music with the character of a call, an address, which assumes an irresistible performative force. Too irresistible, one might demur, but the key point here is not whether the call is coercive, but that to hear expressive music is to be addressed by a call. Even works inherited from eras that conceived of them otherwise may sound as calls when we hear them aesthetically.

In principle, a viable model of subjectivity should be available to anyone who wants it, even though in history it never has been. So it is important to spell out what the understanding of subjectivity as addressed and addressing does and does not involve, musically and otherwise. That comes next.

CONCEPTUAL INVENTIONS

Assuming that the address form has to be reckoned with in any account of music composed since the mid-eighteenth century, and perhaps since the mid-sixteenth,[16] just how is this form put to work—conceived, deployed, enacted, sustained? And if one addresses oneself to music from an antisubjective or posthuman standpoint, what happens to the sense of music as an extension of living subjectivity that arose within the era of the grand history? Was it just an illusion? Why does it still compel us, as it surely often does? Would not even a model of subjectivity divorced from the era's widely criticized conception of a privileged, autonomous, self-possessed subject, the exclusionary sovereign *I*, be put out of joint, or at the very least diminished? Would one not have to conclude with van Maas that "musical subjectivity functions, so to speak, 'on top' of an aural-musical event that is more radically indeterminate than any play with subject[ivity] allows us to recognize?"[17]

The answer to the last question is a resounding "Yes and No." *Yes* in the sense that to ignore the cross-current of automatism in the long era of subjectivity would be a serious blunder. But *No* in the sense that the history of subjectivity is full of encounters with automatism, both external and internal to the subject. Subjectivity and automatism are ultimately one concept, not two. We might imagine a sphere of purely automatic or impersonal agency with no relation to subjectivity at all: a seated mannequin leans forward, its eyes turned toward a player piano. But, ironically, we can imagine this privation of subjectivity only as subjects. The privation of subjectivity is one of our inventions. And so is the mannequin, which should already have been recognizable as the Jacquet-Droz organist, an automaton that coaxes us to imagine her as a subject as she breathes and plays.

Consider an automaton of quite another sort—one whose call forms an all-too-determinate "musical-aural" event that asks its designated addressee to become an automaton in turn.

In the third act of Wagner's *Parsifal,* the brotherhood of Grail Knights gangs up on its gravely wounded leader, Amfortas, and demands that he perform his holy office. Amfortas refuses, driven by the unbearable pain of his wound. (He has other reasons too; we will return to Amfortas.) The music for his refusal is savage, equal in excess to Amfortas's surplus agony. Wagner, or Amfortas, pushes this outcry to the point of atonality, which in Wagner's musical language still means sound stripped of meaning, sound as abrasive material, the correlative of pain pushed to the point of impersonality: "Pain torturing itself," as Wallace Stevens later described such an extreme, "Pain killing pain on the very point of pain."[18] The music denies the audience a subjective relationship as Amfortas denies the Knights their magical bread and wine. Denies more than that: he enjoins them to kill him; he wants to deny them the bare possibility of address.

But such voiding of subjectivity can also happen in circumstances that are anything but sublime or tragic. The intensifying repetitions of Ravel's *Bolero,* which also lead to a point of collapse, invite the listener to become mesmerized by a rhythmic mechanism powered by orchestral color. Ravel himself characterized the two themes that alternate throughout as "altogether impersonal" and—also playing on the mechanism of language— described "an analogy between the alternation of these two themes riveted one to the other and the links of a *chaîne* (chain / assembly line)."[19] *Bolero* may be as popular as it is precisely because it offers a release from subjectivity in an abandon of what might be called sensuous automatism. Yet the subject need comply no more with such a perversely seductive machinery of abnegation than with its opposite number, the call that coerces. All one has to do after hearing *Bolero* is walk away at one's own pace in the bolero rhythm and hum the tune.[20]

Where, then, and how does the address form place music in the history of subjectivity and vice versa? I propose to sketch the rudiments of an answer in a series of additional inventions. But before turning to them a little further reflection is needed.

Throughout these inventions there has been and will continue to be a certain free interchangeability among the varieties of auditory expression: voice, speech, music, singing, instrumental sound, call, reply. What makes this fluidity possible is the address form, which operates regardless of what fills it out. The question before us is thus not inherently musical, but a question that music appropriates. Music is traditionally the most idealized vehicle of address, the vehicle most free (so we like to think) from the pitfalls of address in antagonistic or authoritarian speech. Music has been chosen as the aesthetic vehicle in which the ambiguities of address yield to unambiguous pleasure. We can continue to ask our question about address and subjectivity through music, but that is best done in the awareness that the answer we thus call for needs to be sounded more broadly.

The question is how closely our auditory experience ties in, and ties us in, to the address form, and therefore—this should be italicized: *therefore*— becomes the matrix of subjectivity. For, as we have seen, the address form is not something an independent subjectivity may take part in or not. On the contrary, it is the condition of possibility for subjectivity. Subjectivity is something that happens within the address form. Subjectivity is *that which* happens within the address form. Only subjects can be addressed; subjects can only address themselves to and through other subjects.

And what then? Let me suggest two points.

First, the address form holds on to the idea of the subject, not to sustain any notion of a center of conscious knowledge set over against an array of objects, but to provide for the singular, sentient, and reflective locus of human agency. No one escapes the demands of that agency and no one escapes its outcome. The subject is that which dies. Martin Heidegger's conception of the world as "the ever-nonobjective" because it is permeated by concern is relevant here.[21] The subject (not that Heidegger would approve the term) is a transient relay in the "worlding" produced by the operation of concern. The world in Heidegger's sense is neither a "mere collection" of "things that are just there" nor "a merely imagined framework added by our representation to the sum of such given things." Instead "the *world worlds,* and is more fully in being than the tangible and perceptible realm in which we believe ourselves to be at home."[22] Human agency assumes historical and material definition where and wherever occasions of concern give it a world to act in. The person who acts, whom I want to keep addressing as the subject, is one in whom the mechanism of relaying concern is primordially the vital action of listening, calling, and replying. Music (of whatever kind) is both a mirror of that process and a means of it, an example and the thing exemplified. Perhaps that is why music is one of the few true cultural universals.

Second, address concerns listening, not hearing. Its concern is not the event of sonority but the cultural practice of making something of sonority. In relation to language, this relationship is ancient, but in relation to music it is strikingly recent. It is also, however, strikingly potent. Once music takes up the address form, no matter to what era one dates the event, it becomes impossible to separate subjectivity from the experience of music in and through the vicissitudes of address.

But this expressly does not mean "subjectivity" in the sense of the consciously self-possessed master subject, which has an existence far shakier and less idolized than conventional wisdom would have it. (To say this is not to minimize the evils that follow when the addressee is cast as a social or racial inferior in the name of the subject in power—a topic too large to be more than acknowledged in passing here. But I would like to believe that subjectivity can rise above its potential for abuse.) Real subjectivity is volatile, spectral, mutable, contingent, as much unconscious as conscious, impelled to a fascination with the nonverbal by its own linguistic ability. Once invented, subjectivity proliferates; it becomes more expressible by accumulating supplements, artifices, devices, and prostheses, and the more expressible it becomes, the more mercurial it grows. Automatism may sometimes be called on to curb subjective invention. It is methodical in action even when it is anarchic or "glutinous"—the term will come up—in effect. To be sure, this distinction is porous. Subjective agency may contract into a technique of automatism; the technique of automatism may expand into subjective agency. But the tendencies persist. To invoke a distinction that much absorbed Wittgenstein, the character of subjectivity can never be said, only shown. But automatism is sayable, sayable to excess—as the promised inventions will illustrate. Starting now:

"WEAVE A CIRCLE ROUND HIM THRICE..."

The intrusion of automatism into the address form has its own history. Nineteenth-century instances tend to dwell on monstrosity and mortality, especially in conjunction with technology. The twentieth century, as we will see in the next chapter, scaled down to detachment, artifice, and impersonality, although monstrosity and mortality kept breaking through. In most cases, automatism becomes a threat to subjectivity to the extent that it disrupts the address form from within.

For a genealogical perspective, consider a perhaps unlikely trio of nonpersons from the nineteenth century. The first is the title character of Edgar Allan Poe's story "The Facts in the Case of M. Valdemar." On his deathbed, Valdemar consents to be mesmerized in the interests of science—an important point, since it was as science that mesmerism flourished; many of Poe's readers took his fantastic tale as a factual report. The unintended consequence of the mesmerism is to preserve Valdemar's capacity to speak after his death. In particular he, or rather his tongue, answers two questions spaced seven months apart; each answer ends with a self-description that no subject can make: "I am dead."

In the heyday of poststructuralism, this sentence became something of a *cause célèbre,* attracting readings from Jacques Lacan, Barthes, and Derrida, all of whom in different ways regarded "I am dead" as an index of the otherness of language as such.[23] But Poe's emphasis is not on language; it is specifically on speech. "I am dead" is not impossible as language, and certainly not as writing. First-person epitaphs stand at the origin of Western lyric poetry;

the ancient collection known as the Greek Anthology contains an abundance of them, many of which utter the infamous sentence or some variant of it. To take just one example, somewhat abbreviated: "I am an Athenian woman; for that was my city; but from Athens the wasting war-god of the Italians plundered me long ago ... and now that I am dead, sea-girt Cyzicus wraps my bones."[24] Epitaphs like this almost anticipate Derrida's claim that the ability to say "I am dead" is the condition of a true act of language.[25] In any case the sentence is a perfectly good metaphor. But speech and language are not the same, and speech is another matter. "I am dead" is impossible as a *speech act*. It cannot be a constative because if true it cannot be spoken; it cannot be a performative because there is nothing its speaker can do.

Just how impossible it is to endure the illocutionary force of "I am dead" may be gauged from a rare disorder known as Cotard's syndrome or Cotard's delusion, after the French physician who first identified it in 1880. Sufferers from Cotard's delusion sincerely believe that they are dead; they are often incapable of recognizing themselves in the mirror. The delusion is typically accompanied by intense feelings of self-loathing, in Valdemar-like response to the subject's feeling of its own putrefaction. Cotard's sufferers may utter words, but they cannot have real conversations. As an answer to the questions of Poe's narrator, "I am dead" breaks the address form in the very act of conforming to it: making a reply. The sentence, a death sentence condemned to life, shares in the dissolution of the body through which it speaks.[26]

The break comes about because the voice that replies belongs to no subject, or, more exactly, to the no-subject. The reply comes from no one. No one's voice speaks, but it speaks in a voice unlike any other. The source of its automatism is neither death nor life, but undeath, which exceeds them both. "I am dead," which can be spoken only by the undead, lends implicit support not only to Derrida's claim about the true act of language, but also to a more inclusive claim: that true speech has the ability to say itself from a source beyond, behind, any I.

Speech shares this ability with technological supplements that all too easily usurp the place of the subject. Poe's narrator reports that Valdemar's tongue made a "strong vibratory motion" between rigid lips and jaws. The description suggests a telegraph key, popularly known at the time as a "clattering tongue"; the sound it makes seemed to come "from some vast distance." But the sound does more than clatter. The vibrating tongue is also a vibrating string, drawing sound forth from an oracular interior as if from "some deep cavern within the earth." The "intonation" of this voice of the dead, or dead voice, is a decomposing music. It is "harsh, broken, and hollow"; worse, it is "gelatinous" and "glutinous," no longer addressed to the ear—that is, no longer addressed at all—but imposed on touch.[27] As a musical instrument, Valdemar's tongue suggests that music, especially when removed from the naturalness of the voice, is even more than language the medium of the utterance "I am dead."

Poe's associations of dead voice with the remote and the cavernous carry over into the second no-subject on our itinerary. This one is fully musical: it—the pronoun is exact—is Wagner's Titurel, the founder of the grail brotherhood in *Parsifal*. Titurel shares with M. Valdemar the phenomenology of the undead who speak. He dwells in his coffin, kept "alive," if that is the word, only by the administration of the grail, with due ritual, by his wounded son, Amfortas. Wagner would no doubt have hated the idea, but the grail acts here no less as a technological supplement than the mesmerism exercised on Valdemar. And the results are no less creepy.

Wagner's treatment of Titurel is too complex for detailed treatment here.[28] Suffice it to dwell on the exemplary moment when he asks the harassing question "Mein Sohn Amfortas, bist du am Amt?" (My son Amfortas, are you at your office?). The question, like all of Titurel's utterances, comes from a disembodied voice both distant and buried. Wagner's stage directions call for the voice to issue from an invisible source somewhere behind Amfortas; usually this means off or beneath the stage, so that the voice seems to come, like Valdemar's, "as from a vast distance or from some deep cavern within the earth."

As Slavoj Žižek likes to emphasize, Titurel's question is aggressive and punitive.[29] It is all the more powerfully so because it appropriates the grail ritual to the preservation of Titurel's undead state. "Titurel's voice"—that's how Wagner's score refers to it, *Titurels Stimme*—embodies oral greed in the absence of mind. Its question, we might say, is spoken and can only be spoken in the voice of the drive to undeath. As long as Amfortas remains susceptible to it, his own state of living death, the subjective version of Titurel's vacant automatism, is doomed to survive.

We can hear as much in the melody that Wagner invents for the question, which is close to a musical equivalent of M. Valdemar's speech. Until the laden last word "Amt" (office), the melody hews to the tones of the D-flat Minor triad. (See example 9.) But with "Amt" it becomes mortifying in the original sense of the word, rising to a close on the augmented fourth D♭-G. The effect goes beyond the tritonal dissonance; it assumes a "glutinous"

EXAMPLE 9. Wagner, *Parsifal*, Titurel's voice.

morbidity by corrupting the A♭, the fifth scale degree, on which the key depends for its tonal life. In response or extension—it is impossible to say which—the timpani beats out a brief tattoo on E♭, which leads to a long dead silence. The addition of E♭ to G portends an outburst of E-flat-Minor that will come from the orchestra during Amfortas's reply, but its immediate effect is to inhabit the tonal noplace opened by Titurel's question. Its E♭ will come to be animated, but for the present it is neither that nor the contrary. It is only the place held by the sonority of the timpani, which, "harsh, broken, and hollow," extends and suspends Titurel's question in its automatism. The sound of the drum is the resonance of the sepulcher from which the question issues and the echo of M. Valdemar's tongue "rolling violently" between the stretched skin of his lips.

Parsifal is famously an opera with a message, "Durch Mitleid wissen" (to know through compassion). It is a message reiterated through one of the very few leitmotifs in Wagner to echo the singing of the words. Both the words and the music are a call to assume a subject-position, and what both Parsifal and Amfortas discover is that to heed the call may be more agonizing than any subject can bear. It may lead into an abyss of sentient automatism—embodied in Amfortas's wound—that only a miracle can cure. It should be no surprise, then, that Wagner reinvented M. Valdemar as Titurel to hold a place in that abyss and to give the call an abyssal sound and shape. At one stage in his work on the opera, Wagner even considered having Titurel briefly revive—and sing—during the final grail ceremony in which Parsifal takes over Amfortas's office.

We can be glad he decided to pull the plug; the Valdemar-like moment would really have spoiled the party. What could Titurel have sung except "I am dead"? But the idea is revealing. Within just a few years, Titurel himself would be reinvented in the form of another coffin-dweller of great age kept alive only by a parody of a sacred meal. *Parsifal* premiered in 1882; Bram Stoker published *Dracula* in 1897. Even the technological supplements supporting the undead state are similar. In the novel, the vampire-hunting heroes form a grail-like brotherhood through the then-new technology of blood transfusion. Their aim is to cure the first victim Dracula claims from them: to heal the wound that threatens to turn the living subject into the no-subject of undead substance.

Their effort fails, but the bond it forms is indispensable later as the group tracks down the vampire with the help of hypnotic passes—shades of M. Valdemar again—over the unconscious body of the novel's heroine, Mina Murray. Mina has suffered her own kind of blood transfusion. She has been forced to drink Dracula's blood, producing a telepathic sympathy with him that enables her, when questioned in her Valdemar-like state, to emit clues to the vampire's whereabouts. And not just any clues: Mina *hears* what Dracula does. This auditory communication over a vast distance gives the play of subjectivity and automatism in Mina's body a quasi-musical force. It even becomes a kind of leitmotif as Mina repeatedly speaks, or the speech that issues from her tells, of the sound of "lapping waves and rushing water."[30] The fluidity of the sound epitomizes the dissolution of boundaries as Mina's subjectivity and Dracula's lack of it appropriate each other in a strange game of telephone.[31]

The series of automatized subjects from Poe through Wagner to Stoker reverses the appeal of the eighteenth-century androids we started with; M. Valdemar and company can be thought of as the degenerate forms of Vaucanson's flute player and his kind. For the nineteenth-century avatars, music is no longer proof of life—though it should be. These figures expose a horror latent in the address form but they do not break with its appeal, in both senses of the word: attraction and plea. Both *Parsifal* and *Dracula* can be said to end by restoring the bond between subjectivity and address. But this new train of metaphors does urge the recognition that both subjectivity and automatism depend on invention, and even on their invention of each other. In the largest sense, that is the import of Derrida's maxim that the only possible invention is the invention of the impossible, the invention that lets the other arrive.

What needs to be added is that music has a prominent historical role in this call to invention. Music itself has recurrently suggested just that, as the inventions offered here have sought, and in a moment will seek again, to show. The question that music raises, both in general and in a host of particulars, is not an either/or between subjectivity and automatism, and certainly not a feeble both/and. It is a question of separation: of how, when, and whether to tease apart the possible and the impossible, sensibility and mechanism, the reply and the call, music as virtual feeling and music as resonant matter. And so on: the question itself is subject to endless reinvention as it moves within and between styles and genres, well beyond my smattering of classical samples, and within and between the cultural tropes that music shares in and helps to animate. And so—on.

DER DREIMALIGE ACCORD

I. Reader, I . . .

It is another famous moment of address, this time from English poetry (Brontë would have known it). But it is not just *an* other, not just one:

> I met a traveler from an antique land
> Who said: "Two vast and trunkless legs of stone
> Stand in the desert. . . . Near them on the sand,
> Half sunk a shattered visage lies, whose frown,
> And wrinkled lip, and sneer of cold command
> Tell that its sculptor well those passions read
> Which yet survive, stamped on these lifeless things,
> The hand that mocked them, and the heart that fed;
> And on the pedestal, these words appear:
> My name is Ozymandias, King of Kings,
> Look on my works, ye Mighty, and despair!
> Nothing beside remains. Round the decay
> Of that colossal Wreck, boundless and bare,
> The lone and level sands stretch far away."[32]

The speaker is (not exactly) Percy Shelley, who, however, has little presence in the text beyond the grammatical "I" that, with some irony, stands at its head. What is most resonant about this poem for present purposes is its multiplication of address. Ozymandias, King of Kings, addresses himself to the mighty via the writing on his pedestal but his message goes awry even before it is sent, rewritten (because well read) by the sculptor whose tacitly ironic version belatedly reaches the traveler in (then from) an antique land who in turn relays the message as speech to the "I" of the poem who (both "as" Shelley and for him) transmits it to subsequent generations of readers, including, dear Reader, you, yourself, right here and right now.

The voice of Ozymandias (only ever transcribed) echoes across the millennia but only in depersonalized, ironic, negated form. This voice is a lifeless thing that yet survives amid the many lost voices of "Ozymandias," a poem that, itself, ironically replicates the monumental ruin of the colossus. The poem has voices but it has no voice. It is full of addresses but never reaches the address to which it is sent—though it has never failed to arrive, not to this very day.

Those who intercept this postcard of a poem with a musical bias might find in its imagery a recollection of a shattered colossus in the desert of Egyptian Thebes. From antiquity through the nineteenth century the statue was popularly said to represent the mythical Ethiopian king Memnon, son of Eos, goddess of the dawn—and the subject of a song by Schubert. According to the second-century Greek geographer Pausanias, "This statue was broken in two by Cambyses, and at the present day from head to middle it is thrown down; but the rest is seated, and every day at the rising of the sun it makes a noise, and the sound one could best liken to that of a harp or lyre when a string has been broken."[33]

The text of Schubert's song, by Johann Mayrhofer, turns on another change of address: the statue's sound is mournful but strikes mortal ears as lyrical. The song redresses—readdresses—the unwitting irony by treating it as a transformation wrought by art; the setting of the last stanza ecstatically grants the wish, the reunion with E(r)os, that the text says cannot be granted. But the rerouting does not proceed without marking the witting irony of taking subjective pleasure in an automatism's "expression." In the penultimate stanza the song brutally warps its own melodic voice to imply, as I put it elsewhere, that "the subject named Memnon is and must be absent from the scene of pleasure."[34]

II. O Friends . . .

Another iconic moment of musical address, but this time with surrogate voices. Classical surrogates: the pastoral pipes that speak for and as the shepherd swain who alternately plays them and sings. The scene is the pastoral frame of the slow movement of Hector Berlioz's *Symphonie fantastique*. At the start, the calls of an English horn find their distant answers in the return call, at once echo and reply, of an offstage oboe. The invocation (take the term literally) of real rather than metaphorical space turns the episode into an allegory of music as call, of an address by one sentient and sensitive being to another. (Lover to beloved here, of course, but also more; hovering behind the scene is Rousseau's famous observation that animals have voices but only humans sing; when he hears a singing voice he knows he is in calling distance of another sentient being like himself.[35] His impulse to call to this other is that of a subject on the knife-edge of nonsubjectivity; without the other whose song is the index of likeness, the listener would have no self to be like.)

At the end of the movement the English horn call goes forth again. But this time the oboe is silent. Perhaps it has gone elsewhere, or has been called away by fate, or was just not listening, or has changed its mind. We don't know; there is no answer. But yes, there is, only not the answer called for: the answer comes in the form of rumblings for four timpani, sometimes together, sometimes apart. The immediate effect is topical; the drums betoken distant thunder. The symbolism is plain, and so is the allusion to Beethoven's *Pastoral Symphony*. But there is more at stake. The drum sounds constitute the material form of the loss of address, the palpable absence of an answering voice for lack of which the call of the first voice carries into a void where it too is lost. The loss of address brings with it the loss of subjectivity; the drums, ironically replying only to each other in a travesty of calling and answering, negate the call with the mutter (not its symbol, sign, or signifier, but the actual sound) of the mute, the inarticulate, the unvoiceable. If he could recognize anything, Titurel would recognize this.

And? This isn't famous at all but perhaps it should be. Among Vivaldi's many concertos is a brief one in E Minor for Cello and Bassoon. Writing it was odd to begin with; in Vivaldi's day both instruments, especially the bassoon, were primarily workhorses assigned to the bass line rather than bearers of melody. (Vivaldi wrote other concertos for each, but dragging them up together from the basso continuo was something else again.) But the oddness continues. The first movement begins, not with a ritornello, but with a somber duet for the concertino. When it comes, the ritornello for strings is an intrusion. It is a violently agitated passage that interrupts the cello and bassoon as they cadence and proceeds with complete indifference to the music it has elbowed away. The movement as a whole consists of a spasmodic alternation of these two elements, the concertino evolving, the ritornello not. It is as if the ensemble were switching arbitrarily between two entirely different pieces.

The result is the mirror inversion of what happens in the recitative-inflected movements by Haydn and Mozart. The concertino does not present itself as an address, or if it does, it is an address between the instruments rather than from the duo to a listener. (The partners are unequal, so there is a subdued drama going on; the cello's superior melodic capacity increasingly asserts itself. In the slow movement and finale it will dominate completely.) But when the ritornello blusters in, the concertino *becomes* an address. The ritornello's indifference becomes a trait that provokes; its lack of either "objective" or "subjective" reference forms a disturbance reflected back upon itself in the music's agitation. Heard against this not at all pleasant "toy," as Sulzer might have called it, the concertino assumes the character of an appeal. It becomes an expression that has just discovered its own expressiveness and the corresponding need to be recognized for what it is. The music discovers the possibility and therefore the necessity of a subject by exposing itself to the force of bare automatism.

In its dual singularity this obscure jeux d'esprit stumbles onto the broader collision between subjective address and automatism that in varying proportions will subsequently constitute—and therefore will have become what had always constituted—the art of Western music.

EPILOGUE. TRANSITION. LIKE A MAN THAT'S DEAD.

But what Western music? The music in this chapter, and this book, is "classical," but if the argument of the chapter is credible it should apply to other kinds of music as well (best discussed by those who know them better than I do). Consider the blues, as invoked in the poem by Langston Hughes that figures in the train of metaphors started in the introduction. Hughes's narrative voice is perfectly explicit about hearing the blues performance as a call. The bluesman makes the piano sing and its voice comes "from a black man's soul." But this subjectivity is shadowed by its opposite:

The singer stopped playing and went to bed
While the Weary Blues echoed through his head.
He slept like a rock or a man that's dead.[36]

The Weary Blues becomes an earworm, emptied of soul. The musician's stony sleep is a death in life because his own weariness comes not simply from hours spent playing at a Lenox Avenue nightspot, but from centuries of racial oppression.

But how does the narrator know? He can only know through the music. He knows because he shares the musician's history and the music makes him feel it. His own subjectivity gives a temporary home to the bluesman's and his poem reenacts the man's performance and his call. But the burden remains—literally the burden of the man's song, which says he can't be satisfied. Subjectivity is necessary but it is not enough.

By 1926, when Hughes published "The Weary Blues," classical music had reached similar conclusions, but for different reasons. Moved by other historical urgencies (and largely ignoring the one that burdened Hughes), classical music took the tension between vitalism and mechanism in a new direction. That direction is the subject of the next chapter.

SIX

Waltzing Specters

LIFE, PERCEPTION, AND RAVEL'S "LA VALSE"

> There comes a time when the waltz
> Is no longer a mode of desire, a mode
> Of revealing desire and is empty of shadows.
>
> Too many waltzes have ended.
>
> —WALLACE STEVENS

INSTEAD OF OPPOSING MECHANISM TO ORGANIC LIFE, early twentieth-century modernism connects it with artificial life, that is, with organic expression as acknowledged artifice. Hoffmann's and Offenbach's Olympia is succeeded by Stravinsky's Petrushka; the mute Pierrot of Parisian pantomime finds a voice in the Sprechstimme of Schoenberg's *Pierrot lunaire*. As these passing allusions suggest, to recognize the artifice is not necessarily to refuse its enchantments. Maurice Ravel might be said to have built his whole career on that possibility. The forms of pleasure he affords range from the mechanisms of farce to the mechanics of dream, as evidenced in the fascination with clockworks shared by the comic opera *L'heure espagnole*, in which clockworks chime with sexual hijinks, and the piano piece "Le vallee des cloches," which animates the valley of its title with multilayered pealing.[1] But the fascination can also become terror—or Grand Guignol *frisson*—as it does in another piano piece, "Le gibet" (The Gallows, from *Gaspard de la nuit*), which famously incorporates a clock tower's death knell, a continuously repeated octave, from start to finish. Ravel is exemplary in treating the artifice of life as a cultural rather than a physiological or biological mechanism.

The Enlightenment project persists for him, or more exactly revives, but cut off from its roots. The object of simulation is the life of—simulation.

THE SPECTERS OF SOUND RECORDING

Part of the responsibility for this development rests with the phonograph. The evolving soundscape of Ravel's career coincided with the rise in prominence and credibility of the new medium. Most of his music was recorded during his lifetime, and in 1931 he noted with pleasure that the technology of the phonograph was rapidly improving, far outstripping that of radio. ("Spare me the radio!" he said; "it is painful to hear my music so distorted.") Ravel observed that a recent recording of "Bolero" was "completely satisfactory" but added that "it is more difficult to record 'La Valse.'. . . In spite of the improvements, microphone recordings still aren't ideal."[2]

But sound recording also resulted in a queasy relationship between live and "mechanical" music. Listening to a recording might leave one feeling "astonished and somewhat terrified," as it did Sir Arthur Sullivan in 1888. Mark Katz notes Sullivan's remark as one of many: "Amazement and even fear were not uncommon reactions to the technology of sound recording in the late nineteenth century and the early twentieth."[3] If the invention of sound recording severed the tie between voice and life, as the previous chapter began by observing, its technological improvement soon did more. When it became possible to record music, the tie between music and life was severed too. The fact that music no longer needed a live performer to be heard allowed it to assume a strange spectral life of its own that was also a kind of afterlife. Like the voices that could now speak despite belonging to the dead, the music could go on sounding despite having vanished in the moment of being made. The music on a recording was neither an imitation nor a simulation. It was really "there" in an uncanny new form, vital and mechanical at the same time.

At least it was so for a little while. Like the cinema, to which it would be joined after a few decades, recorded music was something to which people soon became habituated. During its earlier years, however, the consequences of its arrival were unsettling. They became something for later music and, as we'll see, for cinema to reflect on as an index of modernity. The poem quoted in my epigraph, Wallace Stevens's "Sad Strains of a Gay Waltz" (1936), makes that reflection as well:

Too many waltzes—The epic of disbelief
Blares oftener and soon, will soon be constant.[4]

The story will eventually lead to the waltzing specters of my title, but it begins with the complement to sound recording's severance of music from life: silent cinema's severance of sight from sound. This separation gave new prominence to an asymmetry (noted in chapter 2) that had long haunted the history of perception. Since ancient times the experience of sound without sight has carried a romantic allure. Live acousmatic sound, the natural sound of voice or music or song separated from its origin, is a medium of fantasy. Just saying the words makes the call resound: music in the air, voices from afar. The appeal of Homer's sirens despite foreknowledge of the danger they represent is already ample testimony to the romance of sound at a distance, out of range of the eye. Unseen sounds can also startle, of course; they can elicit anticipation or excitement or fear. But they rarely, if ever, elicit diffuse anxiety. That is more often reserved for their complement: sight without sound. Even miming commonly carries a fringe of something disturbing, from the dumb show in *Hamlet* to the ballets of haplessness spun out by the sad, white-faced Pierrots I referred to earlier. When vision is muted for reasons other than mere miming the effect can be deeply troubling. Silence in excess is uncanny.

But I spoke of the *history* of perception. Acousmatic sound was already a familiar theatrical device when the invention of the telephone made it a part of everyday life. The telephonic effect of disembodied voice did make some early users uneasy but it was naturalized with remarkable speed, perhaps because, unlike recorded voice, the voice on the phone is still "live." Telephonic voice is extended presence; it becomes disturbing not by being heard but by going unheard; it becomes uncanny in the solitary voice that addresses it, responds to it. In Jean Cocteau's play *La voix humaine* (1930), a monologue for a desperate women speaking over the phone to the lover who has just abandoned her, it is precisely the unheard voice on the phone line that becomes a "terrible weapon," a condition reenacted in Francis Poulenc's operatic setting in 1959. Perhaps not until the invention of cinema did unseen speech engender a significant measure of unease, carried by the voice over, the voice off, the *acousmétre*—even, at times, over the phone.

Cinema, however, went much further in the opposite direction, exposing the queasy effect of moving images without sound by doing everything possible within the limits of available technology to avert them. No doubt the persistence of musical underscore in narrative film derives partly from the history of the medium; music was the first available means to avert genuinely *silent* movies and its use survived its obsolescence in that role. But its survival is more than a relic or a mere habit. Even endowed with speech and ambient sound, film without music quickly seems to fall into a certain void. It is a void that has often been used creatively, but the norm has been, and still is, to keep it filled up and thereby to keep it at bay. The void of sight without sound thus becomes a distinctive feature, the dark horizon, of modern visibility.

Sometimes, however, the same void becomes a feature of modern *audibility*. Sight without sound becomes audible, not really paradoxically, in music that re-creates its effect on the observer. This perceptual twist might seem unlikely at first, even impossible; how is music supposed to embody its own inaudibility? The answer depends on a shift in the angle of hearing, the auditory parallel to point of view. The music re-creates the effect of sight without sound *from the standpoint* of the missing sound. The condition of going unheard cannot be simulated musically, but music can represent it metaphorically by painful distortion—the condition, to Ravel's ear, of music on the radio. It is as if the act of severance injured sound as much as it undercut sight. In hearing the music, what we hear is the pain of being silenced.

In what follows I want to examine this effect and its cultural meaning in two well-known compositions: primarily "La Valse," which I take to be a reflection on modernity as a condition of perceptual disarray, and secondarily the scherzo of Mahler's Symphony no. 2, which predates the cinematic revolution but not the mechanization of perception from which cinema develops. Both works will turn out to have affinities with a film about uncanny dislocation that can be read as a reflection on the conditions of cinematic perception: Carl Dreyer's *Vampyr*. The film is also about bringing the dead to life, or more exactly making them undead. So is the music. M. Valdemar and Titurel, visited in the previous chapter, are not far off. These affinities are the more suggestive for being unplanned; they are strikingly close.

"LA VALSE" AND ITS INTERTEXTS

"La Valse" is a candid study of perception in collapse. It is music that veers gradually but inexorably from the not yet heard to the no longer hearable. It is unique in Ravel's output for its auditory violence. The reasons why begin with the First World War, but they do not end there.

Composed in 1919–1920 with the war barely over, "La Valse" is distinguished by its gradual transformation of alluring waltz themes into a grotesque cacophony. The music immediately suggests an attitude of bitter disenchantment. It sounds like a French appropriation and repudiation of one of the dead Hapsburg Empire's cultural jewels. But although the darkness of the piece is brutally evident, its import depends not on antagonism to the waltz as emblem of an enemy culture but, on the contrary, on solidarity with it. That much is evident from the music, in which the waltz functions not as an agent but as a victim. The dance is coaxed to return to life from a bygone time and then systematically, but slowly, so slowly it does not notice until too late, it is maimed, lamed, tripped up, disfigured, defaced.

This is what befalls "the waltz," the genre, the aesthetic social contract only represented by the varied waltzes that spin through the piece. For that reason there is no point in going over the music blow-by-blow (as I just said, it does that itself: really, blow by blow); there will be no "analysis" here to make the piece seem less cruel and anomalous and yet for all that—it's a popular piece; always has been—pleasurable. Here is what we need to know:

The piece is a frame structure. It begins with a lumbering mass of sound that splits the inchoate waltz rhythm between deep bass sonorities. It ends with a violent outburst in which already distorted reminiscences tumble down in a heap. In between the waltz takes tentative shape, comes to vivid life for a while, and then begins to mutate, vacillating between raw, truncated bursts of energy and spells of sensuous refinement (not to say indulgence) carried by a highly discriminated orchestration. In the end the refinement exhausts itself and the energy becomes a bludgeon. End of story, end of era, the end, period.

It was not supposed to turn out that way. "La Valse" was conceived as a straightforward homage under the title "Wien" in 1906. Although the eventual work is virtually the opposite, it nonetheless retains the traces of the younger Ravel's "deep sympathy with these wonderful rhythms, and ... the joie de vivre expressed by the dance."[5] In an interview given in 1922, Ravel denied that in "La Valse" he was making a "symbolic" statement about Vienna; the subject was purely the intoxication of the dance, carried to an extreme that, we seem meant to suppose, is immanent in the genre. But it is hard to extricate the self-consuming musical narrative of the music from the self-immolation of Europe in 1914–1918. The dance does represent a collective madness, a cultural juggernaut. But its focus is less on the trauma of the war per se (audible only in the over-the-top violence of the closing episode) than on the underlying disorder of which the war was the horrific symptom.

In the pre-war years Ravel seemed to think of the Viennese waltz as the repository of a certain European grace and simplicity, qualities reflected, though with a difference, in his piano suite "Valses nobles et sentimentales" (1911). As Ravel observed, the title "sufficiently indicates" music written in emulation of Schubert, who published separate sets of "noble" and "sentimental" waltzes for piano.[6] Schubert's waltzes are not dance music. They are character pieces in which the waltz, abstracted from dancing bodies in social rituals, acts as an ideal—no matter, in this context, of what.

Almost a century later, the nobility and sentiment retain their appeal, but no longer their substance. They can be enjoyed only with the help of an affectionately ironic framing, a sophisticated reinscription. Their qualities are reminiscent, perhaps, of those rare idyllic moments in the poetry of Baudelaire—not far removed from Schubert in time but utterly remote in spirit—set on the threshold of a corruption that is left, for the moment, palpably in abeyance. Ravel greatly admired Baudelaire, whose "Harmonie du Soir" offers a virtual model. The poem was set by Debussy; Ravel imitated its unusual form in the second movement of his own Piano Trio (1915):

> Voici venir les temps où vibrant sur sa tige
> Chaque fleur s'évapore ainsi qu'un encensoir;
> Les sons et les parfums tournent dans l'air du soir;
> Valse mélancolique et langoureux vertige!
>
> Now comes the hour when trembling on its stem
> Each flower exhales its vapor like a censer;
> Sounds and perfumes turn in the evening air,
> Melancholy waltz and dizzy languor![7]

Ravel's framing plays out at the levels of both form and waltz rhythm. Most of the waltzes are in continuous ternary form with varied reprises; the suite raises the form to a higher order by ending with an extended epilogue that reworks and combines themes from the earlier waltzes. The essential action at both levels is reflective, a waltz-like turning of expression back on itself. Similar turnings twice partner one waltz with another: no. 3 ends with a segue into no. 4 and the introduction to no. 7 is based on the A section of no. 6.[8] No. 7 introduces a moment of false—nostalgic?—closure by reprising its own A section literally, only to usher in the greater turn, or overturning, of the epilogue. The trope of turning continues throughout the treatment of the waltz rhythm, the model of turning par excellence, which Ravel continually refines and abstracts. The result is a tranquil sense of observation at a distance that will return in distressed form in "La Valse." It permits the dance scenes evoked by the waltzes to be visualized like fond memories and at the same time renders their visualization spectral. The music appropriates obsolescence as pleasure without for a moment forgetting that this pleasure no longer has an object. Ravel's score accordingly dedicates its waltzes to "the delicious and ageless pleasure of a useless occupation."

At the same time, and in a contrary spirit, Ravel retained the sensuality and sexuality from which Schubert, setting a precedent for a long line of concert waltz composers, abstracted the dance. At one time the waltz was scandalous because dancing it required close bodily contact and its distinctive turning motion was widely felt to be a barely veiled surrogate for something still more intimate. In 1813 Lord Byron even wrote a long satirical poem on the subject:

> Waltz—Waltz alone—both legs and arms demands,
> Liberal of feet, and lavish of her hands;
> Hands which may freely range in public sight
> Where ne'er before—but—pray "put out the light."
> Methinks the glare of yonder chandelier
> Shines much too far—or I am much too near.[9]

The closing lines of this extract uncannily anticipate an image that Ravel would set at the center of "La Valse."

Richard Strauss had of course revived the sensual and sexual force of the waltz with a vengeance in *Der Rosenkavalier*, which premiered in January 1911, the same year Ravel wrote his waltz suite. When Ravel subsequently orchestrated the latter as a ballet score, *Adélaïde*, the scenario he provided was a love triangle set in the demimonde of the 1820s and furnished with an improbably happy ending. The plot involves symbolic gifts of flowers, as its subtitle, "Le langage des fleurs," suggests.[10] The ballet is a miniature *Rosenkavalier* for a fin-de-siècle Paris nostalgically backdated, like Strauss and Hoffmansthal's Vienna, to a remote era. The atmosphere of the work is simultaneously innocent and corrupt, which is one way to gloss the semi-ironic phrase "noble and sentimental."

Strauss's waltz suite from *Rosenkavalier* furnishes a revealing contrast to "La Valse" as well, one that it is hard to imagine that Ravel left to chance. The modernity of the *Rosenkavalier* waltzes takes the form of their indeterminate vacillation between irony and nostalgia, each of which repeatedly becomes the occasion—or the pretext—for the other. Strauss uses framing devices, elaborate self-reflective orchestration, and travesty to stake out his historical position. So does Ravel. Near the end Strauss lets the orchestra run riot with a heavy, galumphing tread. He does not quite revisit the irony of the fatal waltzes in *Salome* and *Elektra,* but the memory is there. Nonetheless, he allows the music to remain caught in its perpetual indecision—that too a token, one token, of the modern condition. Ravel's conclusion is more violent, and its import more decisive. Though fully acknowledging the allure of nostalgia, he shows it, or lets it show itself, as a destructive machine. He gives free rein to its corrosive effect on the possibility of perception. Too many waltzes, Ravel seems to be saying, have not yet ended. They have not ended *enough.*

Both the gracefulness of the waltz and its contrary body heat reappear in "La Valse" but they return there in exacerbated form, as travesty, in a "dance" of empty signifiers. The noble becomes the blatant, the sentimental the languorous. But the music retains enough of the original qualities to lure us into what proves to be a trap. The less than noble and more than sentimental are not, until the very end, entirely divorced from a certain pleasure in which the traces of lost simplicity and useless occupation still lurk.

The result is a strange hybrid of the kind that the poet Francis Ponge, in an equally strange hybrid titled *Soap,* called a *momon:*

> A *momon* [phonetically identical with *moment*] is a masquerade, a sort of dance done by masked figures, ending in a challenge delivered by them. Its radical is the same as in mummery. One ought to be able to so name, by extension, any work of art including its own caricature, or one in which the author was to ridicule his means of expression. Ravel's *La Valse* is a momon. The genre is peculiar to periods in which rhetoric, dying, examines itself.[11]

Like Ponge's book, itself a *momon* that dances verbally around the foamy stuff of its title, Ravel's composition perpetually slips away from itself. But its dancing bubbles turn out to burst with a sting—unlike the waltzes of the *Rosenkavalier* suite, which leave a film behind. Ravel's *momon/moment* holds itself at arms' length like a dance partner embraced with skepticism or dislike. Its waltz rhythm, straining to hold on to pleasure in sound and movement, collapses on itself and mocks itself but without ceasing to stumble on. In the end one partner falls flat, but it is impossible to say which one.

What remains is the ghost of an absent dance. This statement is meant to be taken literally. Important in any concert performance of "La Valse" is the bit of lore recalling that the music was originally written for Serge Diaghilev to stage as a ballet. Diaghilev, however, rejected the score as undanceable. It was, he said, not a ballet but a "portrait of a ballet, ... a painting of a ballet."[12] Ravel was so offended that he never worked with Diaghilev again, but Diaghilev was not wrong to see the distance built into the music. Ravel himself did the same, however grudgingly. He attached to the score of "La Valse" a scenario of spectral waltzing from the previous century, a distorted trace of the visual that lingers in concert performances of the piece as a kind of impossibility. No one can dance to these dances, so the "scene" floats in visual tatters around the deformed waltz music.

The scenario reads like a small prose poem:

> Swirling clouds afford glimpses, through rifts, of waltzing couples. The clouds disperse little by little: one makes out a vast hall populated by a whirling crowd. The scene grows progressively brighter. The light of the chandeliers bursts out at the *fortissimo*. An imperial court, about 1855.[13]

In an autobiographical sketch dictated in 1928, Ravel reaffirmed that he had "conceived of this piece as a kind of apotheosis of the Viennese waltz, mingled with ... the impression of a fantastic, fatal whirling."[14] The waltz idea is obvious, and so is the fatal whirling; what needs elucidation is their mingling.

The place to begin is the language of Ravel's gloss, which is almost entirely visual in its orientation. The waltzes are something seen, not something heard; there is no reference to sound at all until the *fortissimo* is said to coincide with the chandelier's outburst of light, almost as if the music were an electric switch. (The anachronism of my metaphor is deliberate; the topic will return in a moment.) The translation is not from light to sound but from sound to light. The effect of the chandeliers is not to let the music burst out along with the light but to make the scene recognizable as an imperial court ball and to date it—presumably by costume and decor—to 1855. The music of "La Valse" is the soundtrack for a scene of seeing, not the substance of something heard.

As the music, of course, says on its own behalf: no one could mistake its dances for authentic period waltzes. Ravel even complained once that "they don't play ['La Valse'] well in Paris. They make it sound too much like a Viennese waltz."[15] These dances are stylized replicas, formal caricatures. They are auditory captions that might just as well read "Ceci n'est pas une valse." Like the virtually aerial scene they frame yet leave invisible, the waltzes of "La Valse" present themselves at a distance.

This distance is temporal as well as perceptual. "La Valse" does not stay in the past occupied by the waltz scene to which the introduction leads it back. Instead the music increasingly disengages itself from the scene it nominally supplements. It moves inexorably into the present, the decisive arrival of which coincides with the outburst of dissonance and distortion and the collapse that ensues; the music fades into a present in pieces. This temporal separation is what brings about the irremediable and as it were doubled severance of sight from sound in the work. By the close, and really long before, the scene has become not only invisible but impossible. This contretemps may have been the feature that troubled Diaghilev. His complaint that "La Valse" was a "picture of a ballet" suggests that the derangement enacted by the music could not be danced; real bodies could not represent it adequately. And despite the fact that Bronislava Nijinska did choreograph "La Valse" for Ida Rubenstein in 1928, followed by George Balanchine in 1951 for the New York City Ballet, Diaghilev was probably right. "La Valse" is exactly what Ravel decided to call it, a "choreographic poem for orchestra"; it is dance that can only be heard, not seen.

The process of temporal separation in the music is inexorable but it is not dramatic. It happens continuously; the frame around it is clear but with fuzzy borders, so that it is impossible to say exactly when we cross from one epoch, one frame of reference, to another. There is a point of formal division about halfway through when the opening returns, after which the waltzes that have been heard intact return in fragments. But it is impossible to say whether this reflective movement is a cause or a consequence of a point of no return in the passage from past to present. The waltzes are still waltzes—or almost; traces of the past persist in them as long as their distortion does not overcome all their appeal. Only when the waltz rhythm itself finally collapses do we know for sure that time has caught up with us without remedy.

The temporal movement, fused with the literal duration of the music, thus becomes an acoustic allegory for the transition to modernity from the old dispensation signified by the arbitrary date of 1855. The fatal whirling is the experience of epochal time, and in particular the experience of epochal time as traumatic—not just shocking, as in Walter Benjamin's celebrated analysis, but pathogenic.[16] This fatality, moreover, is presented without rationalization. It has no content, just facticity, no expressive meaning, just a rhythmic frenzy. Propulsive rhythm, of course, is itself a common signifier of modernity in terms both negative (speed and mechanism) and positive (bustling energy, new styles of popular dance). The question of rhythm, already invoked by Ravel in relation to "Wien," will return again—as so many things seem to in this context, almost as in a waltz.

The conjunction of gloss and music in "La Valse" looks both back to the distorted dancing that preoccupies Mahler's scherzo (1888–1894) and ahead to a scene of waltzing shadows early in *Vampyr* (1931). The connections are symptomatic, not allusive; the hobbled waltzing and severance of sight and sound in these works testify not to specific cross-references but to a persistent modern reworking of the traditional image of the dance of death—something that would also turn up in Jean Renoir's film *The Rules of the Game* (1939) to the waltz strains of Saint-Saëns's "Danse macabre."

Ravel, as it happens, perhaps hoping to avoid being lumped with Saint-Saëns, disavowed the association, but both the music of "La Valse" and Ravel's gloss for it speak louder. The scene described in the gloss could have come right out of Edgar Allan Poe's "The Masque of the Red Death," which (Poe being a favorite of the French Symbolists, especially Baudelaire) is a not-unlikely source, perhaps together with Baudelaire's poem "Le Jeu":

> It was a voluptuous scene, that masquerade. . . . [But] at each lapse of an hour, the musicians of the orchestra were constrained to pause, momentarily, in their performance, to hearken to the sound [of the clock]; and thus the waltzers perforce ceased their evolutions; and there was a brief disconcert of the whole gay company; and while the chimes of the clock yet rang it was observed that the giddiest grew pale. . . . But the echoes of the chime die away. . . . And now the music swells, and the dreams [the waltzers] live, and writhe to and fro more merrily than ever, taking hue from the many-tinted windows. . . . And the revel went whirlingly on, until at length there commenced the sounding of midnight upon the clock. And then the music ceased.[17]

Sous de sales plafonds un rang de pâles lustres
Et d'énormes quinquets projetant leurs lueurs
Sur des fronts ténébreux de poètes illustres
Qui viennent gaspiller leurs sanglantes sueurs;

Voilà le noir tableau qu'en un rêve nocturne
Je vis se dérouler sous mon oeil clairvoyant.[18]

Beneath the soiled ceilings a pale line of lamps
And huge chandeliers projected their glare
On the gloomy brows of illustrious poets
Who came to waste what sweating blood had won.

Such was the black tableau of a dream one night
I saw unfurl to my clairvoyant eye.

Aside from a passing reference to the tinkle of jewelry, Baudelaire makes no reference to sound, so that the scene he invokes, like the scene in Ravel's gloss, unfurls for the most part in uncanny silence. There is nothing strange, in this context, about the affinity between what "La Valse" makes of its imaginary ball and an episode in a horror movie.

But perhaps the script credit should go to Mahler. Anticipating Ravel's strange rendition of what it is like to *hear* the experience of seeing without hearing, Mahler heard the scherzo of his Second Symphony as transcribing in sound the experience of a dance scene rendered horrific by silence. Dreyer would do much the same; we will come to that.

MAHLER'S DANCE SCENE

Mahler likens the effect of his scherzo to the "gruesome" (*grauenhaft,* "gruesome," "atrocious," "bloodcurdling") experience of watching "the billowing of dancing figures in a brightly lit ballroom that you gaze into from the outside in the dark—from so great a *distance* you can *no* longer hear the *music!*"[19] In a parallel comment made at about the same time, he adds that the distant "whirling and bustling of the couples," watched through a window, "seem weird and senseless, because the rhythmic key to them is lacking."[20] This music is one of those pieces that have absorbed my attention repeatedly. Having discussed it at length elsewhere,[21] I return to it here from a different perspective. The dance devoid of rhythm has a peculiarly mechanical quality, something it shares with both "La Valse" and, as we will see, *Vampyr.* The senselessness of the dance feels like the senselessness of a life gone awry in the mechanical revolutions of its "gear" *(Getriebe):* "incessantly moving, never resting, never intelligible."

It is just as important to take note here of what Mahler does *not* say as of what he does. (And what, moreover, he does not say publicly. He made his remarks in a pair of letters; what he describes is not what his listeners are supposed to understand but what they are supposed to feel.) For Mahler the scherzo does not *depict* the experience he describes but *resembles* it. Hearing this music resembles an alienated and furtive form of gazing—from the distance, in the dark night. Not unlike, therefore, the distanced, beclouded gaze at the start of "La Valse." And not unlike a gaze at moving images framed by the distant window of a film screen in the dark.

But the resemblance too is alienated, a kind of stumble. It is not an analogy but an inversion. For the sight of dancing couples stripped of the rhythmic sound that gives their motion a sense, we get the sound of a rhythm so stripped of sense that no dancing couple could move to it (it would crush them together or tear them apart). The music embodies the senselessness that results when sight is stripped of sound, but *from the perspective* of the fugitive sound.

Like "La Valse," the Scherzo combines proliferating travesty with touches of allure, though with a more immediate sense of debasement; Mahler's dance hall is not Ravel's Imperial ballroom. Like "La Valse," the Scherzo grows more grotesque as it continues, more twisted in orchestration, more gawky in rhythm; increasingly fractured dancelike rhythms recur throughout under the twisting and turning of the melody. And like "La Valse," the Scherzo presents this deformity, which marks it as modern, sundered from a past it cannot quite let go, without rationale or explanation but, instead, as a haunting but unarguable fact, a perceptual absolute.

Philippe Lacoue-Labarthe hears Mahler's Scherzo as a demonstration that the visible acquires a sense only in the hearing of a rhythm: "Rhythm, of a specifically musical (acoustic) essence here, is prior to the figure or visible schema whose appearance ... it conditions."[22] One might say that this priority is precisely what Mahler and subsequently Ravel discover, but discover as a perceptual condition only insofar as it is a historical condition. By breaching the integrity of rhythm, and specifically by driving dance rhythm to self-parody, Mahler and Ravel create the musical equivalent of an immanent critique of the historical order of perception. That may sound like saying too much, but not if one allows the music to bypass one's defenses and present itself in all its brutality.

Lacoue-Labarthe further suggests that, beyond its specifically musical dimension of "pulsation and interruption, cadence and measure," rhythm is the device that "establishes the break between the visible and the audible." In this respect it should be understood, in "a Derridean sense," to "resist ... the hold of such partitions" (199). For Jacques Derrida, the break between the visible and the audible would also be the means of their connection, the "spacing" that disorients their proposed mutuality but that in doing so establishes the condition in which they can appear.[23] Rhythm in this framework would appear as that which shows this break, this gap, but only in the act of closing it, filling it, healing it up regardless of the faint scar that will necessarily be left as a trace thereafter. But it is precisely rhythm in this sense that Mahler and Ravel harass to the point of its collapse, exaggerate to produce its reductio ad absurdum.

DREYER'S WALTZING SPECTERS

Or perhaps just one step short, if we judge from the further reduction found in *Vampyr*. The plot turns on the discovery of a vampire in a French village, but the film is less concerned with telling a horror story than with forming a lavish parade of spectral images. Paramount among these, especially early in the film, are images in which shadows become animate, separating themselves from the bodies that cast them. The separation is neither interpreted nor explained. Perhaps the most pertinent reading of it would take a hint from Mahler and understand the shadows as forms voided of sense: souls that are not meaningless because they are dead but dead because they are meaningless.

In any event the film treats the separation of the shadow from its body as the mark of a primary maiming or hobbling. The intimation is progressive: First we get glimpses in silhouette of a man with a scythe and then of a shadow making digging motions; the man digging remains unseen, his existence only a supposition. Then we follow the movements of a shadow without a body but with only one leg, as he, it, appears in a labyrinthine old chateau and climbs a ladder. A moment later we discover that the shadow "belongs"—though the word here is equivocal—to a wooden-legged soldier. That shadow sits down across from the motionless body on a bench and momentarily assumes its proper place. After another moment a summons is heard and the shadow and the body hobble away from each other. The camera's gaze, like the protagonist's, follows the shadow, but what it meets with next is the waltz.

Like their unseen counterparts in "La Valse," the waltzing shadows of *Vampyr* expose the always-latent gap between the auditory and the visual and disclose it as a condition of modernity. Though seemingly incidental, these shadows form a pocket allegory of both the film's substance and its medium. Visually, the turning motion of the waltzers links them to the rotary motion of the film projector, the magic circle of modern perception; at the same time their motion is not graceful but jerky, mechanical, so the dancing shadows look something like the images in a zoetrope. The setting enhances this affiliation with mechanism or automatism; before the camera eye finds the dancers it lights on a swinging pendulum, and as it leaves the dancers behind it comes on a vast hall with wheels suspended from the ceiling. The imagery prefigures the end of the film, in which the vampire's mortal helper is buried alive by grain showered down on him by the rotation of a giant mill wheel.

On the auditory side, the music for the waltz of the shadows, like the music of "La Valse," is divorced from the scene of the dance. We hear an ominous symphonic underscore as the protagonist prowls through the chateau to make a reconnaissance. Just before he catches sight of the waltzers, the underscore breaks out—shades of Mahler!—into a vulgar waltz. The two musical styles alternate several times without transition and with no change in point of view. The effect is to leave the waltz music audible but absent; it remains hemmed in by the underscore, as cut off from the dancers as they are from their bodies. There is no coordination between the rhythm of the music and the movement of the shadows, so even if they "hear" the waltz—and they might; we do catch a glimpse of the shadow musicians—their hearing is a kind of deafness. At the end of the scene the vampire (an old woman) enters the hall and cries, "Silence," and a dead silence follows—but what the cry silences is the symphonic music, not the waltz.

Meanwhile, and most importantly, the protagonist seems to hear nothing but the brief sound of barking dogs outside. The dance is as silent to him as to Mahler's night wanderer, and as senseless. But it is not senseless to us. Because we in the audience do hear the waltz, we not only see the event of seeing without hearing but also, as it were, hear ourselves seeing it. We hear the junction between music and sight as tenuous or fictitious. We join with the two senses as they enter a "fugue" state by flying off the hinges. We reel as the music lurches from one foot to another and the protagonist's gaze detaches itself from him like a shadow and passes through the scene on its own.

This separation opens an ontological vertigo that captures both the shadows and their observers. And because the shadows are phantoms of mechanism, what Ravel might have called their "fantastic, fatal whirling" becomes identified with the mechanization of perception. The subject becomes modern by becoming a sensory machine. As Jonathan Crary has documented, the reduction of organic sense to machinic action was a primary means of theorizing perception in the later nineteenth century. It is no accident that this line of thought overlapped with the invention of cinema.[24] As an event in the history of perception, cinema figures not only as a new visual medium but also as a medium that renegotiates the perception of the visible. The moving image makes apparent, as if for the first time, a general necessity in the visible for an auditory supplement. Without sound, the seen tends to become impalpable, itself a kind of image.[25] The moving image reveals a gap in the visible that the auditory supplement seeks to fill. The sound covers what the images expose. But ambient sound alone cannot cover the gap fully enough, or for long enough, to hold it in check. For that, music is required. And even music, in the end, can only reobscure the gap, not fill it.

In "La Valse" Ravel exposes the same gap from its other side. He composes a music that turns the normal concert experience of hearing without seeing into an act of hearing *against* seeing. The turn—another waltz step—is all the more spectral and haunted because of its narrative scheme. Much of the central dance scene is as clear and distinct a vision as the ghost of Descartes might wish. Too much so, even: the music draws on an archive of images of elegance and romance that had already passed into cliché. But the dance scene is framed between two impossibilities of vision: before, the nebulous cloud that blocks the gaze, and after, the grotesque churning that exceeds or defeats the gaze. Before, organic sense suspended; after, machinic action in overdrive. The shadows of the film do not know it, but they are really dancing to "La Valse."

In Benjamin's account the cinema initiates a new regime of perception by means of a double lack. The mechanical reproducibility of films means that they lack *aura,* the quality of irreplaceable singularity in an object or event. They thus have a weightlessness that comes out in the way they deflect attention. Films can be apprehended only in a state of distraction—a state that Benjamin, following the sociological model of Georg Simmel and others, takes as a primary trait of modernity.

The narrative of *Vampyr* can be read as an allegorical reflection of a similar idea. It unreels as the passive protagonist is continually sidetracked by portents and apparitions—or, from another perspective, by cinematic gimmicks. Among those distractions are the shadows, the negatives of aura. Like the observer of Mahler's deaf dance scene, the pallid wanderer of *Vampyr,* almost a shadow himself, is lost in the night of distraction. And he is joined there by "La Valse," which can, almost must, be heard as an allegory of distraction, but with the waltz itself and all it portends taking the place of the distracted subject and his aura-less shadow.

ENTR'ACTE

The trope of the house occupied only by dancing specters had also occurred to Thomas Hardy in his poem "The House of Silence" (ca. 1916). The nexus between lost time and a dance to silenced music seems to have arisen without direct connection in multiple venues:

> "That is a quiet place—
> That house in the trees with the shady lawn."
> "—If, child, you knew what there goes on
> You would not call it a quiet place.
> Why, a phantom abides there, the last of its race,
> And a brain spins there till dawn."
> . . . .
> "Morning, noon, and night,
> Mid those funereal shades that seem
> The uncanny scenery of a dream,
> Figures dance to a mind with sight,
> And music and laughter like floods of light
> Make all the precincts gleam."[26]

Is Hardy's narrator nostalgic or deranged? It is hard to tell the difference, assuming there is a difference to be told here. The spinning dance becomes an artifact of the spinning brain, another instance of perception disfigured by modernity. Like Ravel's, Hardy's scene becomes flooded with light, but the light is more blinding than revealing and does nothing to mitigate the "funereal shades" that frame it. The horror of the scene, only implicit here, assumes a lurid, Poe-like form in William Butler Yeats's late play "Purgatory" (1938). The play replaces the doomed romance of the waltz with a full-fledged Freudian primal scene, culminating in a lullaby that the onlooker sings to his long-dead mother.

"LA VALSE," KARL KRAUS, AND THE VIOLENCE OF MEMORY

The separation of hearing and seeing in "La Valse" is both a fatality and a pathology. The more the music of the phantasmal Imperial ballroom comes back to life, the more grotesquely distorted it becomes. The more it can be heard, the less it can be seen. If the music of the waltz scene of 1855 is regarded as the mark of the scene's aura, merged with the brilliance of the ball and the glamour of an epoch, then "La Valse" is a demonstration of what happens when aura is lost. But it is a demonstration made *from the perspective* of aura itself. What one gets in the music is not a discredited object or genre but the auditory specter of its aura, a debased form of the singular that is the ghost that haunts modernity.

The turning point in this demonstration is the division of "La Valse" by the disfigured return of its opening. The division is a symbolic watershed. It marks the moment at which the estrangement of perception decisively becomes the index of modern skepticism, Stevens's blaring "epic of unbelief." The waltz tunes that emerge from the murk of the opening are already in decline; as one succeeds another in a long train, the series of tunes sounds like an attempt to imagine the music that fits the ball scene of Ravel's scenario. The attempt does not work, at least not for more than an instant or two at a time. The music remains the sound that is *not* heard; too many waltzes have ended, and this is their phantasm. Moreover this inaudibility, not so much a silence as a blockage, assumes a sound of its own. The various waltzes are crosscut by a surplus of sounds—runs, churnings, splotches, excesses of orchestration—that give positive form to the failure of the waltzes to be heard. The pressure exerted by this residue increases as the music progresses, and after the return of the opening the increase accelerates until the music breaks down like a machine run amok. Prior to the point of division, we might say, the waltzes contain the residue; after that point the residue contains the waltzes, until in the end it contains nothing at all.

The effect of modern perception on the past is to destroy its mystique; too many waltzes have ended. But does the music regret that? Or does it, instead, take a savage pleasure in scourging the illusions of luxury and pleasure to which it still feels a certain attraction?

The same question haunts yet another *momon*, or rather a whole series of them, assembled by the Viennese satirist Karl Kraus. Starting in 1926, Kraus cast himself in a series of one-man shows, including radio broadcasts, based on the operettas of Jacques Offenbach—music from the era of Ravel's dance scenes. Kraus felt that Offenbach's music transfigured the vapidity of his operetta plots without disguising it. In Offenbach, he wrote, "the satire of the follies of state and mankind . . . cannot be divorced from the brilliant music." The operettas inhabited a "fantastical" world in which "causality is abolished and everybody lives happily under the rule of chaos."[27]

But by the 1920s the operettas could be no more than exercises in the same fatal nostalgia that had overtaken the waltz. Kraus's presentations of them are acts of creative disfigurement. They replace the orchestra with a piano and singing with recitative *(Sprechgesang).* They are ghost operettas. For Benjamin,

> The voice of Kraus speaks, rather than sings, [Offenbach's] inner music.... It hums, like the wind in the chimney, a requiem to the generation of our grandfathers.... For where this fickle voice is heard, the lightning flashes of the advertisements and the thunder of the Metro cleave the Paris of the omnibuses and the gas flames.[28]

But the voice ends in exhaustion. Benjamin says—rightly or wrongly; some of the radio broadcasts are available online, so one can judge for oneself—that "by extending its boundaries further and further it finally enfeebles itself, dissolving into a merely animal voice."[29]

Ravel does something very similar in "La Valse," but with the important difference that he does it with enhanced rather than diminished music. He stays within the medium of transfiguration in order to negate it and, worse, to negate it by showing its innate self-destructiveness and impulse to self-corruption. Ravel redefines the nature of nostalgia, the appeal of which he nonetheless does nothing to deny, by turning its exercise into an exorcism in which the waltz dances itself to death. But there is no decline to a merely animal voice. Rather like the abhorred Saint-Saëns in *Danse macabre,* Ravel keeps the music at a sufficient distance from what it depicts to sustain pleasure in the artifice of the depiction, although whether its violence belongs inside or outside the virtual quotation marks thus created remains an open question.

Taken together, Ravel, Dreyer, and Kraus suggest a turning point in the long development of artificial life in media. What begins in the Enlightenment as an attempt to simulate animation becomes in modernity an attempt to find in simulation the technology of reanimation. The vampire, as undead, is a primary metaphor of this process, in which cinema, as Dreyer's vampire demonstrates, takes pride of place. Ravel's dancers and Kraus's Offenbachian farceurs are all virtual vampires, the walking or waltzing spirits of the Europe destroyed in the Great War.

"La Valse," framed by fantasy and catastrophe, is more than a desublimating retraction of Ravel's earlier waltz idea and its motif of innocent pleasure. The piece turns that retraction into a musical indictment of European modernity as a form of noise, that is, of sound as violence. The indictment is not typical of Ravel, who generally took pleasure in being modern without ambivalence. It does seem to be an effect of the immediate postwar moment, but it cannot be reduced either to an indirect comment on the war's devastation or to a nationalist change of heart about the Viennese waltz. It was perhaps to avert such reductions that Ravel insisted that the destructive energy of "La Valse" was immanent in the idea of the dance. The agent of negation was the very rhythm that the younger Ravel found "wonderful." If the piece is an indictment, the rhythm is its writ.

Like Mahler, Ravel heard the loss of the "rhythmic cue" as both disconcerting and symptomatic. Like Mahler, he expresses this rhythmic lapse by exaggerating the dance rhythm until it falls apart or explodes. A single element, a somewhat overemphatic downbeat, already present at the outset in the inchoate thuds of the double basses, becomes a disfigurement. Eventually, especially via the excess repetition of a single melodic fragment, it becomes punishing, then monstrous. The fact that the waltz tunes in the middle of the work are genuinely attractive is not simply a sign that something admirable has gone bad, but part of the essential instrumentality of destruction. It demonstrates that one's own investment in the corrupted or, as Slavoj Žižek might say, the "obscene" pleasure of the music is what permits the catastrophe at the close.[30]

Unlike its counterpart in the noble and sentimental waltzes of the previous decade, the frame of "La Valse" is broken. The opening is an obfuscation, distraction spread like a veil over the ear; the close is the running-down of a machine like one of the toothed millwheels in *Vampyr*. The connection between them is lost, as if a phone line had been cut. The whole conception, including the prose-poem scenario, is cinematic, but it is cinematic in pieces, with sounds on the sprockets instead of images and the images held in suspension at too far a remove. If only Ravel could have phoned it in, "La Valse" might have been a siren song without the brutal outcome, a beautiful summons (a summons to the beautiful?) like the one that ends Debussy's "Images" for Orchestra, a telephonic retelling of the fable as a fairy tale.

This is no joke, but a recognition of the telephonic mode as a primary medium of modern perception. It speaks to why music is used—not well, of course, in fact annoyingly, but the thought is there—to placate people on hold. The early telephone shared the spectral character of early sound recordings. There are famous literary instances in both Proust (the narrator speaking with his grandmother in *The Guermantes Way*) and Joyce (Leopold Bloom imagining a phone line to the grave in Ulysses).[31]

In his *The Post Card*, since Lacoue-Labarthe has brought up the name, Derrida notes a strange, as if unconscious, exception, though we really need to speak here of something consciously unconscious, knowingly unaware, to the rule of mischance that haunts all communication. That rule—that a letter may always not reach its destination—is what Derrida calls the postal principle. It shapes the destinies of an era of the post extending, as his subtitle has it, "From Socrates to Freud and Beyond." The exception comes over the telephone. It comes, more specifically, from the late twentieth-century landline, happily immune from dropped calls. The phone in this sense recurs as the alternative, if ever elusive, channel of communication between the speaker (a thinly veiled autobiographical persona) and the unnamed addressee of the love letters that make up the bulk of the volume: "*28 August 1977.* You just called. You asked me if I had heard you call me? Is that a question? I stayed silent. The idea that you might 'call' me and that I might not answer overwhelms me. So much telephone between us." "How nice it is that you called back immediately. I caressed your voice." "You just hung up (the intermittent hissing that always follows: it drives me crazy enough to kill)."[32] Each of these quotations reflects the anxiety that arises when one becomes aware of a medium that is normally expected to disappear into its use. The phone is supposed to bring the voices, and thus the persons, into contact, almost literally into touch, in a way that writing can never do, but the slightest glitch can turn the medium itself into the noise that always follows. Nonetheless, unlike the woman and her lost love in "La Voix humaine," Derrida and his beloved addressee recurrently find "love at a distance" through the "teleorgasmization" of their voices.[33]

Too bad Ravel could not get to a phone!

In the end what is broken along with the frame is memory, for the frame is ultimately nothing but memory itself. The opening of "La Valse" shows a wish to remember, the close a need to forget. But what kind of memory is this? It is not documentary, not an archive of the waltz, and it is not subjective, nothing like the rich flood of sensations released by an unexpected trigger such as Proust's famous *petite madeleine*—though it might well be a travesty of that. It is more like a haunting memory, a nagging, obsessive idea that will not leave the mind alone. A haunting memory; a tune stuck in the head. One way to *hear* modernity is as the time of haunting memories. (The twentieth century was littered with them.) What "La Valse" choreographs is an attempt to work through the haunting, to discharge it by letting its implacability rise to a point of catharsis. Or rather what the music choreographs is the failure of that attempt. When we listen we know just what's coming, but a good performance will find us as vulnerable to it as we ever were—every time. "La Valse" is a siren song after all in the form of an imaginary dance that treads our desires and illusions under foot.

SEVEN

The Musical Biome

IN *FRANKENSTEIN,* MARY SHELLEY TRACES the genesis of self-awareness in the creature no sooner brought to life by Victor Frankenstein than cruelly abandoned by him. The creature is "born" fully grown but must learn to become something other than an empty vessel. Shelley had a famous precedent for this primal coming-of-age story in a text we encountered early on, the *Traité des sensations* (1754) of Étienne de Condillac. As we know, Condillac's treatise tells the story of a statue brought to life as a tabula rasa but drawn by sensation into learning how to become human. Drawn to the same end, Frankenstein's creature must be affected in both body and mind. What affects him the most, and forms the bridge between body and mind, is the sound of a musical instrument that we later learn is a guitar. Shelley implicitly continues the long train of metaphors that identifies the musical vibration of a string with the vibration of a nerve:

> The young girl ... took something out of a drawer, which employed her hands, and she sat down beside the old man, who, taking up an instrument, began to play, and to produce sounds, sweeter than the voice of the thrush or the nightingale. It was a lovely sight, even to me, poor wretch! who had never beheld aught beautiful before.... [The aged cottager] played a sweet mournful air, which I perceived drew tears from the eyes of his amiable companion, of which the old man took no notice, until she sobbed audibly; he then pronounced a few sounds, and the fair creature, leaving her work, knelt at his feet. He raised her, and smiled with such kindness and affection, that I felt sensations of a peculiar and over-powering nature: they were a mixture of pain and pleasure, such as I had never before experienced, either from hunger or cold, warmth or food; and I withdrew from the window, unable to bear these emotions.[1]

The music becomes the medium in which the creature discovers that he is truly alive. It twines him into life as the young girl's hands knit or sew or embroider in parallel with the old man's twining together of musical sounds on the strings.[2]

This chapter asks what might happen if we were to take the equation of music and life with complete seriousness, understanding it to inhabit the wavering, uncertain space between real and metaphorical agency. The objects of the inquiry are J.S. Bach's *Goldberg Variations* and a novel by Richard Powers that carries almost the same name. The distinction between the music and the book will quickly begin to waver, along with the difference between literal and metaphorical life. The life in question, moreover, is the expression not of an indefinite vital force but of the genetic code; this is a story about DNA. But this project requires a pair of detours before it can get going. The first concerns translation, which may seem remote from the matter at hand but actually bears on it closely. The second concerns the distribution of agency among nonhuman actors. Both involve the discernment of something lifelike in nominally nonliving things.

LIFE, TRANSLATION, AND ACTOR-NETWORK THEORY

In "The Task of the Translator" (1923), Walter Benjamin links the translation of classic texts that formed one of the foundations of humanism with a radically expanded concept of life. Benjamin disengages life from biological forms and attaches it to history instead: "That one should not ascribe life to organic corporeality alone was suspected even in times of the most biased thought.... Rather only if life is accorded to everything that has a history... does the concept of life come into its own. It is history, not nature, that ultimately determines the sphere of life."[3] Chief among those things with histories are works of art, which derive those histories and thus that life from being translatable, even if they are not translated. Their "life and living-on," moreover, "is to be understood with a wholly unmetaphorical objectivity.... Is not at least the living-on of works incomparably easier to recognize than that of creatures?"[4]

By works of art Benjamin primarily means works of literature, which it may seem difficult to experience as literally or almost-literally alive. We have seen abundant evidence, though, that it has been easy, really almost inevitable, to experience music in that way since the train of metaphors we have been following was set in motion. The interchangeability of music and life is characteristic; the interchangeability of translation and life, or language and life, is idiosyncratic. One reason for this difference is that music, to be heard at all, must be "translated" by performance; music must be *sounded*. It's a simple and obvious fact but it has long been the crucial one. Benjamin elsewhere suggests that sound, "the pure formal principle of language," is the "symbol" of the power of human language to translate our "material community" with things into purely mental or spiritual apprehension. This view puts Benjamin in direct opposition to Hegel, who thought the opposite and who maintained that the expression of subjective interiority was hampered when music relied too exclusively on the materiality of sound.[5] Benjamin wanted to find in the written word the kind of life that the "vital materialist" Jane Bennett would later identify as the "vibrancy" inherent in matter itself.[6] But the life he was looking for does not belong to paper, print, and binding, but to a "work" with little or no sensory presence.[7] Music has that sensory presence in abundance. The question that music poses is not *whether* it is vibrant but how, in any given case, it *becomes* vibrant, and to what ends. What translates musical sound into life?

So ends the first detour. The second goes by way of two recent philosophical trends that extend Benjamin's initiative though without invoking it: actor-network theory and object-oriented ontology. Actor-network theory is largely the brainchild of Bruno Latour, who began developing it with reference to the history of science in the 1980s. Latour has since reframed the theory with a still more expansive one, based on what he calls modes of existence, but like J. L. Austin's distinction between performative and constative speech acts, actor-network theory has so far led a life independent of its incorporation into a more inclusive body of thought.

Central to actor-network theory is a principle of ontological leveling, by which familiar distinctions between subjects and objects, mind and matter, and human and nonhuman agents cease to be decisive, even if they do not exactly disappear. What Latour calls matters of concern require the orchestration of action—that metaphor is mine, not Latour's—by a plethora of human and nonhuman actors that stand to one another on equal footing, the distinctions between them not always clear.[8] Ontological leveling is also a key feature of object-oriented ontology, which stems primarily from the work of Graham Harman. OOO, as it is called, reduces the difference between living and nonliving things by understanding both as participating in the same fundamental process of withholding themselves from full comprehension or exposure. Their being consists in that process. Objects, a category that includes any and every identifiable phenomenon, are ontologically prior to their relations.[9] Harman resembles Benjamin in envisioning a world of endless striving for translation, and differs from him in emphasizing what cannot be translated as opposed to what can be. "The objects of object-oriented philosophy," he writes, "are mortal, ever-changing, built from swarms of subcomponents, and accessible only through oblique allusion."[10] That, perhaps, is why Benjamin emphasizes life whereas Harman emphasizes being.

The purpose of these brief glances at complex modes of thought is to provide a preliminary rationale for asking just how far it is possible to go with the equation of music and life. How does each translate the other, and at what point, by what means, does this translation affirm an overlap, fusion, or mingling, metaphorical and otherwise? The agents before us in this matter of concern are Bach and Powers, in an encounter assumed to be reciprocal regardless of chronology. The chapter will travel back and forth between the two, but its starting point is Bach.

BACH: LIFE AND THE HARPSICHORD

At about the same time as Denis Diderot was composing his metaphor of the human nervous system as a harpsichord, Johann Sebastian Bach was doing much the same thing—on the harpsichord. The occasion was the composition of the *Goldberg Variations,* music that is unusual in at least three respects other than the extraordinarily complex patterning that turns it into something very like a network populated by independent actors—or the map of a genome. First, Bach arranged for the work to be published during his lifetime (most of his music was not) and he participated in the process of publication. Second, the publisher utilized hand-engraved copper plates rather than movable type. Third, the music was specifically written for a two-manual harpsichord, and each of the variations specifies whether it is to be played on one keyboard, on both, or on either one or both at the performer's discretion.

These details suggest an effort to establish the score as a living monument on the model, derived from the Roman poet Horace (Ode 3:30), of the poem as a medium of memory capable of outlasting brass and stone because of the infinite repeatability of writing—in Bach's case the infinite repeatability of performance embedded in the engraved writing. In English the best-known instance of this trope is from Shakespeare's sonnet 55: "Not marble, nor the gilded monuments / Of princes shall outlive this powerful rhyme."[11] The key word here is "outlive." Gilded monuments can be destroyed, but texts can be reprinted and rhymes repeated. The gilding is an idle boast, but whoever reads performs an act of reanimation. The idea of vying for immortality with princely power is already present in Horace, who speaks of his verse monument rising higher than pyramids. It asserts itself further in Bach through both the text and the typography of his title page: "**ARIA** with diverse variations for harpsichord with two manuals, composed ... by **JOHANN SEBASTIAN BACH,** Composer for the Court of Poland and the Electoral Court of Saxony, Kappelmeister and Director of Choral Music in Leipzig."

From the perspective of actor-network theory, Bach is as much the beneficiary, or even the servant, as he is the master of the instrument that makes the music possible. The harpsichord, together with the social and institutional actions that have shaped its construction, imparts something essential to each variation by either directing the agency of the performer (play this on two keyboards; play that on just one) or liberating it (play where you like). The complexity of the score becomes a projection of the complexity of the instrument and the interweaving of its parts, its keys, its stops, its vibrations. Bach composes for this instrument not only in the sense of requiring its use but also in the sense of writing (and engraving) on its behalf. Bach translates the instrument no less than the instrument translates Bach. Or, in terms more suited to Powers's novel, to which I now turn, the composition of the *Goldberg Variations* enables the two-manual harpsichord to come revealingly to life. The instrument does not "take on a life of its own," as one commonly says, but instead asserts a lifelike disposition to act that has always been immanent to it. Centuries later, Powers elucidates that disposition by discovering, literally and figuratively, its DNA.

POWERS: BACH'S MUSICAL GENOME

Powers's novel is called *The Gold Bug Variations*. The pun in the title neatly concentrates the book's conceptual or metaphorical basis—it is hard to tell them apart. Powers apparently assumes that everyone will catch the allusion to Bach's *Goldberg Variations,* and that his American readers, at any rate, will recognize the reference to Edgar Allan Poe's story "The Gold Bug." The story is about a search for treasure that requires the deciphering of a substitution code; the treasure sought in the novel is the key to deciphering the code governing genetic sequencing. The *Goldberg Variations* preoccupies two of the novel's chief characters (one from each of its two romantic couples, like base pairs in a strand of DNA). As they hear it, the whole work seems to be spun out from the descending bass of its first four measures, G-F#-E-D, suggesting an analogy to the composition of life from the base-pair sequencing of DNA's four component nucleotides, G, A, T, C: guanine, adenine, thymine, cytosine. The question in both cases is how life happens.

The novel proceeds to build the answer into its own DNA, metaphorically splicing the genes of the *Goldberg Variations* into the genome of its narrative. (This metaphor is as much Powers's as it is mine.) One has to read this novel with the *Goldberg Variations* in one's ears. Anything less is not reading it.[12] One has to hear the music, as the characters learn to do, in musically informed terms, but only to decrypt the sources of the vitality it shares with the text. The term "vitality" should be taken literally. *The Gold Bug Variations* comes about as close to being one of Benjamin's books with a life as a book can get.

Powers's novel unfolds the way it claims the *Goldberg Variations* does; the narrative starts with a simple premise and submits it to luxuriant elaboration. The action turns on a puzzle: Why did one of the protagonists, Stuart Ressler, give up a potentially brilliant career in DNA research to appear, twenty years later, as a night shift worker minding the computers of a giant corporation? The puzzle absorbs the interest of Ressler's young coworker Franklin Todd, together with Jan O'Deigh, the research librarian Franklin enlists to look into Ressler's life. Jan is also the narrator of the later parts of the story, which are set in the early 1980s; an old-fashioned omniscient narrator takes the late 1950s.

Like Ressler and his fellow researcher Jeanette Koss decades earlier, Jan and Franklin slide from research to romance, and the variations in the relationships among these four figures, these two couples, comprise the events of the novel. "Strand by strand," Powers has said, "these two love stories twist about each other in a double helix of desire."[13] But the events are less important than the two principles on which they operate. The first principle is that the novel's treatment of the four characters corresponds with Bach's treatment of the four notes from which all of the *Goldberg Variations* supposedly stem. The second principle is that the music's elaboration of these four notes corresponds with the pairing, in the double helix, of the four nucleotides that form the base pairs of DNA. Powers's text strongly suggests that these correspondences should not be understood metaphorically. They form something like the ontological alphabet of life.

In what follows I will examine three of Powers's paraphrases of the *Goldberg Variations*. The first concerns the composition as a whole—aria, variations on a ground, and the return of the aria. The second and third concern specific variations: number 10, a fughetta, and its contrary, number 30, a quodlibet, that is, a contrapuntal medley of popular tunes. The choices are really Powers's, not mine; these are the variations he dwells on most. The contrast between the rigor of the one and the quirkiness of the other defines the space within which the novel sets life, love, and music into motion intertwisting like the strands of a double helix. But in each case my question will not be what Powers or his text do, or think, or would have us think, but what the unleashing of Bach's musical energies in the text affords us the opportunity to do and think in return.

The turning point in the young Ressler's life occurs when Koss, a married woman, unexpectedly shows up at his apartment bearing a gift: Glenn Gould's famous LP recording from 1955 of the *Goldberg Variations*. The music and the woman quickly become Ressler's two great loves. Although the novel treats the music as possessing an ideal, independent existence, Ressler takes possession of it only through Gould's performance. He does so, however, not through the performance *on* the recording, but through the performance that *is* the recording. As Nicholas Cook has argued, recordings are performances in their own right, and Ressler treats Gould's recording as a performance not only of the music but of the performer's absorption in the music.[14] This performance is as much bodily as it is conceptual. It is marked by audible traces: Gould's breathing and vocalization and the squeak of his piano stool. The traces eventually extend to the LP itself, which Ressler virtually scribbles over with the pops and clicks that come from endlessly repeated playing under a diamond needle. Paradoxically, however—paradoxically but not, perhaps, exceptionally—the performance makes the music available to Ressler in what feels like unmediated transparency and fullness. More specifically, and in this it *is* exceptional, the performance makes the music available to Ressler as the unique embodiment of a sublime rationality shared only by the genetic code. The music embodies the power to turn matter into life.

The role of the music in the narrative begins to exceed its premises over the question of that power. What might Powers's bridge to Bach lead us to say independent of the novel's representations? Powers himself is willing to raise the question. He has Ressler joke defensively about the folly of listening to Bach for insights into the genetic code while at the same time what Jan calls the "closet gnostic" in him—and in her—will not let him (who? Ressler?

Powers?) stop. Jan becomes Ressler's de facto pupil both to discover and to uphold the properties of the music that make it the "best model of the living gene."[15] Her conclusions aim to demonstrate that understanding the music retrospectively as a model of biogenesis and hearing it anachronistically as an expression of one's intimate personal history are simply different aspects of the same reasonable process. "Under the pressure of evolutionary restlessness, [the variations] simply spread out across the map of available biomes, unearth some of the embedded germ material, bring some as yet unrealized alternative—similar to all others, only different—into existence.... The variations are the working out of that instruction, buried deep in the Base string, that commands itself to translate, to strain against the limits of its own synthesis, to test the living trick of Perhaps, to love" (584–585).

The living trick of Perhaps applies to far more than the next act of musical invention, and so, of course, does love. "Darwin," Jan goes on to say, "might have found his elusive pangene [the particle bearing inheritance], if only he'd looked in the right place." Darwin did not lack genius; he lacked Bach. The right place to look was the one where "the investing metaphor at the heart of life" couples the "infinitely pliable four-note theme" with the primal quartet of nucleotides (585).

Jan's interpretation of what Ressler hears, and what he makes available to hear, rewrites the history of modern knowledge in an effort to humanize it. The effort is as old as modern science, the byproduct of the splitting of knowledge into separate compartments—empirical, conjectural, moral—that Jürgen Habermas took to be the core problem of modernity.[16] Powers, however, does not identify the humanizing project with overcoming this fragmentation. His novel humanizes by narrating. It links knowledge to life by telling a story of life under the conditions of modern knowledge. *The Gold Bug Variations* represents knowledge grounded in scientific rationality not as distanced from passion, selfhood, and love but as a medium for them, both saturating and saturated by them. Humanizing such knowledge thus means recognizing that it has always already been humanized, and that its progress takes the form, not of discarding older modes of rationality, but of discovering their presence in later modes. It follows that the connection between the logic of Bach's music and the logic of the genetic code, and between both logics and a pair of love stories, should not be surprising—though of course it is.

What, then, of the passions of rationality? Is something of them latent in Bach's variations?

BACH: LISTENING TO REASON

The historical Bach's model of rationality is Pythagorean, mathematical, "analytic" in Kant's sense of framing a truth by reason alone. In other words this is a classical rationality removed from the empirical world, something already anachronistic in Bach's day but still echoing as late as 1805 in Wordsworth's poetic autobiography, *The Prelude*. Inclined to melancholy, the young Wordsworth turns to the study of geometry:

> Mighty is the charm
> Of those abstractions to a mind beset
> With images, and haunted by itself,
> And specially delightful unto me
> Was that clear synthesis built up aloft
> So gracefully... an independent world
> Created out of pure intelligence."[17]

As the quotation testifies, the numerically based perfection of this mode of rationality is divorced from the body. It does not depend on sensation and perception; instead it is a cure for the burdens they bring. Its pleasures come from proportion, which echoes the underlying order of all things.

Bach intimates a similar attitude in the design of the *Goldberg Variations*, which is strictly numerical—indeed, as we'll see, almost geometrical. The full title of the work says so directly: "Clavier Ubung / bestehend / in einer Aria / mit verschiedenen Verænderungen / vors Clavicimbal / mit 2 Manualen. / Denen Liebhabern zur Gemüths- / Ergetzung verfertiget von / Johann Sebastian Bach." [Keyboard Exercise / consisting / in an Aria / with diverse variations / for harpsichord / with 2 manuals. / For connoisseurs to their spirit's / refreshment composed by / Johann Sebastian Bach.] On the title page of the original edition of 1741, the statement about form and instrumentation is separated visually from the statement of purpose. Whoever reads the title moves in doing so from one domain to the other. (See figure 1.) The first statement runs about halfway down the page and tends to draw away from the margins of the ornamental frame. The second statement is dominated by the visual inversion of the first. It begins with *Denen Liebhabern zur Gemüths* (running from margin to margin), draws in to complete the thought of refreshment, and then expands to the margins again with the composer's name in large type. To study and perform this music, which is Bach's stated concern, is to move from bodily exertion to spiritual renewal. The signature seals the lesson with a flourish.

FIGURE 1. Title page, J. S. Bach, *Goldberg Variations*.

The novel does not want to hear the music in these terms, but it does want very much to hear the music, and it takes the music's design as part of its basis—or, to use a term that will become increasingly important, its "Base." Every third variation of the *Goldberg* set is a canon; the sequence begins with a canon at the unison and proceeds one step at a time to a canon at the ninth.

THE MUSICAL BIOME · 153

The titles of the pieces mark this progress. Once Powers has introduced the music into the narrative, he writes nine segments, titled "Canon at the Unison" through "Canon at the Ninth," and distributes them at intervals across the remainder of the text. Bach, however, famously breaks the chain when it comes to a canon at the tenth. Powers does too. As we will see, the consequences are decisive for both the music and the novel.

Meanwhile, what the novel hears in the music has consequences of its own. The import of Bach's ninefold design creates a subtext revealingly at odds with the proto-biochemical logic that Powers finds in it. Bach's canons demarcate groups of three variations; each group ends with a canon. The canons thus compose nine trinities, or three times three threes, a trinity of trinities, a two-level affirmation of the sacred number. This grouping accounts for twenty-seven variations, which seems like a lot. Why not stop there?

Perhaps because twenty-seven is a meaningless number. Bach adds an additional triplet to make up the perfect number ten and thus to produce the full design of thirty plus two pieces, with each piece consisting of thirty-two or twice thirty-two measures, a microcosm to the full set as macrocosm. Only by this means can the work, by its own lights, create an independent world out of pure intelligence. The relationships involved are complex but not esoteric; unlike the genetic code, they are not hidden, not a mystery. The novel has to make a mystery of them—to make the *Goldberg*s a *Gold Bug*—in order to find a mystery it can solve. The music becomes a model of the genetic code, not as it is, but as the intellect wishes it to be: a system that will become fully transparent to the right kind of learning and attention. For Ressler, the music satisfies the desire for knowledge that the real genome continually frustrates, so much so that when the key to the code comes within reach, he renounces knowing it. He has his chance, but chance is exactly the trouble. The genome ultimately depends on chance in a way that the music does not. Nonetheless, the object of desire is the same for both. And like the object of desire in Poe's story, it is treasure.

Something similar holds for the bass line, minus the number symbolism. Powers relies heavily on Ralph Kirkpatrick's analytic reduction of the bass and its punning respelling as the Base.[18] He acknowledges but largely ignores the bass one actually hears, which does not recur literally but by approximations and intimations following the demands of genre and expression within each variation. The friction between abstract form and concrete presentation finds a degree of reconciliation in the recurrence of Bach's initial moment of transparency. Most of the variations do begin over some form of the descending tetrachord G-F#-E-D spread over four measures. Most thus restate the nucleus of the variation process that for Powers anticipates the sequence of four nucleotides. Most, but not all: the work does promise "diverse variations," and Bach's Reason is not unreasonably insistent. Still, the tetrachord recurs. It recurs more than often enough to be recognizable as the source of a "clear synthesis / built up aloft" and thus to guide the work's self-proclaimed mission. The recurrence of these four notes within the framework of nested threes traces a quasi-ritualized passage from the senses to the intellect; the sequence of tetrachords forms the base of the spirit's refreshment. In Powers's novel, the same sequence traces the passage from mere matter to living bodies. Heard in that way, the logic of the variations does more than prefigure the logic of life; it anticipates the production of life. It is almost more alive than it knows. The code that refreshes spirit from body finds its modern revival but also its consummation in the code that elicits life from matter. Both codes ascend, but to different peaks. Powers's characters seek to arrive at the place from which Bach seeks to depart.

In other words, the body that is only a means for Bach is an end for Powers. The novel registers this disparity by focusing on Gould's piano as opposed to Bach's harpsichord. By specifying the use of one or two manuals for most of the variations, Bach's score highlights the mechanical source of the music that refreshes the spirit. The usually unremarkable fact that the harpsichord cannot change tone or volume in response to touch becomes a source of unaccustomed significance. Bach reminds us that the instrumental mechanism literally comes between the body that plays and the spirit that hears. He even builds the reminder into the sequence of variations by omitting the keyboard designation of one—just one—of the variations, no. 21, the canon at the seventh.[19]

The novel inverts this emphasis by dwelling on the materiality of Gould's piano recording, which redoubles his expressive touch at the keyboard. The music cannot be separated from the worn record and the low-fidelity record player, which, however, the intensity of Ressler's listening surmounts and even transfigures. Powers thus hears a miraculous but wholly natural transition from mechanism to animation, from the insensate to the sentient. Bach seems content to keep these realms separate, and he has divine warrant for doing so. The sequential form of his variations refers, not to the world, but to outside the world. This orientation holds good, however, only up to a point—a late point, at which we too will arrive later.

The novel's observations about Bach's musical geometry are latent in what was once, and perhaps still is, the conventional wisdom about him; they are consistent with the cliché of Bach as the preeminent composer of "pure music." But they are rescued by their incorporation into a narrative that must change them to keep them. The novel links the mode of rationality embedded in Bach's technique to the lived urgencies of both pairing (the romantic couples, the narratives a quarter century apart) and sequencing (the nine narrative canons). The affinity between Bach's numerical symmetries and the pairing and sequencing of the genome acts not as a charming abstraction but as the life force of the narrative. It has life-and-death consequences. The novel makes the cliché interesting again and then leaves it behind.

What takes its place? One answer is the phenomenon we began with many chapters ago: simulation. The novel does not want to *see* Bach's variation process as a symbol for the process of biogenesis. It wants to *hear* the variations, and wants us to hear them, as a simulation of life both in biogenesis and beyond it: life as made and life as lived. But there is more than one way to do that, each of which, so to speak, has its own sentient keyboard.

Powers has Jan observe that Ressler's understanding of the variations differs fundamentally from Bach's in one key respect. Although the music is wholly secular, it bears traces of the religious worldview that led the composer to inscribe his scores with "the triplet SDG" (586), the Latin abbreviation for *Soli Dei Gloria* (To God alone the glory). In Ressler's ears, the same music transcribes a purely materialistic conception: "Even this secularly commissioned [entertainment] possesses the religious wonder at being joyously articulate, alive to extend the pattern. But in Ressler's hierarchy of transitional rungs, the thing beyond the composer, on the other side of the threshold from articulate breath, was only dumb designless matter" (586). For Ressler the life in the music forms a bulwark against a formless void that for Bach does not exist. Jan hears things differently, which does not make Ressler wrong. But Jan's version of the music's life also differs from Bach's—how could it not?—though it differs less drastically. The "religious wonder" that she hears in the variations supports the joyousness of immediate living experience, including the experience of listening to this very music in the act of "extend[ing] the pattern." It is hard to say no to this account, and there is no reason to, but Bach's own description nonetheless indicates a purpose that

Jan does not acknowledge. On Bach's stated terms, what his score simulates, or rather, perhaps, rehearses, is the process by which the ultimate immateriality of life reveals itself through the application of bodily discipline—keyboard exercise. The music's simulation of life as made and lived is a later discovery. Bach has his own solution to the mind-body problem.

In Bach's own day, before the experiments in simulation traced in chapters 1 through 3, the musical representation of life was typically occasional, comic, and above all animal. A typical example is Georg Philip Telemann's "Alster Overture" (1725), which includes movements titled "The Swan's Song" and "Frogs and Crows in Concert." In this milieu, the music of the *Goldberg Variations* has nothing to do with life—at least not until the penultimate moment when the sequence of canons breaks in favor of the quodlibet. This is the exception that proves the rule, and we will come to it.

Birdsong aside, most eighteenth-century animal music consisted in the mimicry of animal bodies. The mimicry took two forms. First was life as voice, for which the Telemann overture is again a good example. The voices involved were not "articulate breath" but, precisely, inarticulate. They traced their descent to Aristotle, for whom voice was an animal trait that became human only with the advent of language.[20] A striking later example is the clucking hen in Haydn's Symphony no. 83. Although Haydn, unlike Telemann, did not assign the name, the symphony came to be known as "La Poule," and with good reason. Second, there was the mimicry of animal life on the familiar basis of movement without external force. The Haydn symphony known as "The Bear," again with good reason but without the composer's authority, belongs to the same set that includes "La Poule."

Haydn subsequently, and notoriously, did compose explicit imitations of animal life in his oratorios *The Creation* and *The Seasons*. These pieces, however, especially *The Creation*, mark a shift in orientation that bears on Powers's Bach revival. The carnival of the animals in *The Creation* presents a musical depiction of each animal's typical sound or motion, and hence its life, as first given by the divine hand. We hear the lion, the tiger, the stag, the horse, cattle, insects, and the worm, as well as numerous birds from the eagle to the nightingale. The pageant exemplifies the typological mode of thought characteristic of Enlightenment reason, its faith in classification as a principle of order.[21] This mode of rationality is as important here as the amusing animal ventriloquism that it supports. It is also a far cry from Bach's mode. Because it depends on observation, it literally belongs to a different world. It differs just by belonging to the world. In Powers's novel this typological thinking returns in a new form, as the permutations of the genetic code rather than the table of observed types. As the novel repeatedly says, to understand the message one needs the grammar of the code, not its vocabulary.

But the concept of that grammar is not present in Bach except in Powers's metaphor of the *Goldberg* Base and the DNA base-pairs. The novel asks us to hear the purely hypothetical segmentation of the tetrachord Base as a secret code, a latent form of the genetic code before the genetic code was thinkable. But we might respond by observing that the role of the Base in the music, or rather the role of the less idealized bass that we actually hear, is the very opposite of encoding. Granted, Bach's ground bass is not quite a transparency. It is not as crystalline as the sequence of canons. But the continuity among the many reiterations of the bass is not hard to hear, or at least to feel. There is no need to reduce the bass to a single ideal form.

Powers can no more reduce to system the vitality he finds in the continuity of the bass/Base than Bach can. What he can do, and does do, is expose the impulse to try. Ressler is candid about this dilemma, but he never gives up listening for the secret that he knows may be his own fabrication rather than either Bach's or the world's: "I listened to these miniatures for a year, pulled out of them the most marvelous genetic analogies. But at the end, the music refused to reduce, and it hurt worse than before" (193). The only cure for the hurt is to repeat it, either by oneself or in the person of someone else, in this case Jan, who preserves Ressler's vision of the variations as the acoustic image of a life that always escapes its code: "Ultimately the *Goldberg*s are about the paradox of variation.... By the time the delinquent parent aria returns to close out the set, the music is about how variation might ultimately free itself from the instruction that underwrites it, sets it in motion, but nowhere anticipates what might come from experience's trial run.... What Ressler listened to in that tightly-bound, symmetry-laced catalog of unity was how nothing was the same as everything else. Each living thing defied taxonomy. Everything was its own, unique, irreducible classification" (585–586). Heard in this way, the *Goldberg*s make it possible to think of life not as something that, assuming it is well lived, leads upward to transcendence, but as transcendence itself. The music meant for the spirit's refreshment instead refreshes the life it embodies. What remains unthought is the possibility that the music's virtual genome is actually a product of the life that Jan and Ressler hear in it rather than the other way around. No one in the book will quite admit the possibility that life at this level emerges without a code—but the book admits it. The only recourse is a retroactive dream of cosmic order; Bach can provide it. In admitting dissonances such as this, Powers's novel willingly says more than it knows.

POWERS: LISTENING TO BACH

Does the same apply to Bach? What happens when we flip our previous question and ask what the *Goldberg Variations* may "say" about the novel that purloins something of its title independent of the music's own representations? These questions yield their most revealing answers when asked of the specific variations chosen by the novel for close description: numbers 10 and 30.

Powers associates the four equal contrapuntal voices of the tenth variation with the four characters of his love quadrangle, following in a novelistic lineage that includes, among others, Goethe's *Elective Affinities,* Lawrence's *Women in Love,* and Faulkner's *Light in August.* But one of the four characters, Jeanette Koss, is a virtual shadow, or cipher, for most of the first 250 pages. Before we can account for her presence in variation 10, we need to account for her absence.

Only Ressler, Jan, and Franklin hear the epitomizing tenth variation together. Jeanette emerges as a fully realized character only in the form of an "apparition" that crosses Ressler's threshold to reverse his sensation of her absence: "He lies in bed . . . feel[ing] his legs because they do not touch hers, and her, because she is not any of this, not his, does not touch any of these parts that can *feel* her imprint, so conspicuous is her solidity in her absence next to him" (277). Ressler, Jan, and Franklin form the human equivalent of a codon, a three-nucleotide sequence specifying a single amino acid, a single building-block of life. The codon reverses the classic love triangle; it is a source of generation and regeneration, not of disruption. It is a perfect match for the three-variation sequences that compose the *Goldberg Variations.*

The core of the book is another such codon, a three-part invention in the form of a snowbound weekend in the country that Ressler, Jan, and Franklin spend together. The weekend appears at the very beginning of the narrative and recurs throughout. Jeanette is mainly a negated and negating presence until the secret motives of her affair with Ressler come out belatedly during the course of that all-important weekend. Earlier Jan associates Jeanette with the first variation in the minor mode, number 15, which ends, she says, "in a terminal descent to obscurity, broken only by a last, four-note, densely pitched, failed attempt to lift itself before the final fall" (332). The perfect symmetry, the fearful symmetry, of the music and the nucleic acid chain, found in the tenth variation and lost in the fifteenth, does *not* carry over into the fiction. Does not, that is, until those late disclosures, when the discovery of a long, fiercely introspective letter from Jeanette to Ressler proves to be the sharpest revelation of character in the book and the key to the entire narrative. The letter is a long goodbye. The missing symmetry arrives in the wrong form, a terminal descent into obscurity on the model of variation 15—the midpoint of Bach's journey.

Variation 10 thus comes to embody a perfect four in one that life will not allow. Bach's descent proves not to be terminal, but Ressler will never be the same. The difference between the life simulated by the music and the life lived in the world is the intervention of chance, sheer chance. The music allows for a modicum of chance in its keyboard alternatives but the long arc passes beyond it. The world does not afford the same privilege. It just so happens that Koss gave Ressler the record that changed his life and it just so happens that her marriage made their union impossible. In the novel's long arc, Ressler will respond by contriving to have chance revoked on behalf of Jan and Franklin; at least one pair will get formed. As it turns out, variation 30 will provide the means to do it. The ideal remains variation 10, but the two have to work together for life to prevail.

Ressler is drawn to variation 10 by the perfect symmetry of its form, which exemplifies both the rationality of the variation cycle as whole and its link to biogenesis. The form is all made of fours, as DNA is and as the romance should have been: four entries of the fugal subject answered by four more in phrase units based on multiples of four, and all brought to closure by a harmonic knot tied four-in-hand, which astonishes Jan. "During that forty seconds [of listening]," she says, "I first felt the resonant, connecting joints holding together this experiment in reversing the randomness of inert matter. . . . For forty seconds, I understood that all evolution was accomplished by juggling only four voices. In the fughetta: SATB. In us listeners, in the fughetta-writer himself: GATC" (209–210; example 10 shows the fughetta in full).

What else does this fictional forty seconds make audible? Another feature of the tenth variation (mentioned in passing by Powers) is the running counterfigure in the bass in the first eight measures of the variation's second half.

EXAMPLE 10. J.S. Bach, *Goldberg Variations,* no. 10 (Fughetta).

This independent figure ripples there under the first and second entries of the fughetta subject; it is the sole extraneous element in the tightly woven texture of the variation. The third fugal entry curtails the rippling figure, so that the musical texture returns abruptly to pure fugal counterpoint and stays with it to the end. The return is perhaps responsible for Jan's wonderment at the conclusion. The music curtails the figure as if to insist on essentials, to remain intent on the primal process of pairing strands. And one has to know the music to get the point: the simulation of vital process must be *heard*. It requires the sensory abundance the description necessarily lacks. Similarly, when Jan also marvels at the concluding fusion of counterpoint and harmony, those who can read the score might observe how the same third entry, with the subject in the bass, unobtrusively changes the submediant harmony to ii from its previous II (V/V), thus setting up the cadential ii-V-I progressions through which the final entry leads the variation to a close.

In the novel's terms, the rippling figure comes from outside the code. Why there? One reason might be that the figure fills an empty space and therefore fills a need. Everything in this piece depends on the elective affinities between its strands of sound. If the second half, like the first, were to begin with an unaccompanied entry, what Jan calls the randomness of inert matter might make itself felt. Absence as potential could become absence as negation; the "dead time" latent in spacing could intrude itself. The counterfigure is protective coloration. It clings to the contrapuntal threads and holds them together until they no longer need it. The voices, sufficiently juggled, go on to complete their evolution on their own. They mirror themselves backward, forming musical base pairs as the entries of the first half, bass/tenor, soprano/alto—BT SA—half replicate themselves as soprano/alto, bass/tenor—SA BT—in the second.

But the music also exceeds its code, as Ressler finds out that life does too. Each half of the variation is built of four four-measure phrases, each of them associated with the entry of a different fugal voice. In the second half, the transition between the second phrase and the third—the point at which the rippling figure stops—delivers a small jolt. The parallel point in the first half has a clear line of demarcation marked by a light but firm tonic cadence. The demarcation blurs in the second half; the third phrase begins on V/V with the help of an inner-voice note tied over from the previous measure. The music briefly parts the curtain to show the impulse driving its logic. Although this sort of change is not unusual in itself in Bach's thirty-two-measure form, it assumes real import here because of the clarity with which the fughetta combines its strands.

What does all the symmetry of variation 10, slightly disrupted to be fully affirmed, imply about the larger work it seems to mirror? What does the full sequence of variations want? Whatever the answer, it has to reckon with the contrary motion that Powers singles out: Bach's break with rational symmetry in favor of conviviality. The break comes in variation 30, the "Quodlibet," a form both convivial in itself and supposedly a favorite pastime of the Bach family after meals. The tunes we can still identify by their lyrics speak plainly to the point, combining the strands of hunger and love: *Kraut und Rüben haben mich vertrieben. / Hätt mein Mutter Fleisch gekocht, so wär ich langer blieben* (Cabbage and beets drove me away. If my mother had cooked meat I'd have stuck around) and *Ich bin so lang bei dir gewest. / Ruck her, ruck her, ruck her* (I've been apart from you so long. Come back, come back, come back).

Life, says the quodlibet, needs nourishment, which comes in many forms. One of them comes from the meeting of social and animal forms in the ritual that links earthly life with earthy life: the shared meal. One can emphasize either side of this pairing. David Yearsley has suggested that the quodlibet is literally concerned with taste, that is, with the culinary basis of the metaphor of "taste" in art. He refers this music to the barnyard.[22] Powers takes the social vivacity of the meal as an extension, but also a correction, of the genetic counterpoint that produces life by animating matter. The genetic code and music unite in the work of animation but the work is not complete until people sit together around a table and sing about it. Yearsley's quodlibet refers to a humble place in the plan of divine creation. Powers's quodlibet imparts higher-order vitality to a mundane human act.

THE QUODLIBET: REFRESHING THE BODY

The introduction of the quodlibet reintegrates the overarching system of rationality with the messiness of human relationships. For Bach, this reintegration marks an impasse in the system. As we know, the quodlibet appears where the expected canon at the tenth should have been, but the failure of the canon to appear is actually the solution to a problem. If Bach had written a tenth canon, his trinity of trinities would have been lost. If he had stopped after nine canons, the cosmological structuring around the number thirty-two would have been lost. The quodlibet thus marks the point at which human life defaults on the perfections of reason, the point where fallibility and mutual dependency emerge as equally necessary. Counterpoint becomes party noise becomes counterpoint. The quodlibet is a joke, to be sure, but not a frivolous one. The laugh, if there is one, is on us.

The novel helps make this dimension of the music audible, and it needs to. The narrative needs what the quodlibet has to offer. The turn from the exercise of rationality to the raw essentials of human relationship is one that the novel's characters repeatedly fail to make successfully. In the end, the quodlibet enters the narrative to mend the things that can still be mended. It acts as the connecting link between the two modes of life that the variations are asked to simulate: life in the sense of the genome and life in the sense of an injunction by Henry James that Jan alludes to later in the narrative: "Live all you can; it's a mistake not to" (625; James's narrator fails as matchmaker where Ressler succeeds). In turning to the quodlibet, Powers reconceives the variations as a kind of messenger RNA linking life as produced to life as lived.

This reconception goes further, and brings us back to Benjamin's notion of the real life of literary works, by treating life as an emanation of language. Powers's medium thus binds its strand to Bach's. From its title onward, *The Gold Bug Variations* incorporates a vast tissue of quotations, allusions, and verbal echoes, many of which come from Jan, who, like the author, is a virtuoso at what she calls "the impossibly complex goldberg invention of speech." That phrase itself is an example. Its "invention" refers to a category of rhetoric as well as to the musical form made famous by Bach, while its "goldberg" refers not only to Bach's variations but also to the bizarre contraptions known generically as "Rube Goldberg machines." Late in the narrative, at a pivotal moment, Jan suddenly realizes that this medium, her medium, is literally a lifeline: "I had thought that words . . . enforced a separation, banished me to the nowhere of descriptions. Crossing the Park, I realized that no living piece of tissue could keep its head up above the Second Law [of Thermodynamics] without the power of speech. In shape, function, unfolding: they were all shouting, speaking, feasting on words like lichen on rocks" (632).

The speaking melodies of the quodlibet do likewise; they nourish the weird aliveness of the piece. The quodlibet represents a desublimation of the tenth variation. The fughetta distills attraction and generation to their shared elemental form, an abstract *pas de quatre* for two couples, two pairs. But the flesh and blood realization of these imaginary relationships must wait until the break with code, the act of farewell delivered like Koss's letter. Love has to wait for the arrival of the quodlibet, when the system of rationality has run its course and when the structure offered to refresh the spirit—now as if having no choice—consummates and abolishes itself in the same gesture.

Powers's narrative echoes this outcome by turning from the formal dimension of the quodlibet to its affirmation of bodily bonds. Jan, usually insightful, goes a little too far in interpreting this variation. She sets the familial warmth aside and hears the outline of the Base "underneath the flurry of simultaneous quotes" as a symbolic self-reflection and critique, parried at last only by the return of the aria: "Bach's apology for not being a better cook. Molecular evolution excusing itself: had I been a little more skilled, I might have spared the world all this terminal variety. [But] no matter: the theme is back for good, in the left hand of the quodlibet, incarnate in the material of this last, apologetic child whose parent could in no way have foreseen it" (630). From this point on Jan's experience outstrips her understanding; the final knowledge she gains through the music is not conceptual. Instead, she lives the bodily release granted by this variation in an act of symbolic homecoming. For it is the sound of this music, engineered to come, of all things, from an ATM, that reunites Jan with Franklin after a long separation and cancels the bilingual pun on Franklin's last name: Todd as a variation of *Tod*, German for "death," in a book devoted to the code of life. "I knew the piece," Jan recalls, "before it even started. I knew the [four] melod[ies] at once ... a gathering of old friends, as easy to me, as familiar and close as my own name" (629).

These remarks found a real-world echo in 2020 when the pianist Lang Lang, who had just made two recordings of the *Goldberg Variations,* was asked by an interviewer about the return of the aria at the end:

> Without this variation [the quodlibet] I think the Aria would be so much harder to play, after those fireworks: After the Adagio, Variation 25, you have four variations that are fast and virtuosic. It's just impossible to get back to the Aria. But when you have this family reunion song in the 30th, you suddenly realize that you are getting older.[23]

Time starts pressing; it is time to come home.

Jan's welcome to the family reunion song, just in time, helps tie together the loose strands of the novel and the music. Bach's declared aim of refreshing the spirit by the exercise of rational art succeeds only when it incorporates a grain of the irrational that, following the imagery of the quoted songs, satisfies the appetite but has been away for too long. The quodlibet marks success with sabbatical. Its convivial counterpoint to reason models the inverse of carnival, a return, not a farewell, to flesh. For once the music just sends out a message, plain as day—and as Jan O'Deigh listens, its echo ends the book: love me, welcome me home, bring me back to earth, but please, O please, leave out the cabbage.

Epilogue

SOUND AND THE FORMS OF LIFE

THE INTERWEAVING OF MUSIC AND LIFE TRACED in this book is one chapter in a larger story of sound and life. As I sought to show in *The Hum of the World: A Philosophy of Listening*, the book preceding this one, sound has long been the medium in which life makes itself known and promises to continue. "Sound," as I wrote there, "is the measure of life."[1]

This does not mean, however, that sound is uniquely indicative of some preexisting phenomenon called "life." Once the entanglement of sound and life has been recognized, once it has become something to be thought through, what we mean by "life" changes in scope and substance. No longer confined to living things, life becomes available to experience and susceptible to history. Accordingly the aim of this book has been to show how we can understand music to simulate not the form but the *forms* of life. Underlying this aim is the premise that these forms typically become accessible to us through certain vicissitudes of sound. This auditory unveiling is by no means confined to the arts. The invention of the stethoscope revolutionized medicine by making the body cavity audible. The first thing we want to experience when a baby is born is the sound of its cry. In terrible circumstances, sound may be the last thread that links us to life.

In his Holocaust memoir, *Night* (1958), Elie Wiesel describes such a thread in musical form. After a death march in the dead of winter, through heavy snow, one young man, a violinist, manages to play a passage from "a Beethoven concerto" on the night before dying. He plays even though he fears that the guards will break his violin. Life, embodied by this venerated music, reproaches the death strewn all around it. The reproach extends to the Nazi murderers who falsely represent the tradition that lives on in the music.

There is a controversy about this account. Apart from questions of its adequacy—doesn't it just sentimentalize a cliché that clarifies nothing?—there are questions of its possibility. In the brutal circumstances, from exhaustion and emaciation to the weather, neither the man nor the violin would have been able to play anything from *the* Beethoven Violin Concerto. So is Wiesel just making it up? Is he fabricating, or relying on a false memory, or remembering something with unconscious embellishments, or making up an allegory or morality play that he thinks *should* have happened and would have been meaningful if it had?

Whatever the answer, the symbolic value of the episode is not in doubt. Wiesel's reliance on Beethoven is not surprising, even banal; poor Beethoven has been burdened for so long by the mantle of exemplary heroic musical genius that it would be funny if it were not so wrongheaded. More important is Wiesel's reliance on sound, for which the music becomes only the medium. Apart from darkness and silence, there is nothing but this sound, which is first "as if" alive and then simply a form of life: "All I could hear was the violin, and it was as if Juliek's soul had become his bow. He was playing his life. His whole being was gliding over the strings." In the morning, the instrument as well as the player was dead: "trampled, an eerily poignant little corpse."[2]

Wiesel's text has the nexus of music and life, music and lost life, in common with Arnold Schoenberg's cantata *A Survivor from Warsaw* (1947). The latter's narrative, entirely spoken rather than sung, deals with a double body count: of those dragged out of the sewers of the Warsaw Ghetto and killed on the spot, and those left alive to be carried off to the gas chambers. Speech has been cut off from life; its sound has become fatal. Sound can snip that vital thread as well as spin it. As in Wiesel's narrative, the countervailing force comes from an act of music-making. At the last minute, the doomed Jews spontaneously begin singing the *Shema Yisrael,* the prayer at the very core of Jewish identity. Precarious life once again calls on music to release its sound, to let it resound. Unlike the sound of the violin in Wiesel, the sound of this singing is thunderous. A male chorus loudly intones the prayer in unison; words and melody lose themselves amid the harsh volume and timbre for several uninterrupted minutes until the prayer, and the piece, come to an abrupt end.

None of the music studied in the preceding chapters addresses circumstances so dire, whatever violence may be embodied in *The Battle* and "La Valse." But these limit cases suggest the remarkable durability of the ties linking music, sound, and the forms of life. How do these relationships play out in what we like to think of as more normal circumstances?

Music, and not just the classical music studied here, is an especially concentrated and potent form of the life in sound and the sound of life. Perhaps for that reason, its vivacity is both exceptional and commonplace. We live today in a music-saturated world, so much so that we barely notice most of its soundtrack; we take music for granted or relegate it to the background. Yet we continue to demand that certain musical events move and inspire us beyond the ordinary: to come alive for us in a more than metaphorical sense.

The music we resort to for this transport is the music we value for its aesthetic accomplishment. It is the music we want to hear again and again. But the power of this music does not rest with its artistic design alone. The power also comes from the music's ability *through* its design to enhance our susceptibility to the more primary power of sound. To go back to the starting point of chapter 1: the big loud chord in the slow movement of Haydn's "Surprise" Symphony is more, not less, surprising when one knows it is coming. The anticipation is pure pleasure, in part because we know that our senses are about to be aroused, that the force of the sudden isolated *fortissimo* is about to reach our nerves and our bellies as much as our ears. The touch of violence in the chord will do no harm. The sound is robust. It may remind us that the receptivity of life to sound is also its vulnerability, but for now there is—isn't there?—only exuberance. If you listen in that frame of mind, the effect always exceeds the expectation on which it nonetheless depends. When you hear me, says the chord, as if sotto voce, in advance, you will know what it is you have been hearing to this point in the symphony and what you will hear afterward.

When the symphony was written, and for a long time thereafter, this experience would necessarily have been "live." The fact that the bodies of the musicians and the listeners share the same resonant space magnifies the feeling of vitality. So what happens with recordings, now and long since the most likely venue for hearing the music? Can the life in music be recorded? Or is music truly alive only when its performance is?

The question thus put is inevitable but badly framed. To ask it usefully we need to replace the *is?* with a *when is?* For the characters in *The Gold Bug Variations,* the life in music is absolutely present on a recording, and on one recording in particular, the LP from 1955 devoted to Glenn Gould playing Bach's *Goldberg Variations* on the piano. The reasons why, however, are not acoustic (the record even wears out). The reasons are narrative, and not only because they stem from the novel's plot. They stem even more from the stories the characters are trying to tell to and about each other. Life starts or stops with the story as well as with the music. Life wants to sound, but it has to have a path to sounding. In Aldous Huxley's novel *Point Counterpoint* (1928), a recording of the slow movement of a Beethoven String Quartet not only fails to transmit life but portends death because it cannot sustain the story that a desperate character wants to tell. The recording reproduces the notes, every single one, but it also emits "a faint scratching and roaring that mimick the noise of Beethoven's . . . deafness."[3] The recording petrifies the sound it seeks to vivify.

Whether live or recorded, then, music makes life audible to us when we can follow its path to sounding. That has been what this book is about. Yet the "liveness" of live music must still make a difference, at least potentially. The reason why Vaucanson's flute player became so celebrated and debated is that it gave live performances. If an android could play the flute—really play it, not just imitate playing—then was the flute player merely a machine, or any more a machine than a person was? Was life a product of mechanism or an escape from it? This book has sought to show that once this question became pressing, music was used to frame it and music learned how to ask it. As Powers's novel suggests, we no more know the answer today than we did in 1737. We just know better what we don't know. But we do know the music.

What live performance can add to the life of music, especially to the classical music that as a matter of genre constantly wants to be reanimated in a relatively stable form, is uncertainty.

Heard live, classical music is always in rehearsal in both senses of the word: something gone over reclaimed, recaptured, and something in preparation. It feels alive, not only because its composition embodies the workings of life, and not only because it fits the story that we need or want to tell, but also because its live re-creation in real time occurs in the face of contingency, fallibility, vulnerability, and potentiality. The object of simulation goes beyond the process of life to the practice of living.

Of course all performance shares in this uncertainty. Fallibility, the chance that things may go wrong or fall flat, is the very condition of possibility for performance itself. Anyone who hums a tune or sings a song, any tune, any song, engages with that possibility. Hence the popularity of song contests from *Tannhäuser* and *Die Meistersinger* to *American Idol* and *Eurovision*. But when we *attend* to the way a piece of music comes to life moment by moment in the act of its performance, an event that recording media can document but never capture, we poise ourselves on a moving edge of sound. The music forges ahead not by accepting but by embracing the vulnerability of its condition and the openness of its horizon. It is hard to imagine anything more lifelike than that.

NOTES

INTRODUCTION: MUSIC AND THE LIFE OF STATUES

1. Act 5, scene 3. *The Pelican Shakespeare,* ed. Alfred Harbage (Baltimore: Penguin, 1969), 1367.
2. Condillac, *Logique,* in *Oeuvres philosophiques,* ed. Georges Le Roy (Pans: Presses Universitaires de France. 1947), 11; qtd. in Daniel Leonard, "Condillac's Animated Statue and the Art of Philosophizing: Aesthetic Experience in the *Traite des sensations,*" *Dalhousie Review* 82 (2002): 493–513, at 496.
3. "Mag das Gehirn einmal als ein zusammengesetztes Kunstwerk aus vielen tönenden Körpern gedacht werden, die in einer zweckmässigen Beziehung (rapport) stehen. Wird einer derselben von aussen, durch das Mittel der Sinne, angestossen, so erregt sein Ton den Ton eines anderen, dieser wieder einen anderen; und so wandelt die ursprüngliche Erregung in mäandrischen Zügen und nach bestimmten Kraft verhältnissen durch die weiten Hallen dieses Tempels fort, bis ein neuer Stoss den vorigen Zug aufhebt oder mit dem selben zusammenfliesst und dem vorigen eine andere Richtung mittheilt. Diese Beziehungen der Theilenden Seelenorgans unter einander sind auf ein ebenso bestimmte Vertheilung der Kräfte im Gehirn und dem gesammten Nervensystem gegründet." Reil, *Rhapsodien über die Anwendung der psychischen Kurmethode auf Geisteszerrüttungen* (Halle: Curtschen Buchhandlung, 1803), 46 (via Google Books), my translation.
4. On the connection between the Prometheus narrative and the symphony, see Kramer, "*Eroica* Traces: Beethoven and Revolutionary Narrative," in *Musik / Revolution,* ed. Hanns-Werner Heister (Hamburg: von Bockel Verlag, 1997), 2:35–48; and Ellen Lockhart, *Animation, Plasticity, and Music in Italy, 1770–1830* (Berkeley and London: University of California Press, 2017), 1–4. Lockhart further links Vigano's ballet to one by Gasparo Angiolini explicitly subtitled "La statua di Coindilliac *[sic]*" (1782) while tracing a widespread preoccupation with Condillac-style living statues in Italian theaters in the years covered by her book.

5. Annette Richards, "Automatic Genius: Mozart and the Mechanical Sublime," *Music & Letters* 80 (1999): 366–389. See also David Yearsley, *Bach and the Meanings of Counterpoint* (Cambridge: Cambridge University Press, 2002), 174–181.

6. Jacques Rancière, *The Politics of Aesthetics: The Distribution of the Sensible*, trans. Gabriel Rockhill (London: Continuum, 2004), 4–5, 91, and throughout. See also Giorgio Agamben, *The Man without Content*, trans. Georgia Albert (Stanford: Stanford University Press, 1999).

7. Stevens, "Peter Quince at the Clavier," in *Collected Poems of Wallace Stevens* (New York: Knopf, 1954), 89–90.

8. Hughes, "The Weary Blues," in *The Collected Poems of Langston Hughes* (New York: Knopf Doubleday), 50.

9. Graham, "Mind," from *Dream of the Unified Field: Selected Poems, 1974–1994* (New York: Harper Collins, 2002), 14.

10. Kathleen Higgins, *Music between Us: Is Music a Universal Language?* (Chicago: University of Chicago Press, 2012), 18; quoted in Holly Watkins, *Musical Vitalities: Ventures in a Biotic Aesthetics of Music* (Chicago: University of Chicago Press, 2018), 1.

11. David Chalmers, "Facing Up to the Problem of Consciousness," *Journal of Consciousness Studies* 2 (1995): 200–219. On the hard problem and classical music, see Kramer "The Hard Problem: Classical Music and the History of Consciousness," in *Classical Music in a Changing World: Crisis and Vital Signs*, ed. Lawrence Kramer and Alberto Nones (Wilmington: Vernon Press, 2021), 63–77.

12. Gert-Jan Lokhorst, "Descartes and the Pineal Gland," *Stanford Encyclopedia of Philosophy* (Fall 2020 Edition), ed. Edward N. Zalta, https://plato.stanford.edu/entries/pineal-gland/#PassSoul.

13. My "used to be" acknowledges not only the questions raised by the development of artificial intelligence but also the recent philosophical trend that claims that something like consciousness is an inherent property of matter. See Steven Shaviro, "Consquences of Panpsychism" (2010), https://pdfs.semanticscholar.org/8cea/280650f6d0de2f1a1d754298be7a0275c5ed.pdf.

14. Richmond Lattimore, *The Iliad of Homer* (Chicago: University of Chicago Press, 1951), 18.417–420, p. 386. Quoted in connection with the history of animation in Kramer, *The Hum of the World: A Philosophy of Listening* (Berkeley and London: University of California Press, 20019), 75.

15. Ovid, *Metamorphoses*, book 10, ll. 10.250–251, 10.291–294, my translation. Latin text from https://en.wikisource.org/wiki/Translation:Metamorphoses/Pygmalion_and_Galatea. Most translations of ll. 250–251 ascribe a look of modesty to the statue, but Ovid's term, *reverentia*, primarily means "awe" or "diffidence"; the suggestion is that the statue looks as if it were aware that it could not assume life but had to be given it by divine agency, in this case courtesy of Venus.

16. A further resonance comes from the fact that the other tales sung by Orpheus involve transgressive desire in both gods and mortals; only the desire of Pygmalion for his statue ends well.

17. Lockhart, *Animation*, 12. Rousseau was in part writing in reaction against Jean-Phillippe Rameau's one-act opera-ballet *Pygmalion* (1748). For more detail on

Rousseau's *Pygmalion* and its relationship to the period's iconography of the myth, see Victor I. Stoichita, *The Pygmalion Effect: From Ovid to Hitchcock* (Chicago: University of Chicago Press, 2008), 111–128; on the work's relationship to automata, see Wendy C. Nielson, "Rousseau's *Pygmalion* and Automata in the Romantic Period," in *Romanticism, Rousseau, Switzerland: New Prospects,* ed. Angela Esterhammer, Diane Piccitto, and Patrick Vincent (London: Palgrave Macmillan, 2015), 68–83.

18. Kazuo Ishiguro, *Never Let Me Go* (London: Faber and Faber, 2005).

19. Ludwig Wittgenstein, *Philosophical Investigations,* 2nd ed., trans. G.E.M. Anscombe (New York: Macmillan, 1958), 89–105.

20. See in particular the trilogy on musical understanding: *Interpreting Music* (Berkeley and London: University of California Press, 2010); *Expression and Truth: On the Music of Knowledge* (Berkeley and London: University of California Press, 2012; and *The Thought of Music* (Berkeley and London: University of California Press, 2016).

21. Wye Jamison Allanbrook, *The Secular Commedia: Comic Mimesis in Late Eighteenth-Century Music* (Berkeley and London: University of California Press, 2014), 10.

22. Watkins, *Musical Vitalities,* 3. *The Android's Flute* is less concerned with nature than *Musical Vitalities* is, but the two books are clearly on the same wavelength, not least in the conviction, as Watkins puts it, that "the axis along which most studies travel, with social meaning at one end and the autonomous realm of 'music itself' at the other, excludes [a host of] wider resonances from consideration" (43). On undoing that rigid axis, see Kramer, *Musical Meaning: Toward a Critical History* (Berkeley and London: University of California Press, 2002), 1–9. For more on the triangulation of nature, technology, and music, see Richard Leppert, *Aesthetic Technologies of Modernity, Subjectivity, and Nature: Opera, Orchestra, Phonograph, Film* (Berkeley and London: University of California Press, 2015).

23. On affordances in music, see Eric Clarke, *Ways of Listening: An Ecological Approach to the Perception of Musical Meaning* (Oxford: Oxford University Press, 2005), 36–38; Nicholas Cook, *Analysing Musical Multimedia* (Oxford: Oxford University Press, 1998), 93–97; and Kramer, *The Thought of Music,* 163–168. The concept originated with James J. Gibson; see Gibson, "The Theory of Affordances," in *Perceiving, Acting, and Knowing: Toward an Ecological Psychology,* ed. Robert Shaw and John Bransford (Hillsdale, NJ: Lawrence Erlbaum, 1977), 67–82.

24. Mary Shelley, *Frankenstein: The 1818 Text* (New York: Penguin, 2018), 42.

CHAPTER ONE: FROM CLOCKWORK TO PULSATION I

1. Daniel Chua, *Absolute Music and the Construction of Meaning* (Cambridge: Cambridge University Press, 1999), 92–93; see also the full chapters on biology and the body, 92–104. For more on this topic, see Elisabeth Leguin, *Bocherrini's Body: An Essay in Carnal Musicology* (Berkeley: University of California Press, 2005), esp. 182–189; and Thomas Christensen, "Bemetzrieder's Dream: Diderot and the

Pathology of Tonal Sensibility in the Lecons de clavecin," in *Music, Sensation, and Sensuality,* ed. Linda Austern (New York: Garland, 2002), 39–56.

2. Emily Dolan, *The Orchestral Revolution: Haydn and the Technologies of Timbre* (Cambridge: Cambridge University Press, 2013), 129, where the remark by Haydn is quoted too. "Enthusiasm" in the eighteenth century, in both Germany and England, carried a much stronger sense that it does today. Dolan also notes (130) the intriguing fact that Haydn's initial draft of the movement lacked the "surprise" chord. Given his identification of the chord with its drum stroke that grounds it, his decision to add it gives Chua's reference to the human hand a literal meaning.

3. See Anne C. Vila, *Enlightenment and Pathology: Sensibility in the Literature and Medicine of Eighteenth-Century France* (Baltimore: Johns Hopkins University Press, 1998), 3–42; and Charles T. Wolfe, "Sensibility as Vital Force or a Property of Matter in Mid-Eighteenth-Century Debates," in *The Discourse of Sensibility: The Knowing Body in the Enlightenment,* ed. Henry Martin Lloyd (New York: Springer, 2013), 147–170. The relationship of sensibility and excitation produced considerable debate; my concern is not with specific theories on the subject but with the persistence of the categories the required theorizing.

4. G. W. F. Hegel, *Hegel's Aesthetics: Lectures on Fine Art,* trans. T. M. Knox, 2 vols. (Cambridge: Cambridge University Press, 1998), 2:890.

5. My translation of "Die Töne klingen nur in der tiefsten Seele nach, die in ihrer ideellen subjektivität ergriffen und in Bewegung gebracht wird"; Hegel, *Vorlesungen über die Ästhetik,* www.lernhelfer.de/sites/default/files/lexicon/pdf/BWS-DEU2-0170-04.pdf, 1008.

6. Hegel, 1081. My translation of "nicht genötigt, sich hierhin oder dorthin zu bewegen, sondern in ungefesselter Freiheit auf sich selbst beruhend." The subsequent quotation is from the same page.

7. Hegel, 1085: "Die subjektive Willkür mit ihren Einfällen, Kapricen, Unterbrechungen, geistreichen Neckereien, täuschenden Spannungen, überraschenden Wendungen, Sprüngen und Blitzen, Wunderlichkeiten und ungehörten Effekten."

8. David Hume, *A Treatise of Human Nature,* vol. 1, *Texts,* ed. David Fate Norton and Mary J. Norton (Oxford: Clarendon, 2007), 257–290. Most studies deal with drive in accounts of the prehistory of psychoanalysis and the Freudian unconscious. See Jon Mills, *The Unconscious Abyss: Hegel's Anticipation of Psychoanalysis* (Albany, NY: SUNY Press, 2012), 71–72, 82–84, 141–143; Matt Ffytche, *The Foundation of the Unconscious: Schelling, Freud and the Birth of the Modern Psyche* (Cambridge: Cambridge University Press, 2011), 92–93; John H. Zammito, *Kant, Herder, and the Birth of Anthropology* (Chicago: University of Chicago Press, 2002), 95–97, 170–172; and Slavoj Žižek and F. W. J. von Schelling, *The Abyss of Freedom/Ages of the World,* trans. Judith Norman (Ann Arbor: University of Michigan Press, 1997). Günter Gödde traces a "drive-related irrational line" of thought extending from Schelling through Edward van Hartmann and Nietzsche; see Gödde, "Freud and Nineteenth-Century Philosophical Sources on the Unconscious," in *Thinking the Unconscious: Nineteenth-Century German Thought,* ed. Angus Nicholls and Martin Liebscher (Cambridge: Cambridge University Press, 2010), 261–286.

9. Quoted in Zammito, *Kant, Herder, and the Birth of Anthropology*, 317.

10. Herder, *Herders Sämmtliche Werke*, bd. 4, *Kritische Wälder, 4, Wäldchen, 1769*, ed. Bernhard Ludwig Suphan (Berlin: Weidmann, 1878), 161 (via google books), my translation. The statement was prescient, but it came in a text that was not published during Herder's lifetime. In the original (all emphases Herder's):

> Es erschallt *Musik*.
> Hier öffnet sich ein neuer Sinn, eine neue Pforte der Seele[,] und empfindet *Ton*. *Töne, Töne*, die in jedem einfachen Momente das Ohr mit Wollust in sich zieht; *Töne*, die in jedem einfachen Momente auf tausendneue Arten die Seele berühren, und tausend neue, verschiedene, aber innige, unmittelbare Empfindungen geben: *Töne*, die das unmittelbarste Instrument auf die Seele sind. Wogegen also der Ausdruck der anschaulichen Kunst nichts als Oberfläche war, wird hier innigesWesen, das ist die Energische Kraft, das Pathos, wie soll ichs nennen? das Tiefeindringende auf die Seele: die Welt eines neuen Gefühls. Alle unsre Empfindungen werden hier ein Saitenspiel, dessen sich das, was Ton heißt, in aller Stärke einzelner Momente, und schöner Abwechselungen und wiederkommender Empfindsamkeiten bemächtigt.

As Mark Evan Bonds has noted, Herder later extended the idea of listening "with the whole body" to the perception of cosmic harmony. See Bonds, *Absolute Music: The History of an Idea* (New York: Oxford University Press, 2014), 122.

11. Emerson, *The Journals and Miscellaneous Notebooks of Ralph Waldo Emerson, 1838–1842* (Cambridge, MA: Harvard University Press, 1969), 158.

12. Goethe, "Seelige Sehnsucht," https://kalliope.org/en/text/goethe2000082806.

13. Walter Pater, *The Renaissance: Studies in Art and Poetry* (New York: Dover, 2005), 154; condition of music, 90.

14. David Hume, *A Treatise of Human Nature*, sec. 9, "Of the Direct Passions," quotation accessed via Project Gutenberg, www.gutenberg.org/cache/epub/4705/pg4705.txt.

15. Quoted in Charles T. Wolfe, "On the Role of Newtonian Analogies in Eighteenth-Century Life Science: Vitalism and Provisionally Inexplicable Explicative Devices," in *Newton and Empiricism*, ed. Zvi Biener and Eric Schliesser (New York: Oxford University Press, 2014), 223–261.

16. Denis Diderot, *D'Alembert's Dream*, trans. Ian Johnston, http://records.viu.ca/~johnstoi/diderot/conversation.htm.

17. Diderot, *Letter on the Deaf and Dumb*, in *Diderot's Early Philosophical Works*, trans. Margaret Jourdain (Chicago: Open Court, 1916), 185–186 (via Google Books).

18. This passage occurs in a footnote to the statement "La sécrétion se réduit donc à une espèce de sensation, si on peut s'exprimer ainsi" (Secretion is thus reduced to a species of sensation, if one can put it that way). The text reads: "C'est encore ici une de ces métaphores qu'on doit nous permettre; ceux qui examinent ces questions de près, savent combien il est difficile de s'expliquer lorsqu'il s'agit de parler de la force

qui dirige avec tant de justesse mille mouvemens singuliers du corps de l'homme et de ses parties; on ne sait pas même de quels termes on doit se servir pour exprimer, par exemple, certains mouvemens des végétaux et même certaines propriétés des minéraux.... [Georg Stahl] prétendoit que l'ame dirigeoit tout dans le corps animal; quoiqu'il en soit, on peut dire que toutes les parties qui vivent sont dirigées par une force conservatrice qui veille sans cesse; seroit-elle à certains égards de l'essence d'une portion de la matière, ou un attribut nécessaire de ses combinaisons? Encore un coup, nous ne prétendons donner ici qu'une manière de concevoir les choses, des expressions métaphoriques, des comparaisons." Translation repunctuated for clarity. Text accessed at Internet Archive, *Recherches anatomiques sur la position des glands et sur leur action,* http://archive.org/details/recherchesanatomoobord.

19. Sigmund Freud, *New Introductory Lectures on Psychoanalysis,* trans. James Strachey (New York: Norton, 1965), 84; Freud, *Beyond the Pleasure Principle,* trans. James Strachey (New York: Norton, 1961), 72.

20. From the poem "Discourse on Man in Verse" (1738), quoted in Paul Metzner, *Crescendo of the Virtuoso: Spectacle, Skill, and Self-Promotion in Paris during the Age of Revolution* (Berkeley and London: University of California Press, 1998), 165; my translation of "Vaucanson, rival de Prométhée, / Semblait... Prendre le feu des cieux pour animer les corps." The subtitle of *Frankenstein* is *The Modern Prometheus.*

21. For detailed accounts of all of these androids, see Jessica Riskin, "Eighteenth-Century Wetware," *Representations* 83 (2003): 97–125. On the dulcimer and organ players, see Adelheid Voskuhl, *Androids in the Enlightenment: Mechanics, Artisans, and the Cultures of the Self* (Chicago: University of Chicago Press, 2015). On the role of androids in eighteenth-century thought, see Minsoo Kang, *Sublime Dreams of Living Machines: The Automaton in the European Imagination* (Cambridge, MA: Harvard University Press, 2011).

22. See Wolfe, "Sensibility as Vital Force," 233–230.

23. Herder, *Kalligone,* in *Music and Aesthetics in the Eighteenth and Early Nineteenth Centuries,* ed. Peter le Huray and James Day (Cambridge: Cambridge University Press, 1988), 188–189.

24. Here and elsewhere I will use the traditional categories of exposition, development, and recapitulation for clarity of exposition in dealing with movements in "sonata form," though I am increasingly skeptical that the categories, as well as the form they describe, are the best way to say what is at stake in such music. There is, however, no widely accepted alternative outside the technical vocabulary of music theory.

25. See Kramer, *Interpreting Music* (Berkeley and London: University of California Press: 2010), 52–66.

26. Stevens, "The Man Whose Pharynx Was Bad," in *Collected Poems* (New York: Knopf, 1954), 96.

27. Michel Foucault, *The History of Sexuality,* vol. 1, *An Introduction,* trans. Michael Hurley (New York: Random House, 1978), 133–159.

28. Deleuze, *The Logic of Sense,* trans. Mark Lester and Charles Stivale (New York: Columbia University Press, 1990), 160.

CHAPTER TWO: FROM CLOCKWORK TO PULSATION II

1. See Michel Foucault, *The Birth of the Clinic*, trans. Alan Sheridan (New York: Routledge 2012), 200–204; Lauri Siisiäinen, *Foucault and the Politics of Hearing* (New York: Routledge, 2013), 25–31; and Kramer, *The Hum of the World: A Philosophy of Listening* (Berkeley and London: University of California Press, 2019), 198–202.

2. See Elisabeth Le Guin, *Boccherini's Body: An Essay in Carnal Musicology* (Berkeley and London: University of California Press, 2006); J. Q. Davies, *Romantic Anatomies of Performance* (Berkeley and London: University of California Press, 2014); and Youn Kim and Sander Gilman, eds., *The Oxford Handbook of Music and the Body* (Oxford and New York: Oxford University Press, 2019).

3. Writers about musical embodiment generally observe that modern musicology and music theory continued a process of disembodiment grounded in nineteenth-century aesthetics, on the assumption that the relationship between the composer and the listener or performer is what Suzanne Cusick has called "a mind-mind game." The assumption forgets that "these practices of the mind are non-practices without the bodily practices they call for." See Suzanne Cusick, "Feminist Theory, Music Theory, and the Mind/Body Problem," *Perspectives of New Music* 32 (1994): 8–27, at 16. For a recent overview, see Holly Watkins and Melina Esse, "Down with Disembodiment; or, Musicology and the Material Turn," *Women and Music* 19 (2010): 160–168.

4. Oliver Sacks, *A Leg to Stand On* (1984; New York: Simon and Shuster, 1998), 94. Kramer, *Interpreting Music* (Berkeley and London: University of California Press, 2010), 42–45. It is worth noting that Sacks describes his fall (the result of a flight from an alpine bull, and not, as my earlier discussion mistakenly says, from a ski accident) as a cacophony: "One moment I was running like a madman, conscious of heavy panting and heavy thudding footsteps, unsure whether they came from the bull or me, and the next I was lying at the bottom of a . . . cliff" (4).

5. Sacks, *A Leg*, 117.

6. Gertrude Koch, "Carnivore or Chameleon: The Fate of Cinema Studies," *Critical Inquiry* 34 (2009): 228.

7. Mikhail Bhaktin, *Rabelais and his World*, trans. Helene Iswolsky (Indianapolis: Indiana University Press, 1984), 315–320.

8. Daniel Chua, *Absolute Music and the Construction of Meaning* (Cambridge: Cambridge University Press, 1999), 92.

9. Chua, 92.

10. For Mozart and Haydn the simplicity would have suggested sexual innocence, not the nursery. The tune was published by itself in 1761 and again in 1764 with words added from "La Confidence naïve," a poem about the seduction of a shepherd girl.

11. William Carlos Williams, *The Collected Poems of Williams Carlos Williams*, vol. 2, *1939–1962*, ed. Christopher MacGowan (New York: New Directions, 1991), 58.

12. Quoted in Jessica Riskin, "The Defecating Duck, or the Ambiguous Origins of Mechanical Life," *Critical Inquiry* 29 (2003): 599–633, at 601.

13. Lydia Liu, "iSpace: Written English after Joyce, Shannon, and Derrida," *Critical Inquiry* 32 (2006): 515–560.

14. Jacques Derrida, *Of Grammatology*, trans. Gayatri Chakravorty Spivack (Baltimore: Johns Hopkins University Press, 1974), 3–27.

15. Derrida, 68–69; italics in original.

16. Quoted in Anne C. Vila, *Enlightenment and Pathology: Sensibility in the Literature and Medicine of Eighteenth-Century France* (Baltimore: Johns Hopkins University Press, 1998), 59.

17. Vila, 59.

18. Vila, 59.

19. Denis Diderot, *D'Alembert's Dream*, trans. Ian Johnston, http://records.viu.ca/~johnstoi/diderot/conversation.htm.

20. Diderot, *D'Alembert's Dream*.

21. The locus classicus is Rey M. Longyear, "Romantic Irony in Beethoven," *Musical Quarterly* 61 (1970): 647–664.

22. Michel Foucault, *The Order of Things: An Archeology of the Human* Sciences (1966; New York: Routledge, 2002), 303–343.

CHAPTER THREE: FROM CLOCKWORK TO PULSATION III

1. Quoted in Minsoo Kang, *Sublime Dreams of Living Machines: The Automaton in the European Imagination* (Cambridge, MA: Harvard University Press, 2011), 110. See Julien Offray De la Mettrie, *Man a Machine*, trans. Gertrude Bussey et al. (Chicago: Open Court, 1912), 141–142; via Google Books. Kang (146) observes that Jean-Jacques Rousseau (who met Vaucanson at a party) was also familiar with the comparison to Prometheus.

2. Michel Foucault, *The Birth of the Clinic: An Archaeology of Medical Perception*, trans. Alan Bass (London and New York: Routledge, 2012).

3. Hagedorn, "Der Mai" (www.lieder.net/lieder/get_text.html?TextId = 25905); Klopstock, "Die Lerche und die Nachtigall (www.zeno.org/Literatur/M/Klopstock,+Friedrich+Gottlieb); Goethe "Mailied" (www.oxfordlieder.co.uk/song/1993).

4. Michel Foucault, *The Order of Things: An Archaeology of the Human Sciences* (New York: Pantheon, 1970), xv–xxiv. Foucault subsequently replaced "archeology" with "genealogy"; the differences between the two have been the subject of considerable debate. For an overview, see David Garland, "What Is a History of the Present?: On Foucault's Genealogies and Their Critical Preconditions," *Punishment and Society* 16 (2014): 365–384.

5. Denis Diderot, *D'Alembert's Dream*, trans. Ian Johnston, http://records.viu.ca/~johnstoi/diderot/conversation.htm.

6. Daniel Heartz, *Mozart, Haydn, and Early Beethoven: 1781–1802* (New York: Norton, 1999), 466. Heartz is less reticent than Scott Burnham, who refers only to the bassoon's "vulgar klaxon" and seeks to recuperate it formally by suggesting that it is ironically "the very thing that puts this movement back on track and allows it to conclude." See Burnham, "Haydn and Humor," in *The Cambridge Companion to Haydn,* ed. Caryl Clark (Cambridge: Cambridge University Press, 2005), 67–68.

7. In Lacanian terms, the bassoon sound is a stain of the Real on the symbolic order. On this phenomenon, see Slavoj Žižek, "Grimaces of the Real; or, When the Phallus Appears," *October* 58 (1991): 44–68; and Kramer, *Expression and Truth: On the Music of Knowledge* (Berkeley and Los Angeles: University of California Press, 2012), 37–42.

8. Mikhail Bakhtin, *Rabelais and his World,* trans. Helene Iswolsky (Indianapolis: Indiana University Press, 1984), 303–436.

9. New York Philharmonic Leon Livy Digital Archive, https://archives.nyphil.org/.

10. Lessing, *Laocoon: An Essay upon the Limits of Poetry and Painting,* trans. Ellen Frothingham (New York: Dover, 2005), 167.

11. Kant, *Critique of Judgment,* book 2, paragraph 48, my translation from *Kritik Der Urtheilskraft,* ed. Benno Erdmann (Leipzig: Verlag Leopold Voss, 1880), 154 (via Google Books). *Ekel,* the word used by both Lessing and Kant, also means "nausea." For more on the latter in Kant's aesthetics, see Jacques Derrida, "Economimesis," *Diacritics* 11 (1981): 2–25, at 21–25. For later developments of the aesthetic value of disgust, see Jenefer Robinson, "Aesthetic Disgust?," in *Royal Institute of Philosophy Supplement* 75 (2014): 51–84.

12. For more on artificial speech in the period, see Jessica Riskin, "Eighteenth-Century Wetware," *Representations* 83 (2003): 97–125, 105–108, and Kramer, *The Hum of the World: A Philosophy of Listening* (Berkeley and London: University of California Press 2019), 21–22.

13. Michael Thompson, *Life and Action* (Cambridge, MA: Harvard University Press, 2012), 1–14.

14. The novel was published in English as *Memoirs of a Polar Bear,* trans. Susan Bernofsky (New York: New Directions, 2016); the quotation is from p. 208. For further discussion, see Rebecca L. Wallkowitz, "On Not Knowing: Lahiri, Takada, Ishiguro," *New Literary History* 51 (2020): 323–346, at 335–341.

15. Foucault, *The Order of Things,* 127–128.

16. John Locke, *An Essay Concerning Human Understanding,* chapter 27, https://earlymoderntexts.com/assets/pdfs/locke1690book2_4.pdf, p. 114.

17. Locke, 114.

18. From Herder's *Kalligone* (1800), excerpted in *Music and Aesthetics in the Eighteenth and Early Nineteenth Centuries,* ed. Peter le Huray and James Day (Cambridge: Cambridge University Press, 1988), 188–189.

19. Foucault, *The Order of Things,* 232.

20. Robert-Houdin, *Life of Robert-Houdin, King of the Conjurers, Written by Himself,* trans. Robert Shelton Mackenzie (Philadelphia: Porter and Coates, 1859), 159–160 (via Google Books).

21. Emily Dolan, *The Orchestral Revolution: Haydn and the Technologies of Timbre* (Cambridge: Cambridge University Press, 2013), 10, 211–257. For a comprehensive account, see Mark Evan Bonds, *Absolute Music: The History of an Idea* (Oxford and New York: Oxford University Press, 2014), esp. 39–126.

22. See Hamish J. Robb, "Imagined, Supplemental Sound in Nineteenth-Century Piano Music: Towards a Fuller Understanding of Musical Embodiment," *Music Theory Online* 21 (2015), https://mtosmt.org/issues/mto.15.21.3/mto.15.21.3.robb.html.

23. Robb, "Imagined, Supplemental Sound."

24. Or, from the contrary perspective, reconciling bodily mechanism with aesthetic vitality. As Alexandra Hui points out, some advocates of virtuosity appealed for validation to the experimental findings of (primarily German) psychophysics—a science steeped in the musical culture of the period. Hui, *The Psychophysical Ear: Musical Experiments, Experimental Sounds, 1840–1910* (Cambridge, MA: MIT Press, 2013), xiv, 66–80. On the aesthetics of virtuosity, with special reference to Liszt and the piano, see Dana Gooley, *The Virtuoso Liszt* (Cambridge: Cambridge University Press, 2004); Richard Leppert, "Cultural Contradiction, Idolatry, and the Piano Virtuoso: Franz Liszt," in *Piano Roles: A New History of the Piano,"* ed. James Parakilas (New Haven: Yale University Press, 2001), 200–223; and Lawrence Kramer, "Franz Liszt and the Virtuoso Public Sphere," in *Musical Meaning: Toward a Critical History* (Berkeley and London: University of California Press, 2001), 68–99.

CHAPTER FOUR: 1812 OVERTURES

1. Nicholas Cook, "The Other Beethoven: Heroism, The Canon, and the Works of 1813–14," *Nineteenth Century Music* 27 (2003): 3–24. See also Nicolas Mathew, *Political Beethoven* (Cambridge: Cambridge University Press, 2013), 22–30. The aesthetic and political perspectives developed by Cook and Mathew assume further significance in relation to the history of simulation and projection, the technologies of perception that formed the horizon of the real from the mid-eighteenth century through the late twentieth.

2. See Richard Will, *The Characteristic Symphony in the Age of Haydn and Beethoven* (Cambridge: Cambridge University Press, 2002), 188–240.

3. Giorgio Agamben, *Homo Sacer: Sovereign Power and Bare Life,* trans. Daniel Heller-Roazen (Stanford: Stanford University Press, 1998), 35.

4. Walter Benjamin and Gershom Scholem, *The Correspondence of Walter Benjamin and Gershom Scholem: 1932–1940,* ed. Gershom Scholem, trans. Gary Smit and Andre Lefevre (Cambridge, MA: Harvard University Press, 1992), 142.

5. Eric L. Santner, *On the Psychotheology of Everyday Life: Reflections on Freud and Rosenzweig* (Chicago and London: University of Chicago Press, 2001), 25–45.

6. Santner, 36; italics in original.

7. *Childe Harold's Pilgrimage,* canto 3 (1816), ll. 249–252, www.newsteadabbeybyronsociety.org/works/downloads/childe3.pdf. Byron's battle is Waterloo; he pointedly avoids any suggestion of recovery from the havoc he describes.

8. See Maynard Solomon, *Beethoven* (New York: Schirmer, 1077), 132–142.

9. Lawrence Kramer, "Eroica-Traces: Beethoven and Revolutionary Narrative," in *Musik/Revolution,* 3 vols., ed. Hanns-Werner Heister (Hamburg: von Bockel Verlag, 1997), 2:35–48; and Kramer, *The Thought of Music* (Berkeley and London: University of California Press, 2016), 31–43.

10. Cook, "The Other Beethoven," 17–18.

11. Will, *The Characteristic Symphony,* 196.

12. John Spitzer, "Beethoven's Acoustics," *Beethoven Forum* 12 (2005): 212–219, at 214.

13. Cook, "The Other Beethoven," 11.

14. Cook, 16.

15. "Bei jenem Werk ... alle waren eins, es gab keine Kunstler, ja keinen Beethoven mehr ... Das Werk ward lebendig, es ward erschaffen und erlebt." My translation. Quoted in Gregory Maldonado, "Critical Reception of Beethoven's 'Wellington's Victory; or the Battle of Vitoria,' Op. 91," Department of Music, California State University, Long Beach, 2005, 33n.

16. "Wer hat die Schlacht geschlaget, / Wer hat die Schlacht getönt, / Wer hat den Sichelwagen, / Der über das Blutfeld drohnt, / Harmonisch hinubergetragen, / Dass sich der Schmerz versöhnt?" Maldonado, 35n, my translation.

17. Clifton Fadiman, ed., *The Little Brown Book of Anecdotes* (New York: Little, Brown, 2009), no page reference (via Google Books).

18. On the optical and precinematic dimensions of the era's music, see Deirdre Loughridge, *Haydn's Sunrise, Beethoven's Shadow: Audiovisual Culture and the Emergence of Musical Romanticism* (Chicago: University of Chicago Press, 2014).

19. Dead Media Archive, http://cultureandcommunication.org/deadmedia/index.php/Daguerre%27s_Diorama.

20. On the decline of the android, see Christopher R. Clason and Michael Demson, eds., *Romantic Automata: Exhibitions, Figures, Organisms* (Lewisberg, PA: Bucknell University Press, 2017). The situation, however, was not straightforward, especially in the latter half of the century. Despite its lack of humanoid form, the early Edison phonograph (invented in 1877) was sometimes credited with a voice of its own and even with a personality, as if it were a form of artificial life. The reception of the phonograph was overwhelmingly favorable. See Rolf Goebel, "The Soul of the Phonograph," *Humanities* 9 (2020), www.mdpi.com/2076–0787/9/3/82; and Jason Camlot, *Phonopoetics* (Stanford: Stanford University Press, 2019). Threatening automatons also seem to have been rapidly eclipsed by "degenerate" human figures such as Robert Louis Stevenson's Mr. Hyde, Bram Stoker's Dracula, and George Du Maurier's Svengali, all of whom embody the era's well-documented fears of a cultural/evolutionary regression in which the "lower" forms of human life turn out to be more vital than the higher.

21. Walter Benjamin, "On the Concept of History" (1940), www.marxists.org/reference/archive/benjamin/1940/history.htm.

22. All three of us can trace a certain lineage to Beethoven's contemporary A. B. Marx, who, as Mathew puts it, understood *Wellington's Victory* as "turning the *Eroica* towards the world"; see the discussion in *Political Beethoven*, 42–48.

23. Deleuze, *Difference and Repetition,* trans. Paul Patton (1968; London: Continuum 2004), 263.

24. Susan Neiman, *Evil in Modern Thought: An Alternative History of Philosophy* (Princeton: Princeton University Press, 2004), credits the earthquake with permanently changing European thought about the nature of evil—which, however, did not stop it from becoming, like a famous battle, the stuff of popular entertainment.

25. Andrew Robinson, *Earthquake: Nature and Culture* (Chicago: University of Chicago Press, 2012), 36.

26. Stendhal, *The Charterhouse of Parma,* trans. Margaret R. B. Shaw (Harmondsworth, UK: Penguin, 1958), 54.

27. Stendhal, 53–54.

28. Sigmund Freud, *The Ego and the Id,* trans. James Strachey (New York: Norton, 1962), 29.

29. Daniel Tiffany, "Lyric Substance: On Riddles, Materialism, and Poetic Obscurity," *Critical Inquiry* 28 (2001): 72–99.

30. Walter Benjamin, "The Work of Art in the Age of Its Technological Reproducibility" (third version), trans. Edmund Jephcott and others, in *Selected Writings,* vol. 4, *1938–1940,* ed. Howard Eiland and Michael W. Jennings (Cambridge, MA: Harvard University Press, 2003), 266–267.

31. See Friedrich Kittler, *Gramophone Film Typewriter,* trans. Geoffrey Winthrop-Young and Michael Wutz (Stanford: Stanford University Press, 1999), 29–31.

32. Baudelaire, "Le Sept viellards," https://fleursdumal.org/poem/221, my translation.

33. Jonathan Crary, *Suspensions of Perception: Attention, Spectacle, and Modern Culture* (Cambridge, MA: MIT Press, 1999), 261–263.

34. Elizabeth Morgan, "Combat at the Keys: Women and Battle Pieces for the Piano during the American Civil War," *Nineteenth-Century Music* 40 (2016): 7–19; see also Gavin Williams, "Gunfire and London's Media Reality: Listening to Distance between Piano, Newspaper and Theater," in *Hearing the Crimean War: Wartime Sound and the Unmaking of Sense,* ed. Elizabeth Morgan (New York: Oxford University Press, 2019), 5–87.

35. Performances by the Youth Orchestra of Los Angeles had gathered 157; by the Argovia Philharmonic, 226; the 2013 Horse Guards Parade (performed in the presence of Queen Elizabeth), 343; an unidentified performance with scrolling score, 984; and the Berlin Philharmonic (as posted by one BubbaBigDude), 1,600, all as of July 19, 2020. These figures are not in the league of, say, 7,800 "likes" of a

Berlin Philharmonic performance of the *Eroica* (with over a million views), but, undead or alive, *Wellington's Victory* is not doing too badly.

CHAPTER FIVE: "DEAR LISTENER" . . .

1. The recordings are available online from the website of the Thomas Edison National Historical Park: www.nps.gov/edis/photosmultimedia/very-early-recorded-sound.htm. On the recording of the Handel aria, see Kramer, *The Hum of the World: A Philosophy of Listening* (Berkeley and London: University of California Press, 2019), 205–207.

2. Kramer, *The Hum of the World,* 20–22; see also Julie Park, "Making the Automaton Speak: Hearing Artificial Voices in the Eighteenth Century," in *AI Narratives: A History of Imaginative Thinking about Intelligent Machines,* ed. Stephen Cave, Kanta Dihal, and Sarak Dillon (Oxford: Oxford University Press, 2020), 119–143, esp. 133–137.

3. Rolf Goebel, "The Soul of the Phonograph: Media-Technologies, Auditory Experience, and Literary Modernism in the Age of COVID-19," *Humanities* 9 (2020), www.mdpi.com/2076-0787/9/3/82.

4. In light of Edward T. Cone's well-known *The Composer's Voice* (Berkeley: University of California Press, 1974), it is as well to add that the voice I refer to is not the composer's, even when we recognize a composer by style. It belongs to the subject that the music brings to life.

5. For a fuller account see Kramer, "The Mysteries of Animation," *Music Analysis* 20 (2001): 151–176.

6. Quotations from Peter Le Huray and James Day, eds., *Music and Aesthetics in the Eighteenth and Early Nineteenth Centuries* (Cambridge: Cambridge University Press, 1988), 86, 99, 188, and 222–230, respectively.

7. Personal Communication. See van Maas, "Scenes of Devastation: Interpellation, Finite and Infinite," in *Thresholds of Listening: Sound, Technics, Space,* ed. Sander van Maas (New York: Fordham University Press, 2015), 51–69. The volume also contains an earlier and much different version of this chapter, written in dialogue with van Maas.

8. Derrida, "From *Psyche:* Inventions of the Other," trans. Catherine Porter, in *Acts of Literature,* ed. Derek Attridge (New York: Routledge, 1991), 44, translation slightly modified.

9. Roland Barthes, *Camera Lucida: Reflections on Photography,* trans. Richard Howard (New York: Hill and Wang, 1980), 76–77.

10. Derrida, *The Post Card: From Socrates to Freud and Beyond,* trans. Alan Bass (1980; Chicago: University of Chicago Press, 1987).

11. *Pour se jouer 840 fois de suite ce motif, il sera bon de se préparer au préalable, et dans le plus grand silence, par des immobilités sérieuses.* Quoted in Robert Orledge, *Satie the Composer* (Cambridge: Cambridge University Press, 1990), 143.

12. Thus Alex Ross, reviewing a performance in 1993: "Robert Ashley played the piece with meditative concentration; Joshua Pierce found a beguiling, lilting lyricism; Kirk Nurock imported twentieth-century upheaval; Kyle Gann gave the music a marked forward motion; ... and, at the end of the night, William Duckworth played with uncanny steadiness and stillness." Alex Ross, *The Rest Is Noise,* www.therestisnoise.com/2004/10/satie_vexations_1.html.

13. An even more famous instance is the pair of recitatives in the first movement of Beethoven's Piano Sonata no. 17 in D Minor, op. 31, no. 2 ("Tempest," 1802). For commentary, see Kramer, "Primitive Encounters: Beethoven's 'Tempest' Sonata, Musical Meaning, and Enlightenment Anthropology," *Beethoven Forum* 6, ed. Glenn Stanley (Lincoln: University of Nebraska Press, 1998), 31–66, rpt. in Kramer, *Critical Musicology and the Responsibility of Response: Selected Essays* (Aldershot, UK: Ashgate, 2006), 109–144; and Kramer, *The Hum of the World,* 59–60. Bach's Adagio has a parallel in the slow movement of his Violin Concerto in E Flat, BWV 1042, where the overall treatment is somewhat looser but the vocal quality is intensified by the violin's capacity for sustained tones and legato phrasing. Here the solo voice becomes two voices, one lamenting, the other consoling.

14. Judith Butler, *Giving an Account of Oneself* (New York: Fordham University Press, 2005), 30–40.

15. From "Expression in Music" in the second (1792) edition of Sulzer's book, originally published 1771; reprinted in Le Huray and Day, *Music and Aesthetics,* 99.

16. See Kramer, "The Mysteries of Animation," 157–159.

17. Personal communication.

18. Stevens, "Esthetique du Mal" sec. 1, ll. 9–10, in *Collected Poems* (New York: Knopf, 1954), 314.

19. Quoted in Deborah Mawer, "Ballet and the Apotheosis of the Dance," in *The Cambridge Companion to Ravel,* ed. Deborah Mawer (Cambridge: Cambridge University Press, 2000), 156, translation slightly modified.

20. As Mawer (156) notes, in its original form as a ballet score titled *Fandango, Bolero* accompanied a flamenco dance of seduction. One might say that the individual segments of the piece retain the character of subjective address, which is negated, but pleasurably negated—with a kind of benign, perhaps slightly condescending irony—by the prevailing mechanism of repetition.

21. Martin Heidegger, "The Origin of the Work of Art," in *Poetry Language Thought,* trans. Albert Hofstadter (New York: Harper Perennial, 2001), 43.

22. Heidegger, 43.

23. Lacan takes the sentence to epitomize the idea that only the Symbolic stands between the subject and the repellent morass of the Real. See Jacques Lacan, *The Ego in Freud's Theory and in the Technique of Psychoanalysis,* Seminar II, ed. Jacques-Alain Miler, trans. Silvana Tomaselli (New York: Norton, 1991), 231–232. Barthes similarly contends that "The fright and terror [stem from] a gaping contradiction between Death and Language; the contrary of Life is not Death (this is a stereotype): it is Language. It is undecidable whether Valdemar is living or dead; what is certain

is that he speaks, without it being possible to ascribe his words to Death or Life"; quoted by Allen S. Weiss, *Breathless: Sound Recording, Disembodiment, and the Transformation of Lyrical Nostalgia* (Middletown, CT: Wesleyan University Press, 2002), 41. Derrida's view is discussed in text and cited in note 25.

24. J. W. Mackail, *Select Epigrams from The Greek Anthology*, epitaph 15, www.fullbooks.com/Select-Epigrams-from-the-Greek-Anthology3.html.

25. Derrida, in a discussion transcribed in *The Structuralist Controversy*, ed. Richard Macksey and Eugenio Donato (Baltimore: Johns Hopkins University Press, 1975), 156.

26. The condition of undeath also bears on ordinary life insofar as the subject automatically yields to any perceived address. For an account that links this phenomenon to both the Freudian unconscious and the force of law, see Eric Santner, *On the Psychotheology of Everyday Life* (Chicago: University of Chicago Press, 2001).

27. The quotations from Poe are from *Poe: Poetry and Tales* (New York: Library of America, 1984), 833–842; on the "clattering tongue," see Adam Frank, "Valdemar's Voice, Poe's Telegraphy," *ELH* 72 (2005): 635–662.

28. For a fuller account, see Katherine Syer, "Unseen Voices: Wagner's Musical-Dramatic Shaping of the Grail Scene in Act I," in *A Companion to Wagner's Parsifal*, ed. William Kinderman and Katherine Syer (Rochester: Boydell and Broyer, 2005), 177–214.

29. Žižek has made the point in more than half a dozen books; for representative instances, see Žižek, *Tarrying with the Negative: Kant, Hegel, and the Critique of Ideology* (Durham: Duke University Press, 1993), 191; and Žižek, *Opera's Second Death*, with Mladen Dolar (New York: Routledge, 2002), 173. See also Kramer, "The Talking Wound and the Foolish Question: Symbolization in *Parsifal*," *Opera Quarterly* 22 (2006): 208–229.

30. The phrase and its variants occur eight times during the chase, most easily tracked in the searchable text available from Project Gutenberg, www.gutenberg.org/files/345/345-h/345-h.htm.

31. The connection also forms a link between Mina and the phonograph; see John M. Picker, *Victorian Soundscapes* (New York: Oxford University Press, 2003), 134–136.

32. Shelley, *Shelley's Poetry and Prose*, ed. Donald Reiman and Sharon Powers (New York: Norton, 1977), 103.

33. Pausanias, *Description of Greece*, trans. W. H. S. Jones (London: William Heineman, 1918), 1.227.

34. Kramer, *Franz Schubert: Sexuality, Subjectivity, Song* (Cambridge: Cambridge University Press, 1998), 65–66.

35. Jean-Jacques Rousseau, *Essay on the Origin of Language*, in *The First and Second Discourses and Essay on the Origin of Language*, ed. and trans. Victor Gourevitch (New York: Harper and Row, 1990), 287.

36. Hughes, *The Collected Poems of Langston Hughes* (New York: Knopf Doubleday), 50.

CHAPTER SIX: WALTZING SPECTERS

1. A few words on the opera: The narrative takes place in a clockmaker's shop, which is also his house; various men end up hiding in the cases of grandfather clocks to accommodate the numerous infidelities of the clockmaker's wife. The music mocks the mechanism of its plot, and of sexuality, by simulating the mechanism of multiple clocks, each of which runs on its own time. For a full account, see Jessie Fillerup, "Composing Voices and Ravel's *L'Heure espagnole*," in *On Voice*, ed. Lawrence Kramer and Walter Bernhart (Amsterdam: Rodopi, 2013), 179–196.

2. Arbie Orenstein, ed., *A Ravel Reader: Correspondence, Article, Interviews* (1990; New York: Dover, 2003), 474.

3. Mark Katz, "Introduction," in *Music, Sound, and Technology in America*, ed. Mark Katz, Timothy Taylor, and Tony Grajeda (Durham and London: Duke University Press, 2012), 11. The quotation from Sullivan is also on p. 11. For a comprehensive account of the technology, see Katz, *Capturing Sound: How Technology Has Changed Music* (New York and London: University of California Press, 2010). On the astonishment, terror, and uncanniness, see Friedrich A. Kittler, *Gramophone Film Typewriter*, trans. Geoffrey Winthrop-Young and Michael Wutz (Stanford: Stanford University Press, 1999), 21–114; and Steven Connor, *Dumbstruck: A Cultural History of Ventriloquism* (New York: Oxford University Press, 2001), 358–361.

4. Wallace Stevens, *Collected Poems* (New York: Knopf, 1954), 122.

5. Orenstein, *Ravel Reader*, 80.

6. Maurice Ravel, *Valses Nobles et Sentimentales*, ed. Maurice Hinson (Van Nuys, CA: Alfred Music, 1988), 3.

7. Baudelaire, *The Flowers of Evil*, trans. James McGowan (Oxford: Oxford University Press, 1993), 97, translations mine.

8. For more detail, see Hinson's introduction (pp. 5–6) to his edition of the score.

9. *The Works of Lord Byron* (ed. Coleridge, Prothero), https://en.wikisource.org/wiki/The_Works_of_Lord_Byron_(ed._Coleridge,_Prothero)/Poetry/Volume_1/The_Waltz.

10. For a summary, see again Hinson's introduction to the score (p. 5).

11. Francis Ponge, *Soap*, trans. Lane Dunlop (Stanford: Stanford University Press, 1998), 33.

12. Orenstein, *Ravel Reader*, 78.

13. My translation of Ravel's note to the published score: "Des nuées tourbillonnantes laissent entrevoir par éclaircies des couples de valseurs. Elles se dissipent peu à peu: on distingue une immense salle peuplée d'une foule tournoyante. La scène s'éclaire progressivement. La lumière des lustres éclate au *fortissimo*. Une cour impériale vers 1855." Ravel also specifies the precise moments in the music when the ballroom becomes apparent and the illumination peaks.

14. Orenstein, *Ravel Reader*, 32.

15. Orenstein, 423. For a more affirmative view of what it should sound like, see Michael Puri, *Ravel the Decadent* (Oxford: Oxford University Press, 2011), 168–184.

16. Walter Benjamin, "Some Motifs in Baudelaire," trans. Harry Zohn, in *Illuminations* (New York: Schocken, 1969), 155–200.

17. Edgar Allen Poe, "The Masque of the Red Death," www.poemuseum.org/the-masque-of-the-red-death.

18. Baudelaire, *The Flowers of Evil*, 194, translation mine.

19. My translation from Gustav Mahler, *Briefe 1879–1911*, ed. Alma Mahler (Berlin: Paul Zolnay Verlag, 1925), 189, emphases in original: "das Gewoge tanzender Gestalten in einem hell erleuchteten Ballsaal, in den Sie aus dunkler Nacht hineinblicken—aus so weiter *Entfernung*, daß Sie die *Musik* hierzu *nicht* mehr hören!"

20. My translation from Natalie Bauer-Lechner, *Erinerungen an Gustav Mahler*, ed. J. Killian (Leipzig: e. P. Tal, 1923), 23: "Wenn du aus der Ferne durch ein Fenster einem Tanze zusiehst, ohne daß du die Musik dazu hörst, so erscheinen die Drehung und Bewegung der Paare wirr und sinnlos, da die der Rhythmus als Schlüssel fehlt."

21. Kramer, *The Hum of the World: A Philosophy of Listening* (Berkeley and London: University of California Press, 2019), 126–130.

22. Lacoue-Labarthe, "Echo of the Subject," in *Typography: Mimesis, Philosophy, Politics*, trans. Christopher Fynsk (1979; Stanford: Stanford University Press, 1998), 194.

23. Jacques Derrida, *Of Grammatology*, trans. Gayatri Chakravorty Spivak (Baltimore: Johns Hopkins University Press, 1976), 74–75.

24. Jonathan Crary, *Suspensions of Perception: Attention, Spectacle and Modern Culture* (Cambridge, MA: MIT Press, 1999), 11–80; see also Friedrich Kittler, *Discourse Networks: 1800 / 1900*, trans. Michael Metter, with Chris Cullens (Stanford: Stanford University Press, 1990), 206–264.

25. For an account of this phenomenon in early cinema, and its implications for music, see Kramer, "Classical Music, Virtual Bodies, Narrative Film," in *The Oxford Handbook of Film Music*, ed. David Neumeyer (Oxford: Oxford University Press, 2013), also available online. Writing on cinema more generally, Michel Chion has similarly observed that images in the audiovisual field "only take on consistency and materiality through sound"; see Chion, *Audio-Vision: Sound on Screen*, trans. Claudia Gorbman (New York: Columbia University Press, 1994), 63. As John Richardson observes, one consequence of this "synchresis" (Chion's term) is that "When synchronization fails or diverges from the norm, something interesting is likely to happen"; John Richardson, *An Eye for Music: Popular Music and the Audiovisual Surreal* (New York: Oxford University Press, 2011), 20.

26. From Thomas Hardy, *Moments of Vision* (1919), www.gutenberg.org/files/3255/3255-h/3255-h.htm.

27. Quoted from Laurence Senelick, *Jacques Offenbach and the Making of Modern Culture* (Cambridge: Cambridge University Press, 2017), 93, 95.

28. Walter Benjamin, *Reflections: Essays, Aphorisms, and Autobiographical Writings*, ed. Peter Demetz, trans. Edmund Jephcott (New York: Schocken, 1986), 262.

29. Benjamin, 264.

30. See, for example (the theme is ubiquitous in Žižek), Slavoj Žižek, *Looking Awry: An Introduction to Jacques Lacan through Popular Culture* (Cambridge, MA: MIT Press, 1992), 47–60.

31. On early reactions to the phone (extending to its relationship to spiritualism), see Connor, *Dumbstruck,* 387–391. As Connor observes, Bloom (whose famous day occurs in 1904) also conflates the telephone with the gramophone.

32. Derrida, *The Post Card: From Socrates to Freud and Beyond,* trans. Alan Bass (1980; Chicago: University of Chicago Press, 1987), 41, 67, 76.

33. Derrida, 108.

CHAPTER SEVEN: THE MUSICAL BIOME

1. Mary Shelley, *Frankenstein: The 1818 Text* (New York: Penguin, 2018), 98–99.

2. In James Whale's iconic film *Bride of Frankenstein* (1931) the instrument is not a guitar but a violin; so is the instrument that allures Gregor Samsa to his ultimately fatal self-exposure in Kafka's "Metamorphosis"; and so, perhaps at the start of the lineage, is the instrument named in the title of E. T. A. Hoffmann's tale "The Cremona Violin," which replicates the voice of the doomed heroine for whom to sing is imperative—but lethal.

3. Walter Benjamin, "Die Aufgabe des Übersetzers" ("The Task of the Translator," 1923), www.textlog.de/benjamin-aufgabe-uebersetzers.html, my translation.

4. Benjamin, "Die Aufgabe des Übersetzers." *Fortleben,* translated here as "living-on," is an uncommon word, which Benjamin glosses later in the essay as "transformation and renewal of the living." For more detail, see Caroline Disler, "Benjamin's 'Afterlife': A Productive (?) Mistranslation?," *TTR* 24 (2011): 183–221.

5. Benjamin, "On Language as Such and on the Language of Man," in *Reflections: Essays, Aphorisms, Autobiographical Writings,* ed. Peter Demetz, trans. Edmund Jephcott (New York: Schocken, 1978), 321; T. M. Knox, trans., *Hegel's Aesthetics: Lectures on Fine Art,* 2 vols. (Cambridge: Cambridge University Press, 1998), 2:889–892, 904–906.

6. Jane Bennett, *Vibrant Matter: A Political Ecology of Things* (Durham: Duke University Press, 2010).

7. The almost-literal life of (certain) literary characters is a separate issue; Benjamin is thinking of the literary work, read silently. On the sensory element in literary language, see the discussions of "the half heard" in Kramer, *The Hum of the World: A Philosophy of Listening* (Berkeley and London: University of California Press, 2019), 57, 68–69, 197–198, inter alia.

8. Bruno Latour, "Why Has Critique Run out of Steam," *Critical Inquiry* 30 (2004): 225–248.

9. Graham Harman, *Tool Being: Heidegger and the Metaphysics of Objects* (Chicago and La Salle, IL: Open Court, 2002).

10. Graham Harman, "The Well-Wrought Broken Hammer," *New Literary History* 43 (2012): 183–203.

11. "Sonnet LV," The Complete Works of William Shakespeare, MIT, http://shakespeare.mit.edu/Poetry/sonnet.LV.html.

12. Notable precedents for this close, virtually intermedial connection between text and music can be found in two short novels by Tolstoy, *Family Happiness* and *The Kreutzer Sonata*. See the discussions of the first in Kramer, *Musical Meaning: Toward a Critical History* (Berkeley and London: University of California Press, 2001), 42–45, and of the second in Kramer, "Tolstoy's Beethoven, Beethoven's Tolstoy: The *Kreutzer* Sonata," in *Critical Musicology and the Responsibility of Response: Selected Essays* (Aldershot, UK: Ashgate, 2006), 145–162.

13. "The Gold Bug Variations," Richard Powers: American Novelist (personal website), Richard Powers, www.richardpowers.net/the-gold-bug-variations/.

14. Nicholas Cook, *Beyond the Score: Music as Performance* (New York: Oxford University Press, 2013), 6–7, 337–373.

15. Richard Powers, *The Gold Bug Variations* (New York: Harper Perennial, 1992), 579. Subsequent citations are given in the text.

16. Habermas, "Modernity: An Unfinished Project," trans. Nicholas Walker, in *Habermas and the Unfinished Project of Modernity,* ed. Maurizio Passerin d'Entrèves and Seyla Benhabib (Cambridge, MA: MIT Press, 1997), 45–46.

17. William Wordsworth, *The Prelude: 1799, 1805, 1850*, ed. Jonathan Wordsworth, M. H. Abrams, and Stephen Gill (New York: Norton, 1979), 194; 1805: 6:179–187.

18. See the introduction to Johann Sebastian Bach, *The Goldberg Variations,* ed. Ralph Kirkpatrick (1938; New York: G. Schirmer, 1993).

19. The omission is almost certainly not an accident. Bach made extensive corrections to his copy of the first edition of the *Goldberg Variations.* He did not add a keyboard instruction to variation 21.

20. Aristotle, *Politics,* in *The Basic Writings of Aristotle,* ed. Richard McKeon (New York: Modern Library Classics, 2001), 1129.

21. Michel Foucault, *The Order of Things: An Archaeology of the Human Sciences* (New York: Vintage, 1994).

22. David Yearsley, *Bach and the Meanings of Counterpoint* (Cambridge: Cambridge University Press, 2002), 120–122. Yearsley's concern is principally with Bach's reconciliation of popular and learned styles in response to contemporaneous debates on the issue, although as noted in the introduction he elsewhere (174–181) considers the impact of Vaucanson's flute player on the conception of music's tie to life.

23. Quoted in Joshua Barone, "Thunderer Greets Austere Bach," *New York Times,* August 23, 2020, AR 4.

EPILOGUE: SOUND AND THE FORMS OF LIFE

1. Lawrence Kramer, *The Hum of the World: A Philosophy of Listening* (Berkeley and London: University of California Press, 2019), 1.

2. Elie Wiesel, *Night,* trans. Marion Wiesel (New York: Hill and Wang, 2006), 95.

3. Aldous Huxley, *Point Counterpoint* (London: Chatto and Windus, 1954), 595.

INDEX

References to Haydn, Mozart, and Beethoven are too numerous to list individually. Index entries for them are accordingly confined to specific compositions.

actor-network theory, 146–147
address form, 101–103, 109–110, 111–112
Agamben, Giorgio, 81–82
Allanbrook, Wye Jamison, 10–11
androids, 3, 5, 7–8, 11, 22–24, 28, 33, 47, 61, 91, 100, 117
animal life, 157
Aristotle, 157
Austin, J. L., 146

Bach, Johann Sebastian, 10, 184n13, 189n19; *Goldberg Variations*, 10, 145–189; Keyboard Concerto in D Minor, BWV 1052, 107–108
Bakhtin, Mikhail, 35, 57, 71
Barthes, Roland, 103, 113, 184n23
Baudelaire, Charles: "Harmonie du soir," 128; "Le jeu," 133–34; "Les sept viellards" [The Seven Old Men], 97
Beethoven, Ludwig van: *Creatures of Prometheus*, 3; *Egmont* Overture, 80; Piano Sonata no. 5, 27–31, 32; no. 10, 48–50; no. 12 ("Funeral March"), 83–86; no. 14 ("Moonlight"), 30–31; no. 17, 184n113; no. 23 ("Appassionata"), 75–76; Symphony no. 3 (*Eroica*), 3, 83, 86–87; no. 6 ("Pastoral"), 120; no. 8, 60, 71–72; no. 9, 104–105; Violin Concerto, 166–167; *Wellington's Victory*, 78–93, 98–99

Benjamin, Walter, 90, 97, 132, 138, 141, 145–147, 149, 164, 188n4
Bennett, Jane, 146
Berlioz, Hector, 73; *Symphonie fantastique*, 119–120
Bernstein, Leonard, 58
Bonaparte, Napoleon, 78, 79, 82, 83–84, 91, 92, 95, 98
Bonds, Mark Evan, 175n10
Bordeu, Theophile, 20, 22, 24, 32, 43–45, 68
Brahms, Johannes: Piano Quintet in F Minor, 74–75
Brentano, Clemens, 89
Brontë, Charlotte, 104, 118
Butler, Judith, 108
Byron, George Gordon, Lord, 82; "The Waltz," 129

Cage, John, 105
Chalmers, David, 7
chess-playing Turk, 90–91
Cheyne, George, 2–3, 7, 16, 17, 18, 44
Chion, Michel, 187n25
Chua, Daniel, 14, 36, 174n2
classical body, 35, 38, 47, 57
Cocteau, Jean: *La voix humaine*, 125
Condillac, Étienne de, 2–3, 5, 7, 16, 17, 44, 101, 144
Cook, Nicholas, 79, 88, 91, 150
Cotard's syndrome, 114

Crary, Jonathan, 137
Cusick, Suzanne, 177n3

Daguerre, Louis, 90
D'Alembert, Jean Rond, 20, 44
Darwin, Charles, 151
Debussy, Claude, 128, 142
De la Mettrie, Julien, 52, 100
Deleuze, Gilles, 30–31, 92
Derrida, Jacques, 42, 68, 113–114, 117, 135; invention, 103; *The Post Card,* 104, 142–43
Descartes, Rene, 7, 16, 51, 138
D'Holbach, Baron, 10–11
Diaghilev, Serge, 130–132
Diderot, Denis, 11, 20–22, 25, 29, 43–44, 47, 55, 67, 147
diorama, 87, 90–91, 99
Dolan, Emily, 74
Dreyer, Carl: *Vampyr,* 126, 133–134, 136, 138
drive, 18–22
duck, defecating (Vaucanson), 39, 51–52, 54, 55, 58–59, 60–61, 67, 68, 72, 73

Edison, Thomas, 100
Emerson, Ralph Waldo, 19
epitaphs, 113–114

flute player (Vaucanson), 3–4, 12, 23–24, 38–39, 41, 44, 47, 51–52, 55–56, 64, 66, 67, 80, 100, 117, 169
force without significance, 81–84, 87, 92, 94–95
Foucault, Michel, 30, 50, 52, 53, 63, 72–73, 178n4
Franck, César: Piano Quintet in F Minor, 74–75
Freud, Sigmund, 95, 139

Ginsberg, Ruth Bader, 9–10
Goebel, Rolf, 100–101
Goethe, Johann Wolfgang von, 53, 80, 159
Gould, Glenn, 150, 155, 168
Graham, Jorie, 6
Greek Anthology, 113–114
grotesque body, 35, 38–39, 41, 47, 57, 71–72

Habermas, Jürgen, 151
Hagedorn, Friedrich von, 53
Haller, Albrecht von, 24
Handel, George Frideric, 100
Haneke, Michael: *Amour,* 31–32
hard problem, the, 7
Hardy, Thomas: "The House of Silence," 139
Harman, Graham, 146–147
Haydn, Franz Joseph: *The Creation,* 157; Piano Sonata in C Minor (Hob. XVI:20), 25–27, 32; *The Seasons,* 157; String Quartet no. 53 in D Major, op. 64, no. 5, "The Lark," 53–55, 58, 59, 64, 66, 68; Symphony no. 7, 107–108, 109; no. 82 ("The Bear"), 157; no. 83 ("La Poule"), 157; no. 93, 55–58; no. 94 ("Surprise"), 14–16, 17, 18, 25, 28, 36–38, 40–42, 44, 47–50, 55, 93, 168, 174n2; no. 101 ("Clock"), 64–67, 71–72
Heartz, Daniel, 111
Hegel, G. W. F., 17–18, 146
Heidegger, Martin, 112
Herder, Johann Gottfried, 18–19, 24–27, 29, 67, 93, 102, 175n10
Higgins, Kathleen, 6
Hoffmann, E. T. A., 61
Homer, 8, 125
Horace, 147
Hughes, Langston: "The Weary Blues," 5–6, 121–122
Hui, Alexandra, 180n24
Hume, David, 18–19, 20, 21, 29
Huxley, Aldous: *Point Counterpoint,* 169

Ishiguro, Kazuo: *Never Let Me Go,* 8

Jacquet-Droz family, 23–24, 47–48, 67; organist, 48, 58, 61, 66, 110
James, Henry, 164
Joyce, James: *Ulysses,* 142

Kafka, Franz, 81; "Metamorphosis," 188n2
Kant, Immanuel, 60, 81, 84, 152
Katz, Mark, 124
Kaulbach, Wilhelm: *The Battle of the Huns,* 95
Kempelen, Wolfgang von, 90
Kintzing, Peter, 23, 61

Kirkpatrick, Ralph, 152
Klopstock, Friedrich von, 53
Koch, Gertrud, 35
Kotzwara, Frantisek: *The Battle of Prague*, 97–98
Kraus, Karl, 139–141

Lacan, Jacques, 113, 179n7, 184n23
Lacoue-Labarthe, Philippe, 135
Lang Lang, 165
Latour, Bruno, 146
legato principle, 74
Leppert, Richard, 173
Lessing, Gotthold Ephraim, 60
life forms, 22–24, 39, 62–64, 68, 73
Liszt, Franz, 73; *Battle of the Huns*, 95–97
Locke, John, 63, 65, 70
lyric substance, 97

Mahler, Gustav: Symphony no. 2, 126
Mälzel, Johann Nepomuk, 91
Marie Antoinette, 23
Marx, A. B., 74, 182n22
Mathew, Nicholas, 91, 180, 182n22
Mawrer, Deborah, 184n20
Mayrhofer, Johann, 119
Menuret de Chambord, Jean-Jacques, 20, 32, 33, 43–44
metaphors: and knowledge, 22, 33; train of, 5–11, 16, 20, 39, 101, 117, 121, 144, 146
Momon, 130, 140
Motley, Eric, 9
moving anatomies, 3, 22, 52
Mozart, Wolfgang Amadeus: Fantasy for Piano in D Minor, 44–48, 57; Piano Concerto no. 9, 107–108; Symphony no. 39, 67–71, 75; variations on "Ah, vous dirai-je maman," 37, 177n10

Neiman, Susan, 182n24

object-oriented ontology (OOO), 146–147
Offenbach, Jacques, 123, 140–141; *Tales of Hoffmann*, 61
ontological leveling, 146–147
Ovid, 7–8, 172n15

Paer, Ferdinando, 85
Pater, Walter, 19
Pausanias, 119
Pergolesi, Giovanni: *La serva padrona*, 11
phenakistoscope, 72, 97
Poe, Edgar Allan, 91, 117, 139; "The Facts in the Case of M. Valdemar," 113–115; "The Gold Bug," 148–149, 154; "The Masque of the Red Death," 133
Ponge, Francis, 130
Porter, Edwin: *The Great Train Robbery*, 93
postal principle (Derrida), 143
Poulenc, Francis: *La voix humaine*, 125
Powers, Richard, 145, 147; *The Gold Bug Variations*, 148–165
Prometheus, 52, 56, 84
Proust, Marcel, 142, 143
pulse, 5, 20, 32, 33, 43–50, 57, 67–71, 72
Pygmalion, 7–8

Ranciére, Jacques, 5
Ravel, Maurice, 186n13, 123–143
Reich, Steve: "Clapping Music," 12
Reil, Johann Christian, 2–3, 6, 16–18
Renoir, Jean: *Rules of the Game*, 133
Richards, Annette, 4
Richardson, John, 187n25
Richardson, Samuel, 104
Robert-Houdin, Jean-Eugene, 73
Roentgen, David, 23, 61
Ross, Alex, 184n12
Rousseau, Jean-Jacques, 102, 120; *Pygmalion*, 8

Sacks, Oliver, 34
Saint-Saëns, Camille, 133, 141
Santner, Eric, 82
Satie, Eric: "Vexations," 105–06
Schindler, Anton, 89
Schoenberg, Arnold: Five Piano Pieces, 12; *Pierrot lunaire*, 123; *A Survivor from Warsaw*, 167
Scholem, Gershom, 81–82, 83
Schubert, Franz: Impromptu in C Minor, 31–32; "Memnon," 119; String Quartets nos. 14 ("Death and the Maiden") and 15, 76–77; waltzes, 128–129
Shakespeare, William, 1–2, 53

Shannon, Claude, 40
Shelley, Mary: *Frankenstein*, 11–12, 14, 23, 39, 101, 144–145
Shelley, Percy Bysshe: "Ozymandias," 118–119
simulation, 4–5, 23, 30–31, 33, 39, 42, 43, 47–48, 49–50, 51–52, 53, 55, 58, 60–73, 78, 80–81, 91–96, 98, 124, 141, 156–157, 162, 169, 180n1
sonata form, 176n24
spaced texture, 39–43, 44, 48–50, 53–55, 57, 58–59, 61, 64, 68, 75
spacing (Derrida), 42–44, 46–47, 48, 51, 68, 75–76, 86–87, 135, 162
speaking melody, 164
Stahl, Georg, 22
Stendhal: *The Charterhouse of Parma*, 94–95, 99
Stevens, Wallace, 110, 124–125, 140; "Peter Quince at the Klavier," 5–6
Stoker, Bram: *Dracula*, 117
Strauss, Richard: *Rosenkavalier* waltzes, 129–130
Striggio, Alessandro, 12
subjectivity, musical, 101–103; and the address form, 112–113
Sullivan, Sir Arthur: "The Lost Chord," 100
Sulzer, J. G., 102, 109, 121

Tallis, Thomas: "Spem in Alium," 12
Tchaikovsky, Peter Ilych: *1812 Overture*, 98
telegraph, 114
Telemann, Georg Philip: "Alster Overture," 157
telephony, 142–143

Thompson, Michael, 62–64
Tiffany, Daniel, 97
Tolstoy, Leo, 189n12
Tonada, Yoko: *Studies in Snow*, 63

undeadness, 82, 114–117, 126, 141

Van Maas, Sander, 102
Vaucanson, Jacques, 3–4, 12, 22–24, 38–39, 41, 44, 47, 51–55, 58–61, 64–68, 73, 80, 100, 117, 169
Vicq d'Azyr, Felix, 73
Vigano, Salvatore, 3–4
Vila, Anne, 43–44
virtuality, 92
Vivaldi, Antonio: Concerto E Minor for Cello and Bassoon, 120–121
voice, 100–101, 114–115, 125–126, 157; acousmatic, 125
Voltaire, 52, 56, 93

Wagner, Richard: *Parsifal*, 110, 115–117
Watkins, Holly, 11, 173n22
Wellington, Arthur Wellesley, Duke of, 78, 79, 89
Wiesel, Elie, 166–167
Williams, John, 99
Williams, William Carlos: "The Kermess," 38
Wordsworth, William, 152

Yearsley, David, 163
Yeats, William Butler: "Purgatory," 139

Žižek, Slavoj, 115, 142

Founded in 1893,
UNIVERSITY OF CALIFORNIA PRESS
publishes bold, progressive books and journals
on topics in the arts, humanities, social sciences,
and natural sciences—with a focus on social
justice issues—that inspire thought and action
among readers worldwide.

The UC PRESS FOUNDATION
raises funds to uphold the press's vital role
as an independent, nonprofit publisher, and
receives philanthropic support from a wide
range of individuals and institutions—and from
committed readers like you. To learn more, visit
ucpress.edu/supportus.

www.ingramcontent.com/pod-product-compliance
Lightning Source LLC
Chambersburg PA
CBHW030654230426
43665CB00011B/1086